The Girl in Rose

The Girl in Rose
Haydn's Last Love

PETER HOBDAY

Weidenfeld & Nicolson

LONDON

First published in Great Britain in 2004
by Weidenfeld & Nicolson

© 2004 Peter Hobday Productions Ltd

A CIP catalogue record for this book
is available from the British Library.

ISBN 0 297 84747 3

Typeset by Selwood Systems,
Midsomer Norton

Printed in Great Britain by Butler & Tanner Ltd,
Frome & London

Weidenfeld & Nicolson

The Orion Publishing Group
Orion House
5 Upper St Martin's Lane
London WC2H 9EA

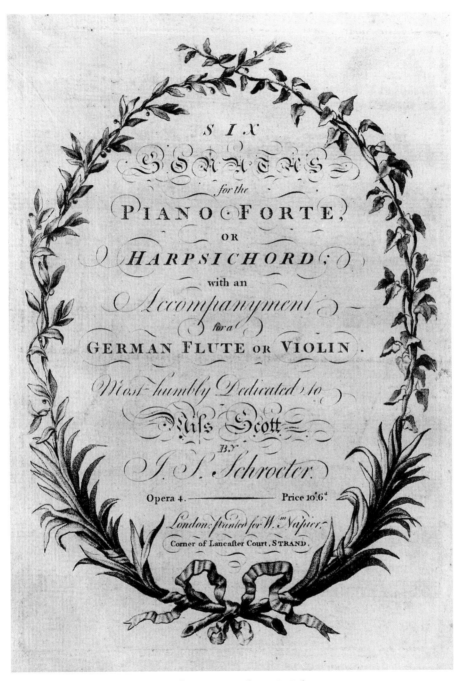

The title page of six sonatas by J. S. Schroeter,
dedicated to Miss Scott, 1772.

Of music Dr Johnson used to say:
It was the only sensual pleasure without vice

European Magazine, 1795

Contents

Acknowledgements

The self-imposed task to discover as much as I could about Rebecca Schroeter began in a radio studio. After I left BBC Radio Four's *Today* programme, I was asked by Tony Cheevers to present a morning programme called *Masterworks* on Radio Three. It was an odd choice on his part because most of my career had been in daily radio and television journalism. I had always loved music, of every variety, but my level of expert knowledge was, I freely admit, rather superficial. Yet here was a music producer willing to overlook such shortcomings. I embarked on a three-year crash course in music. Tony Cheevers was the most demanding producer I have ever worked with. He would never accept less than total commitment. He pushed me to read more and more widely, in order to be able to set the music we played on air in the context of its time. Part of the job of presenting music on Radio Three is to inform as well as stimulate the listener. It is never enough just to say 'Here is Joseph Haydn's second London symphony' and then play the music. Tony, knowing of my love of Haydn, as well as most eighteenth-century music, constructed pro-grammes which gave me the chance to learn more about the most classical of composers. This is how I first discovered the relationship between Haydn and the woman he used to call his 'beautiful English widow'. The interest in the music was mixed with journalistic curi-osity about Rebecca Schroeter and Joseph Haydn. This book is the result.

I have had a lot of help along the way – three wonderful researchers have at times put their talents at my disposal. Abigail Shepherd was the first to trawl through all the relevant archives at Lambeth Palace,

Westminster Library, the Public Records Office, and St Martin-in-the-Fields, while I contentedly went on broadcasting. Then Jim Derriman, a lawyer by training, helped make sense of the Chancery hearings, and with his legal mind warned me, whenever he could, if I was drawing faulty or facile conclusions from flimsy evidence. Finally Christine Baker has worked tirelessly chasing up obscure references in period newspapers at the Colindale Newspaper Archive, or in the romantic novels of the time. While I fully and gratefully acknowledge their contribution, the use I made of their work is my responsibility. They are in no way to blame for any faults. If there is any success, then they must more than share in it. I know that each of them joins with me in acknowledging the help of librarians, archivists, and unsuspecting authors whose generosity and willingness to share their knowledge with us has been the most remarkable feature of this endeavour.

Christopher Sinclair-Stevenson agreed to be my agent at a very early stage, sensing that in a confused manuscript there was a book waiting to emerge. He never lost faith. Jon Jackson, my first editor at Weidenfeld & Nicolson, also helped immeasurably in shaping the final version.

Just after I began to think about Rebecca, I came across an article by Tony Scull, in a musical magazine. It was called 'More Light on Haydn's English Widow'. When we met, Tony told me that he had begun to research Rebecca's life as the possible basis for a television documentary. He could not get any backing for the project at that time, but his initial research was invaluable in opening a window on her life. Professor Anthony Saunders, who teaches keyboard accompaniment at the Royal Academy of Music, was fascinated to learn of Schroeter. When we found some of the music, he spent a whole morning with me playing choice examples and explaining contemporary piano technique. He brought Schroeter to life again after two centuries of neglect.

My family must be thanked. My son John and my daughter Natasha both gave generously of their time to help their father. My wife Victoria has lived with the knowledge that her husband has been fascinated by another woman for the past four years. There have been, as someone once famously remarked, three people in our marriage. Victoria has bravely read, even more bravely, constructively criticised draft after draft. She is now looking forward to listening to music by composers other than Johann Samuel Schroeter and Joseph Haydn.

OVERTURE
Portrait of a Lady

Studying history is like reading by candlelight: it takes time for the eyes to become accustomed to the shadows. The past would look very different if lit by a hundred-watt bulb. But a clear historical image can take time to emerge. In the case of Rebecca Schroeter, it has taken over 200 years before one can arrive at a picture of her, and discover what her life was like and why the most famous musician of his generation, Franz Joseph Haydn, had such fond memories of the woman he called his 'beautiful English widow'.

Rebecca lived in London in the second half of the eighteenth century when, as one of the newspapers put it, there was 'a rage for music'. She had been born into a very rich family, which duly expected her to make a good marriage and land at least an aristocrat. A title in the family was what all aspiring self-made fathers prayed for. Daughters were carefully prepared for their role in life. Among the social attributes expected of a woman like Rebecca was the ability to make music, playing the piano and/or singing some of the popular airs of the day. A young unmarried woman's role was mainly decorative. In society she was expected to entertain the men when they finally joined the ladies after dinner. There is a rather vicious caricature by that keen observer of eighteenth-century manners, Thomas Rowlandson, of an elephantine girl caterwauling to the dismay of the potential suitors her proud merchant father has invited to meet her. Rebecca was the exception. She was beautiful and accomplished. She was passionate about music and had an abundance of talent. Her piano teacher, the most fashionable piano player of the 1770s, Johann

I

Samuel Schroeter, even dedicated – most humbly, as he put it – his early sonatas to her. Rebecca had enough money to allow her to live comfortably and, best of all, to attend the public concerts that took place virtually every night of the season, which featured the greatest names of the day. They flocked to London, where the fees were the largest by far in Europe. That was how she met the greatest of them all, Franz Joseph Haydn. Their relationship began with a simple letter. 'Mrs Schroeter presents her compliments to Mr Haydn, and informs him, she is just returned to town, and will be very happy to see him whenever it is convenient to him to give her a lesson.' The letter is dated 29 June 1791. Haydn accepted the request and so began an affair through which Rebecca achieved her moment of fame.

In the 1800s, during his last handful of years, Haydn was a wealthy man, loaded down with honours and universally respected. Now a widower, he had stopped writing music and, as old men do, he loved to reminisce about his long and eventful life. The son of a poor wheel-wright in rural Bohemia, he had spent most of his life providing music for his employers, the Esterházy family, whose palace rivalled Versailles for its richness and grandeur. Now nearly eighty, he had moved into a small house in the then village of Gumpendorf, just outside Vienna. Here, growing more and more frail with age, Haydn was cared for by Johann Elssler, son of his long-time friend and copyist Joseph Elssler. From time to time he received visitors, though they could not stay too long as it tired the old man. The most regular caller during these last years was Albert Christophe Dies, a landscape painter and amateur musician. He had given himself the task of being one of Haydn's first biographers, 'intending', he writes in his introduction, 'to collect some notes towards a biography rather than to produce myself a work of art that would satisfy all possible demands'. He then goes on to 'justify', as he puts it, 'the method I have chosen. I present to my readers as many sections as Haydn permitted me visits and treat each in the material which the visit yielded. My first visit decided me on this course; I would produce so faithful a representation that every contemporary of Haydn's might find again in the portrait, as if in a mirror, the characteristics of the original.'

Dies's little book was published first in 1810 in German. It was not until 1968, when Vernon Gotwals translated it, that non-German speakers have been able to read the original. Rebecca Schroeter is mentioned only once by Dies – and since then most musicologists have been content to quote the key sentence from the paragraph where this mention occurs, dated by Dies as his twenty-third visit, 18 June 1806: 'Haydn continued to feel well during the warm weather. He took some exercise daily. Haydn showed me another little book of notes. I opened it and found a couple of dozen letters in English in it. Haydn smiled and said, "Letters from an English widow in London, who loved me; but although she was already sixty [*sic*] years old, she was still a beautiful and amiable woman whom I might very easily have married if I had been free then." '

Then Dies adds his own comments:

This woman is the widow, still living, of the celebrated clavier player Schroeter, whose melodious song Haydn emphatically praised. In the letters of the widow, who was a musician herself, one sees that this woman loved Haydn's genius. Often she cannot find words to interpret the feelings that Haydn's music awakes in her. Joined to this is the greatest respect for the man whose genius-laden works are the wonder of the entire world of culture. Haydn enjoyed very pleasant hours in the company of the widow. When he was invited nowhere else, he generally dined with her.

On the basis of that paragraph Mrs Schroeter has been mentioned in every biography of Haydn ever written. You will find her name in sleeve notes on Haydn's famous *Gypsy* trio, which he dedicated to her and in his 102nd symphony in which the second movement features a theme she is said particularly to have liked. While her husband, the pianist Johann Samuel Schroeter, has his own entry in the musical bible, the *Grove Dictionary*, his music has been largely ignored and he only figures in musical history these days as the husband of the 'English widow' who so entranced Haydn during his two highly successful visits to London in the 1790s.

Haydn's music inspires a passion in his listeners: it sounds complete from his earliest works, culminating in the grandest oratorios of his maturity. He composed over a hundred symphonies, dozens of string quartets, trios, sonatas, encompassing virtually every genre known to the eighteenth-century music lover. Through his music one keeps bumping into Mrs Schroeter. Intrigued, I foolishly thought that I would be able to find out enough about this 'amiable' woman fairly easily. History, though, had removed nearly all traces of her. Others had trawled the archives pretty thoroughly, none better than the noted Haydn scholar H. C. Robbins Landon whose pioneering work has shed so much light on the composer's life and works. In 1959 he translated Haydn's correspondence and London notebooks. This allowed a greater insight into Haydn himself and the chance to read Mrs Schroeter's twenty-three letters in context. Even then she was still known only by her married name.

Rebecca was, in many ways, a typical woman of her class. She was rich, pampered and an heiress. She lived in what today might be called a 'male-dominated world'. It is doubtful whether Rebecca Schroeter herself would understand the phrase. That was the way the world was and, in her view, it was unlikely to change – at least not in her lifetime. Men had the power, the prestige and indeed, by law, the right to say what the women in their lives could or could not do. In many ways men and women lived parallel lives. The phrase used was 'separate spheres'. The male sphere was public life. The woman's was in private, with home and family. Yet women of course found ways to circumvent the patriarchal structures, devised strategies aplenty to get their own way, using men's susceptibilities to do and achieve subtly what they had to. The world was changing, too, in Rebecca's lifetime. This is the era of the first real intellectual arguments for women's rights. It is a time when relationships between the sexes are beginning to change. Marriage is changing too. It is more about love and companionship, and less about property and dynasty. Parenthood is also evolving. Children are both seen and heard.

The subject of this biography was not content with the slow changes that were taking place. She grabbed life with both hands.

She refused to live the life that was expected of her. She fell in love with a man her family forbade her to marry, yet married him all the same. She was widowed before she was forty, then fell in love with the most famous musician of the era, Joseph Haydn. She died in her seventies, a widow to the end. The echoes that we have of her, in her letters and in evidence she gave when she sought to recover her dowry that the family refused her, suggest a warm-hearted, loving but determined woman. She had a good brain. She was a talented musician. She was attractive. Most of all, Rebecca was a survivor.

It is difficult to write at some length about a person who existed, without some image of what they looked like. There are many con-temporary portraits that evoke the period, but nearly all are of iden-tified sitters. Having searched everywhere for a portrait, there seem to be none of Rebecca Schroeter herself. The closest is one by Joshua Reynolds of her sister-in-law. There are references to a Reynolds portrait of her brother, but if it ever existed all trace has vanished. It would be surprising if a young lady such as Rebecca did not sit for one of the painters of the day. The rising middle classes who were keen to ape their 'betters' in all things, wanted to hang family portraits on their walls. So Rebecca's likeness probably exists, though the name at the bottom may mean nothing to the present-day owner. There are, though, a surprising number of anonymous portraits. Of these, *The Blue Lady* by Thomas Gainsborough looks at first to be the most likely. The fact that it is by Gainsborough is important. There is circumstantial evidence that Rebecca Schroeter and her husband would have known him. Gainsborough loved music, though his own talents were at best mediocre. Two of his favourite companions in London were Johann Christian Bach, son of the great Johann Sebas-tian, and Friedrich Abel. These two men were among the most suc-cessful concert promoters at the time when Schroeter came to London and they did much to help Rebecca's future husband get established. The painter has left two superb portraits of them. There is also a delightful sketch by Gainsborough of a musical party with two women listening while a man plays at the piano, accompanied by a violin and a viola. This is just the kind of evening that Rebecca, herself an accomplished pianist, would have enjoyed. We know from the descriptions we have of her that she was 'beautiful', 'amiable' and a 'young lady of fashion'. All those words apply to Gainsborough's mysterious lady in blue. If Rebecca should one day be identified as the lady in question, it would solve an artistic mystery. If she is not, then no harm is done because the portrait remains without a name.

Gainsborough's women sitters often have an idealised quality about them. Yet the reality of a changing role for women is subtly reflected in the development of much eighteenth-century portraiture. Early in the century women are often shown in a submissive pose, gazing demurely at the male in the picture. A woman rarely looked directly at the person viewing the canvas. Later in the century the women take on a more distinct pose, standing more as the partner of the man, not his possession. By the end of the century the new woman looks straight out at her viewer.

And besides Gainsborough's portrait of the attractive society girl, there is another contemporary portrait of a 'young lady of fashion' who, despite her anonymity, possesses that more modern strength and vivacity, which outdoes her slightly distant counterpart in blue. This portrait was painted by Nathaniel Hone, a contemporary of Gainsborough's. The looks, social status and attitude of Hone's woman in red wonderfully match the picture of Rebecca Schroeter that emerges from the historical record.

Hone himself was born in Dublin, but after studying in Italy settled in London, where he became a founder member of the Royal Academy. His career, though, was marred by his intense jealousy of Joshua Reynolds. In 1775, the year that Rebecca married, Hone submitted a picture called *The Pictorial Conjurer*, which lampooned Reynolds's love of classical art and also suggested an improper relationship with Angelica Kauffmann, the first female member of the Academy. Hone was forced to withdraw the picture and paint over the offending parts. He retaliated by setting up a one-man show – the first ever recorded – where he exhibited over seventy canvases. Nathaniel Hone died in 1784, just four years before Gainsborough.

The face which the innovative Hone painted is more assertive than

Gainsborough's lady in blue. She looks out with unblinking eyes. Rebecca was a feisty and self-possessed woman. The more the two pictures are compared, the more Hone's vivacious girl in rose seems the truer representation of Rebecca Schroeter who, like him, was a spirited outsider. She was an admirable woman whose life affords some insight into the concerns of her sex in her time, particularly into Georgian England's flourishing artistic life, which captivated her. She in turn captivated the most famous composer in Europe. And no one, now, will ever be able to persuade this author that Hone's charming face from 1770s London is not that of Rebecca Schroeter. That is why she adorns the jacket of this book.

CHAPTER ONE
A Scottish Heiress

At six o'clock precisely on the morning of Saturday, 15 July 1775 a maid knocked and entered her mistress's room in Bedford Row, in London. She had been instructed to wake Rebecca Scott early because, so she had been informed, the family was planning to go out of town that day. To the maid's great surprise she found Miss Rebecca already up and fully dressed. After she had done as she was bid, and seeing that Miss Rebecca had no need of her, the maid curtsied and withdrew immediately. With the curiosity of all servants about their employers' lives she decided to keep watch to see what would happen next. The maid's name was Fanny Wankland. She was a forty-year-old spinster. She had spent all her life in service. It was her job to anticipate the needs of her betters. She had made a lifelong study of the gentry, which is why she was sure that Rebecca was up to something. Nobody else in the family had asked for an early morning call. Women of Rebecca's class did not dress themselves, especially at that hour in the day, unless there was mischief afoot. The maid was as aware as any in the household of the young woman's status. Rebecca was an heiress. Fanny sensed her mistress was planning something that she wished to keep secret from the rest of the family.

With a fortune attached to her name, Rebecca was a valued and tradable commodity in London's marriage market. Robert Scott, her late father, a successful City merchant, had settled £15,000 on her as a dowry, a sum of money worth more than a million pounds in today's values. It was a figure that made doubly sure his youngest daughter should not want for well-born or well-connected suitors. Like so many of the newly rich merchant class, Robert Scott was determined that his family would not only continue to rise in the world, whatever the cost, but also scale the heights of polite society. Social respectability was his aim, for himself and for his heirs and successors. He had spent what was necessary to have her well educated – to increase her marriage prospects. Her parents made sure that Rebecca was well adapted to the demands of polite society. She had come up to London to stay with her married sister, Elizabeth, who was renting the house in Bedford Row for the summer. What the maid had intuitively guessed was that Rebecca, who was just two months past her twenty-fourth birthday, was about to thwart her late father's ambition of a good marriage for his youngest daughter. Fanny watched her tiptoe downstairs to stand with the street door slightly ajar so that Rebecca would see immediately when her fiancé arrived at the top of the street.

At eight o'clock Rebecca planned to marry a man whom she loved, as she put it, 'more than any other'. She may have followed the fashion in most things, yet her marriage plans proved beyond peradventure that she had a will of her own. Not for her the arranged, albeit contented, marriage of her mother. Nor did she want a very conventional marriage like Elizabeth, her older sister, who had fulfilled her family obligations when she had married thirty-eight-year-old Charles Murray, fourteen years her senior. The Murrays and the Scotts knew each other from their business dealings in the wine trade on the island of Madeira. The joining of the two families and their international trading businesses was exactly the kind of alliance that Robert Scott would have wanted. And Murray was just the sort of man he would have wanted a daughter to marry. When another business associate, Thomas Cheap, the then consul, had written to Lord Rochford, the minister of state responsible for the island, suggesting Murray as his replacement, he said Murray had 'a perfect knowledge of the language, laws and manners of this country, and of the interests of His Majesty's subjects who reside in or trade to it, qualifications very necessary in these times'. Rochford replied that His Majesty the King 'was pleased' to accept the recommendation; Charles Murray was duly appointed consul in 1771.

In the spring of 1775 Murray and his family had come back to England on leave. To match his official position in public life, he had rented an imposing town house in Bedford Row for the summer. For Rebecca, who lived most of the year in her widowed mother's fine old place in Blackheath, Murray's home leave provided the perfect opportunity to spend some time in London, see her sister and call on other friends of her age. More important, the visit allowed Rebecca and her fiancé to finalise their plans for a secret wedding. As Rebecca waited all alone by the front door, early that damp, humid and rather cloudy Saturday morning, for her future husband to come in a carriage to take her to the church, she was both elated and nervous. Added to a bride's normal nervousness was Rebecca's knowledge that she was about to give herself to a man whom her family would never have chosen for her. The family was rich and had ambitions to climb the social ladder. The man she had chosen was an outsider, with little class or standing in Britain. He posed a threat, not just to her own position but, by extension, her family's as well.

Rebecca Scott was, in appearance at least, a conventional woman of her times. Of average height, she was judged by all who knew her to be an attractive and handsome young woman. As a member of a wealthy family she was a dedicated follower of fashion, no matter how outrageous. What one wore proclaimed one's status in the world. The *ton* could not, would not, be seen in public in anything but the latest fashion. Women of Rebecca's class had little choice in the matter. In the 1770s she would have had her hair piled high. To the natural hair were added false tresses. The ensuing creation was stuffed with wool, even paper to give it the height society expected. The whole towering edifice was held in place by wire. This hairstyle was so difficult to achieve that many women just left it in place for days. It attracted dust and after a time smelled of candle smoke. It was so heavy that young ladies wobbled as they walked. It made the neck ache. Wits at the time even suggested that birds could nest comfortably and not be noticed by the owner. Rebecca would have had her hair fashioned the day before, and sat up all night so as to look perfect for her wedding. No wonder she was awake and fully dressed when the maid called her at six.

In public Rebecca would have worn a broad-brimmed hat, trimmed with a silk ribbon. The mode was for it to be tilted at a rakish angle. There would be a muslin wrap, or some other fine material over her shoulders, tucked into her tight bodice. Her gaze would be open but demure, exactly the appearance that polite society demanded of a young woman. As her brother-in-law would later describe her, she was 'a young lady of fashion'. Thomas Gainsborough made a fortune painting many of these apparently languid creatures, posing them in a romantic setting, always looking as if they had nothing to do in the world but wait for someone else – their father, or their brothers – to decide what would become of them. Rebecca might have adopted that languid pose on many an occasion but, as her family would soon learn, she was also a determined individual who had decided to wait no longer. For months this seemingly dutiful young woman had carried alone the dangerous secret of her rebellious marriage. Not a single member of the family, nor any of their friends, could have guessed that she had fallen head over heels in love.

Nor dare she tell anyone her secret. The man she had chosen was her music teacher; his name was Johann Samuel Schroeter. There were a thousand and one reasons why she should never even have got close to him, let alone loved him. As one friend later admitted, Schroeter had always shown the 'proper respect and distance'. As her music teacher, he could behave in no other way. Yet despite the distance and the formality of social intercourse at the time, a spark had been struck and a fire now burned. Rebecca believed that by marrying in secret, the family would accept what she had done and, once she was given the chance to explain, they would understand and accept all the reasons why she had chosen this man. She knew that she would have to win her family round, though she firmly believed that the task would not be impossible. Young people in love see only what is good about the object of their affections. It did not matter to Rebecca, that her fiancé was poor. The fact that her family and their friends would want to dismiss him simply as a foreigner on the make made her pity society's small-minded attitudes.

What Rebecca saw was his great talent and she was convinced that he would soon dominate his chosen profession because of it. London in the reign of George III was always ready to laud and reward success. Possibly, at the back of her mind was the fact that at the age of twenty-four, she was getting a little long in the tooth to make a really 'good marriage' in the accepted sense. She dreaded the prospect of some decrepit but titled individual being paraded before her by her anxious family. Even though Rebecca now had the legal *right* to marry whomsoever she chose, she still had to have the *approval and consent* of her brother and mother, who were the executors of her father's will. She knew that if she left the choice to them, they would have wanted a 'gentleman' in the mould of Charles Murray who would help the family's fortunes.

To her friends and neighbours, Rebecca had the best prospects that could be wished for. Not only was she young, good-looking and of an amiable nature, she had the most desirable asset of all: wealth. There were two annuities worth a total of £400 a year under the terms of her father's will. She lived in a fine old house in salubrious Blackheath just eight miles from London. The Scott ladies had servants, their own carriage and the freedom to come and go as they pleased, visiting friends and relatives in London. A journey of eight miles was not an insurmountable barrier even though the roads would be muddy in winter, pitted with wheel tracks and dusty in summer.

Rebecca, while relishing and enjoying the advantages of wealth and position, would have been keenly aware that life was passing her by. The role of obedient daughter and mother's companion was suffocating even in the best of families. While her sister Elizabeth had lived at home, she had had at least someone nearer her age with whom she could chat and laugh and share her adolescent secrets. Her sister had married nearly three years earlier and moved out of the family home. Her ambitious brother Robert, now head of the family, had just moved into a smart house at number 25 Wimpole Street to carry on with his father's business. He took his role as head of the family very seriously. His inclinations, as well as his pressing business affairs, left little time or need to concern himself with his little sister's hopes and ambitions.

Like so many young women of her generation, some of Rebecca's understanding of the world came from the novels and romances borrowed from the circulating libraries. The publishing industry was expanding fast and becoming a huge interlinked operation, with publishers, printers and booksellers combining to satisfy the escalating demand that came from an expanding readership. Moral and religious works dominated, poetry was much in evidence, but the novel was what everyone was talking about. Contemporary male commentators worried that many of the novels then in vogue undermined female modesty and virtue. Dr Johnson believed firmly that 'books have always a secret influence on the understanding'. He was thinking of books written to improve the mind. Others were more cynical, claiming publishers and writers who sought commercial gain would inevitably aim at the lowest common denominator. William Hayley, a minor poet, wrote,

> Beneath the pillow, not completely hid,
> The novel lay – she saw – she seized – she chid;
> With rage and glee her glaring eyeballs flash.
> Ah wicked age! She cries, ah filthy trash.

Heroines served either as models to be emulated, or scorned if they did not conform to the rules of polite society. Rebecca probably saw herself as Pamela from Samuel Richardson's eponymous novel. It was the publishing success of the first half of the century. And as if to confound the cynics, it was a decidedly moral book. It came out in 1740, ran into five editions and, the greatest compliment of all, it was widely parodied and pirated. It was translated into all the main European languages. Of course, Rebecca was of better stock than that heroine. In much the same way she was alone in a hostile world bent on telling young women what they must and must not do. Like Pamela, she knew her duty, but she also knew her worth and she was eager to arrange life to suit her.

Rebecca, like all the fictional heroines, wanted to marry for love. In fiction, just as in real life, young women were pulled in different and conflicting directions. They were difficult to resolve, as Jane Austen showed in her celebrated novel written nearly a quarter of a century later, *Sense and Sensibility*. 'Sense' was doing what was right, what was expected of one, of being humility personified, waiting until you were spoken to, letting men take the lead or the initiative, being, in a word 'dutiful'. First you were a dutiful daughter, then a dutiful wife. 'Sensibility' was the opposite. Sensibility was giving way to passion and emotion. If you loved someone, why wait for him to declare himself as a well brought-up young woman should do? Why not speak openly of your feelings? In fiction, despite appearances to the contrary, the heroine's choice almost invariably fell on a man who turned out to be rich, titled and perfect. The world was taught to believe that poverty was a failing and no young woman, no matter how much she professed to love the man, could really be expected to live without money. For most of her short life Rebecca had been 'sense' personified. She had controlled her innermost feelings – committing them, if she was at all like any of her contemporaries, to her private journal, for which she had more than enough spare time. Today, her wedding day, she was giving in, at last, to her feelings. Therein lay the drama of what was about to happen.

As she waited at the front door to catch sight of her fiancé's carriage come to take her to church, Rebecca could not have stopped herself from thinking about the day that lay ahead and the trouble it might cause. She accepted that she had spent the last few days leading a double life. She knew that if her family had discovered her marriage plans they would have sent her away, maybe to stay with distant relatives in Scotland, until she forgot her folly. Since her arrival in Bedford Row, she had been a model guest. She had properly and genuinely enthused over the success of her sister's marriage; and she had listened at length while her sister talked of the new house she and the consul were building high in the cool hills overlooking the town of Funchal on Madeira. She had gone 'shopping', as the craze was called. Elizabeth and Rebecca had discussed endlessly the latest fashions of the town. Both now had the towering hairstyle then de rigueur.

And there would have been dinners, and concerts, and visits. They had admired brother Robert's fine new town house in Wimpole Street; Georgian London was in the middle of a speculative building boom as the newly rich moved west, out of the stink of the City to the fresher air of Westminster and full-fronted houses up to four floors in height. Much of Wimpole Street today is as it was in Rebecca's day. She had made as much time as she could to visit her friends, the closest of whom was Frances Coutts, the young daughter of the banker James Coutts. In other words, life had been normal, with not a hint of what was to come.

During these regular and largely predictable days, a significant amount of time was taken up with letter writing and diary keeping. All the biographies of the period – from Fanny Burney, Hester Thrale, or the Lennox sisters – remind us that this was a time when prolific correspondence and recording were the norm. People eagerly studied their own behaviour and that of others. Despite the fulsomeness of polite conversation, people were becoming more self-aware and more interested in their feelings than ever before. According to the diarist James Boswell, the human condition was a favourite topic of conversation as much in the chop houses as round the dinner table at home.

Perversely, while people grew more self-aware, masking one's true feelings was still a highly prized skill. Fanny Burney, in her diary, recalls an excruciating time she had at a royal musical evening, when she had to sit in great discomfort for an hour or more with a monstrous toothache, yet ensure that no one noticed. A fetching blush was the most well-bred young ladies were permitted at moments of social awkwardness. At times of great stress, fainting was a useful strategy. But here was a young woman brimming over with love, about to take the most momentous step in her young life, a step that could well sever all connection with her family. It is hard to imagine how Rebecca could have controlled her feelings over those warm and sultry July days under the scrutiny of her sister. Her closest friend, the banker's daughter Frances Coutts, was having to learn to cope with the growing signs of madness in her father and Rebecca would not have wanted to burden her any more.

Rebecca's secret plans were, though, helped by the political climate of the day. The men in the family were increasingly concerned by events in the American colonies. The first rumblings of the American War of Independence were being heard. For merchant families like the Scotts or the Murrays, the possible loss of the American colonies posed a huge threat to their business interests. They probably spent more time in their offices or the coffee house getting the very latest news.

The only other person who shared the secret was, of course, the man she loved – in her eyes the most handsome and most talented of men. And he seems to have been able to carry off the deception with the family equally well. He continued to ride out to Blackheath for her piano lessons, always showing, as one family member recalled, 'proper distance' as a mere music teacher should. Rebecca later insisted that she would have him and no other. Rebecca Scott had become the heroine in her own true story. This was not art but life itself.

As a love story, it certainly did not fit into the pattern of behaviour demanded by the conventions of the age. It was bound to be clandestine at first. After all, the man she now loved, so desperately and completely, was a piano teacher, a foreigner and her social inferior. Had Rebecca's heart not been ruling her head, she would have seen at once what she was asking not only of her family but also of society in choosing him. Any self-respecting Englishman saw music making as something for the ladies and as a profession only to be carried on by foreigners – Germans, Italians or Frenchmen. Lord Chesterfield, who had been a neighbour of the Scotts in Blackheath, wrote, 'Nothing degrades a gentleman more than performing upon any instrument whatever. It brings him into ill company and makes him proud of his shame,' an extreme view with which the celebrated musicologist Doctor Charles Burney would have quarrelled, even though he had to spend the greater part of his life making music a respectable calling. The problem was that most of these foreign music makers were seen as potential seducers of fine young English heiresses.

The man who had won Rebecca's heart, Johann Samuel Schroeter, was a year younger than she. He was German and had the exquisite manners expected of a courtier, learned as a musician in the royal houses of Europe. He had easily won the approval of Rebecca's brother and mother when Rebecca had asked if he could give her piano lessons. Soon he had their permission to come out to Blackheath once or twice a week. Schroeter was beginning to make a name for himself playing the piano rather than the harpsichord. Musical historians would later see him as one of the very first concert pianists in Britain and the man who began the ascendancy of his instrument – an ascendancy that would soon see the piano dominant and the harpsichord all but abandoned. Many, including Dr Burney, liked the music he wrote and the way he played it. Most of the information we have about Schroeter comes from Charlotte Papendieck, who married a member of Queen Charlotte's court. Her memoirs, dictated forty years after the events, are uneven and unreliable. But she certainly remembered Schroeter with a relish that suggests she was, innocently, quite smitten by him. She found him 'fascinating, fawning and suave; a teacher for the belles, company for the mode . . .'

There would have been very few, if any, young men in Rebecca's normal circle of Scottish expatriates and City merchants who would have fitted that description. They would always have been on their best behaviour when meeting her. Schroeter would have been very different in background, outlook and experience of life, so it is easy to understand how a sheltered innocent such as Rebecca could fall for him. Piano teachers can get physically close to their pupils. There are often moments when the teacher's practised hands guide the pupil's hesitant fingers over the keys. There must have been a special moment when, as he leaned close to her, whispering encouragements into her ear, Rebecca heard the voice, not of a teacher but of a man she loved. She would have been chaperoned at first by her mother. But she was an old lady and such chaperones are fallible. Thomas Rowlandson, whose sketches offer unforgettable images of Georgian

Britain, shows in *The Music Lesson* an old man fast asleep, while handsome teacher and pretty pupil are more interested in each other than the piano at which they are both sitting. Old Mrs Scott could well have dozed as the lilting chamber music was played. Rebecca loved music. She was good at it and her choice of a rising young star of the keyboard as her piano teacher certainly suggests that she viewed music as more than just a mere social accomplishment. Music was then and would always be a very important part of her life.

There is an early piano concerto which Schroeter 'most humbly dedicated to Miss Scott' soon after they met in 1772. The music tells its own story of their relationship. It is a quiet and lilting little piece and the gentle melody insinuates itself into the listener's head. Afterwards it just will not go away. If the man was at all like his music, it is obvious how he must have won her heart, quietly and without aggression. That dedication to Rebecca on the first piece of music which Schroeter had published in England, just months after his arrival, suggests that he did not have a richer or more impressive patron to whom to dedicate the music. Music publishers much preferred an aristocratic title on the engraved frontispiece. It was an endorsement that could help sell the piece. The Scott family was not without significance in the world of commerce and they would have been aware of the conventions of the time. It was part of the process of flattering a patron. For Rebecca the dedication must have been like a declaration of his love for her. She probably told her family that she was studying the music, nothing more. The family did not give it another thought and obviously had no suspicions that there was any reason for the dedication other than the respect of a servant for his employer.

Riding out from London once or twice a week to Rebecca's small rural retreat in Blackheath would have been a chore for Schroeter. The round trip would have been about sixteen miles – at least a couple of hours in the saddle depending upon the conditions. He would have got about a half a guinea an hour and, if he was lucky, probably some food in the kitchen before he went back up to town. Rebecca paid the fee – and it must have made quite a dent in her personal accounts.

So right from the beginning it was a relationship fraught with social difficulties – a proud but poor young foreign musician teaching his rich female employer the finer arts of piano playing. Given that she was in a position of authority, it seems logical that she must have given him some initial encouragement. Perhaps there was a glance or their hands touched for longer than was absolutely necessary. Possibly she was so fulsome in her praise of his music that he was made to realise that she felt more than was normal for a student to feel for her teacher.

Whoever made the first move is really immaterial – something happened that prompted Schroeter to know that if he asked Rebecca to marry him, she would say 'yes'. Inevitably, when it became public knowledge, his detractors immediately argued that it was not her beauty that attracted him so much as her £15,000 dowry. They would claim that Schroeter only became serious when sister Elizabeth married Charles Murray in 1772. Murray played by the rules, sought and won the approval required of the executors, and Elizabeth's dowry, also £15,000, was duly invested in government bonds and stocks after the wedding. All this had happened during the time that Schroeter was busy teaching Rebecca at their weekly lessons.

The fortune hunter was a popular stereotype of the period and it is true that many men, especially those who had little financial substance, were cynical about marriage. Heiresses were indeed prizes to be won. Marriage was rarely a romantic union of two loving souls who would live happily ever after. Far from it. The lot of many married women was harsh indeed. If there was not outright physical cruelty, their fortune belonged to their husbands to do with as they wished. The literature of the time is full of such stories. The news-papers even printed a bride's financial status when they carried the news of a society match.

It is inconceivable that the two young people did not discuss Eliza-beth's wedding – after all, it was the first happy family event since the death of her father. It is equally certain that Schroeter must have been aware of the financial arrangements. Was it then that he – or they – conceived of a secret marriage and that by presenting the family with a fait accompli, Rebecca would get the dowry that would make life secure and comfortable? It was obvious that the family would never willingly consent to such a marriage – the social gap and the stigma of his profession would have been too much. But the family might more easily accept the union once the Church had joined them together.

As the minutes ticked away until she stood in the vestry before a licensed curate, it would have been natural for Rebecca to think of all of this and more. She must also have recalled her sister Elizabeth's wedding day eighteen months before in the parish church in Blackheath. The witnesses were her brother Robert and the family's oldest and closest friend, John Pringle. Every family member who could had made the journey to Blackheath. That ceremony was in stark contrast with Rebecca's wedding. There was no last-minute family excitement, no gathering of the clans. There was no one, not even her maid, to help her dress. There was no close relative to give her advice about what a wife's duties were, or explain what a husband's needs involved. She would not have been human had she not felt a pang of fear and insecurity as well as excitement about the prospect before her.

At just after six o'clock at the half-open front door of the tall town house Rebecca kept watch for Schroeter's carriage. They had agreed that it would stop at the top of Bedford Row, away from the house. Then, as now, it was a wide and stylish street, and the carriage could easily have come down to the front door. But that early in the morning a carriage stopping at the front door would have been certain to arouse suspicions. As soon as she saw Schroeter waving to her from his carriage Rebecca ran down the short flight of steps at the front and turned right up towards Holborn where the carriage was drawn up. Hitching up her dress so as to avoid the mud and muck of the pavement, she moved as fast as her heavy skirts and towering hairstyle would allow her towards Johann Samuel Schroeter and her chosen future.

CHAPTER TWO

An Epidemic of Melomania

To exchange the disciplined world of commerce for what would have seemed the much more thrilling and satisfying world of music, as Rebecca was about to do, was a daunting move. One German correspondent told the readers of the *Journal des Luxus und der Moden* that there was at the time an 'universal epidemic of melomania' in London. But loving music and being part of the process that produces it demand vastly different experiences. Even so, Rebecca would have found some similarities with the world she was leaving.

Just as merchant venturers of the time were the precursors of today's global investors, so the modern music business owes a great debt to the musicians, composers and performers of the eighteenth century. These ground-breaking men and women took music out of the private, largely aristocratic sphere into the public concert hall and theatre. To succeed many of them became as commercially minded as the Scotts and the Murrays, and created their own businesses. In many ways they had to be more imaginative than the Scotts and the Murrays. Those merchants traded in physical goods that could be stored, counted and accurately valued. Many of the goods they shipped were essential commodities. The music business traded in talent and ideas, which depended upon the vagaries of public taste and mood to secure any return. A Hamburg-based composer and music critic, Johann Mattheson, said in 1713, 'In these times whoever wishes to be eminent in music goes to England. In Italy and France there is something to be heard and learned; in England something to be earned.' Earning something, though, was a huge challenge, because music was a luxury item. So the nascent music industry quickly developed ways of marketing music and musicians, creating what today we would term 'hits' and 'stars': the bigger the name, the larger were the earnings. These remarkable artistic capitalists traded on the fact that music had no national boundaries; they established that audiences were happy to listen to, applaud and reward foreign talent. The century saw the first musical impresarios who insisted on exclusive contracts with the big-name singers and players. To succeed initially a performer needed to be young, foreign and obviously talented. The newspapers were used to puff up performance and advertise coming events. Newspaper coverage could be bought, or influenced by the amount of advertising placed in its columns. Impresarios and managers had to be hucksters.

A whole industry grew up around music, the excitement of concerts and the cult performers. Concert goers did not just buy tickets. They wanted to make their own music as well. This gave rise to the new instrument makers. The middle of the century saw a huge demand for pianos and there was a steady trade in violins, flutes and oboes. The printing trade did well out of the demand for music; sheet music was sold to the gentry for their family entertainments; beautifully engraved tickets for subscription concerts engaged the talents of artists and engravers like Hogarth, Bartolozzi and Gilray. Candle makers and coal merchants met the huge demand for heat and light in places like the Hanover Square Rooms when concerts were held during the winter months. To heat the largest opera house in Europe, built by Frederick the Great of Prussia, cost £40 a night – that is about £4000 in today's values.

Every night in London there was a perplexing choice of opera, concerts – both public and private – and music played in the theatres and the pleasure gardens like Vauxhall or Ranelagh. Simon McVeigh in his ground-breaking research into *Concert Life in London from Mozart to Haydn* quotes a verse by the playwright James Hook:

> All the modish world appear
> Fond of nothing else my dear

Folks of fashion eager seek
Sixteen concerts in a week.

All this activity made patrons hungry, which in turn created an equally flourishing catering trade. In the pleasure gardens, like Ranelagh or Vauxhall, there were many booths for private supper parties. These events also caught the attention of a class of people for whom music was but the secondary attraction: prostitutes and courtesans prospered mightily, as Orpheus prepared the ground for Eros.

As Rebecca was contemplating her marriage to a German pianist, she no doubt confidently believed that, given the vibrancy and flourishing of musical activity in London, she was not risking very much. What she perhaps did not appreciate was that, ingenious and creative though the foreign artists like her fiancé were, they struggled against huge odds to survive. England then was well along the path to becoming the wealthiest and most powerful nation the world had yet seen. Britannia's triumphs on the world stage bred a tremendous amount of chauvinism. A native-born Englishman had a lot to be proud of and his unalterable view was that God was an Englishman. Even Rebecca's own family, who had come down from Scotland, were mocked for their accents, their clothes and their attitudes. Foreigners, no matter how talented, were scorned as inferior, lesser beings – not just musicians, but diplomats, foreign aristocracy and clerics. The musicians also had to recognise that their religion was often held against them. Many were Catholic and Catholics were not greatly esteemed in Protestant Britain.

The potential rewards of musicianship, of course, far outweighed the probable disadvantages. People would travel a long way in search of success and not the least of the challenges for a musician bent on winning public favour in Britain was physically getting to the country in the first place. Musicians had to put up with riding in bone-shaking carriages for weeks at a time and lodging at roadside inns, which in the main offered dreadful food, dirty bed linen and the likelihood of sharing a room, if not a bed, with total strangers. And whichever way they came, there was always the daunting prospect of a Channel crossing. After waiting for the right wind, the crossing could take up to twenty-four hours if the weather turned nasty. Storms, shipwreck and seasickness were just three of the discomforts on offer.

Among the most travelled musicians of the century were the Mozarts, who arrived in London in the early 1760s. Leopold, the father, kept a meticulous account of his expenses. No matter how much he planned, scrimped and saved, he never seemed to make any real profit from his musical tours, even though he was offering London the chance to hear his two child prodigies, his daughter Nannerl and his son, the extremely precocious eight-year-old Wolfgang Amadeus. London was but one of their early destinations. Before the end of their careers Leopold and his son would have made extensive tours through Italy, France and Germany. Reading the Mozart family letters, one must admire the sheer determination to keep going despite the setbacks, the insults and the hard grind of producing new music day in and day out. The Mozarts were but one family of determined musicians on the road at the time. It was a life that Johann Samuel Schroeter knew well, having travelled with his father and siblings along many of the same rough roads.

This nomadic way of life made the musicians and performers in the eighteenth century a tough breed of people. They needed more than musical talent to survive. They had to be able to deal with the highest and the lowest ranks of society in the countries in which they played. They learned to dissemble with the best of the actors. They knew financial success depended on pleasing people. They quickly grasped how to shape the compliments that would loosen royal and aristocratic purse strings. A sure-fire compliment was dedicating a new composition to the right person. Even the music they wrote was a form of compliment, never too demanding of the amateur who might be tempted to play it at a private party. Rebecca's suave husband-to-be certainly fitted the bill. Entertaining the aristocracy across Europe, being expected to fit in with their way of life, while still keeping the right respectful distance, is the sine qua non of a successful courtier. Musicians were, in the main, courtiers. Those who moved into the public sphere retained many of the tricks of their courtly profession.

These, then, were the type of people for whom Rebecca was planning to abandon her family. She was swapping the dour and narrow confines of Scottish commerce for the debonair but insecure world of international music. She would have been denying her Scottish lineage had she not pondered how she would live with a young musician who was just beginning his career in London. It must be said, though, that of all the peoples who made up Britain in the eighteenth century it was the Scots who were the most prepared to leave their homes and go in search of a better life. Ever since the Act of Union in 1707 there had been a veritable tide of Scottish immigration into London. Rebecca at least believed that she would not start her new life empty-handed. There was her dowry. She knew she would have to fight for that. She probably took comfort from the fact that music dominated society at the time.

The most famous musicians, like the Italian soprano Lucrezia Agujari, could earn hundreds of pounds for a concert. In 1775 she had been filling the Pantheon, which attracted audiences in their hundreds. She had been contracted to give thirteen concerts for a fee of £1200 – that works out at around £100 a night and is twice what a skilled artisan would earn in a year. Rebecca, like most of London, would have known such a fact. The papers were full of details about the celebrities' lives. But Agujari was the exception. A principal player in an orchestra was paid much less. For example, the British violinist John Crosdill received sixty guineas for fifteen concerts, or just four guineas a concert. Given these extremes of fee, the young bride, deeply in love, would obviously firmly believe the man she loved to be closer to Agujari than Crosdill in earning power. So, given the available evidence, Rebecca had many reasons to feel confident that the talented man she was to marry could prosper in the London of the 1770s. The most reassuring fact for her, apart from his looks, his talent and his personality, was his nationality.

Since the turn of the century German musicians had been a major force in musical life in London. They had done well despite the public's love of Italian opera, music and performers. Italian musical talent was in plentiful supply. Italian singers were especially highly rated. For the cognoscenti Italy was the fount from which all great music flowed. The demand for Italian opera, and especially Italian voices, of course, grew out of the increasing numbers of young men who went on the Grand Tour throughout the century. Anyone who had any pretensions to being of a good family went south of the Alps. As Doctor Johnson magisterially observed, 'A man, who has not been in Italy, is always conscious of an inferiority, from his not having seen what it is expected a man should see. The grand object of travelling is to see the shores of the Mediterranean.' This attitude persuaded Italian musicians abroad to become proud and uncompromising. They saw little reason to change their style, their ideas, or their high fees. They were the best and they expected to be paid as such.

The early German composers and performers acknowledged the Italian claim to pre-eminence. They did not try to foist a German style of music on their audiences. Most studied hard in Italy before they came to London. Nearly all were content to compose in the Italian style and employ Italian artists wherever possible to give the authentic feel to the music. Even native-born talent had often to compromise. The singer Nancy Storace, for example, made her name in Italy first, before moving on to Vienna, where she sang the title role in the first performance of Mozart's opera *Le Nozze di Figaro* in 1786. She went on to become a great favourite with London audiences in the 1790s. The German community in England, of course, had one great advantage. Apart from their musical talent, they were bound to prosper in a town where there was a German royal family on the throne. What's more, the Hanoverian royal family were their most enthusiastic sponsors. As Rebecca looked forward to her marriage, she must have calculated that a talented German musician could certainly make his mark in Georgian England, enjoy royal patronage and so provide handsomely for his family. There were many precedents.

One of the first Germans to make a huge impact was George Frideric Handel. After a great success in Rome, where he was known as *Il Sassone* – the Saxon – Handel arrived in London in 1710. Italian opera was already the height of fashion and he produced *Rinaldo* to great acclaim. Two years later he wrote a hugely praised *Te Deum* celebrating the Peace of Utrecht. He also wrote a birthday ode for Queen Anne, who settled on him a yearly pension of £200. When Anne died in 1714, his official employer, the Elector of Hanover, succeeded as George I of England. Some of Handel's earliest music for the new King earned him a doubling of his royal pension. Some claim that the piece that prompted this royal largesse was what is popularly known today as Handel's *Water Music*. It was commissioned to accompany the royal barge on a trip down the Thames. According to the *Daily Courant* of 19 July 1717, the King 'caused it to be played over three times in going and returning'.

Not only did Handel have good relations with the King but the aristocracy liked him as well. For a time he lived in the Duke of Burlington's imposing house in Piccadilly – now home to the Royal Academy of Arts. John Gay, the gossip and playwright, dashed off one of his celebrated verses:

> There Handel strikes the strings, the melting strain
> Transports the soul, and thrills through every vein.

Opera after opera came from Handel's pen; indeed, it is said that he often started one while finishing another. He had a phenomenal work rate. His own house became a music factory, with copyists labouring flat out on the arrangements, singers attending for auditions, tickets being sold to the audiences who flocked to his productions. In between times Handel travelled widely throughout Europe in search of the finest singers. Two of the most famous sang for him to great acclaim: the short, fat, ugly Francesca Cuzzoni and the tall and beautiful Faustina Bordoni. The two women were deadly rivals. How could they be otherwise, given the competitive nature of the musical world? It is no exaggeration to say that they hated each other with as much passion as the mythical heroines whose parts they played on stage. In 1727 they were appearing in an opera written by Giovanni

Bononcini. A fight broke out and the women tried to scratch each other's eyes out. The newspapers of the day had huge fun carrying what they claimed were 'full and true accounts of the most horrible and bloody battle'.

If the women were rivals, so, too, were Bononcini and Handel. The town was split into two almost warring camps. Handel had the backing of the King, while Bononcini had the backing of the Prince of Wales. This rivalry prompted a wit to write the following verse:

> Some say compared to Buononcini [sic]
> That Mynher Handel's but a ninny
> Others aver that he to Handel
> Is scarcely fit to hold a candle
> Strange all this difference should be,
> Twixt Tweedledum and Tweedledee.

London and audiences everywhere loved these artistic rivalries. 'Battles', real or counterfeit, between artists, composers and even theatres set a pattern that was to be repeated endlessly throughout the century. In Vienna in the 1780s, for example, Mozart and a young English-trained but Italian pianist and composer, Muzio Clementi, met in a pianistic duel to the delight of the Emperor. In the 1790s in London, promoters tried to encourage great rivalry between Haydn and a former pupil, Pleyel. Such personal competition was also good for business. Managers and musical promoters exploited it for all they were worth. It sold newspapers, as each claim and counter-claim filled the press and whipped up public interest. Often the printed puffery was paid for, thus providing an extra source of useful income to publishers. Frequently the town was divided into partisan groups of supporters who would turn out in all weathers to cheer on their champion.

The foreigners did not have it all their own way. There were a number of good, sturdy home-grown artists, performers and composers. But most were put in the shade by the extravagant claims of the foreigners. Nevertheless, one of the greatest operatic successes of

1728 was John Gay's *The Beggar's Opera*. It was sung in English, which had all but disappeared from the musical theatre. It had a record-breaking run and for a time pushed Italian opera into the shade. In fact, Gay's opera was a huge send-up of the overblown Italian style, with its set-piece arias brimming over with metaphor and simile. But even this blow for national-culture opera was not solely a British creation. It had nearly seventy short popular tunes, for which Johann Christoph Pepusch, another German musician then resident in London, provided the basses. Pepusch also wrote the overture. He began his London career as a viola player and harpsichordist at Drury Lane Theatre. He was later musical director to the Duke of Chandos. He composed over one hundred instrumental sonatas. Pepusch is another example of a German musician whose understanding of Italian musical traditions gave him a successful career in England. Pepusch, like those who came after him, showed that German composers were prepared to write what was popular regardless of nationality. Therein lay their appeal – for they were notable musicians.

Schroeter would have been as aware as anyone of the success of German musicians in London and for him George Frideric Handel would have seemed an ideal role model. He was a big man in every sense: bombastic, overbearing, short-tempered, but immensely popular nonetheless. He could be very witty on occasions, even though he never lost his thick German accent. It does not do to look too closely at all the music he wrote, because quite a lot of it he stole from other composers. He was not the only composer at the time to do this and this was, after all, an age before any enforceable laws of copyright were on the statute books. But one writer has suggested that Handel was rather like the honey bee, taking pollen from thousands of flowers and then, in its magical laboratory, turning it into something radically different. That was what Handel did: he borrowed ideas which, once filtered through his musical brain, came out as something unique.

Bach said of Handel that had he not been Bach he would have wanted to be Handel. Beethoven saw him as the master of all musicians, so did Mozart and Haydn. Nor was Handel above recycling his own material when the occasion demanded it. One has to recognise that most music written at the time was likely to be performed only a few times at most. Music was an ephemeral art form. Despite his tremendous energy, and vast output in almost every genre, Handel could not fight market forces. He put £10,000 of his own money into an operatic venture at the King's Theatre in the Haymarket; but the attractions of a rival company based at Lincoln's Inn Fields proved irresistible and Handel lost his money. He was virtually bankrupt in 1737. It was also the year he became very ill – some kind of stroke, it is said – and he suddenly discovered religion. It is possible the two events have some connection.

His new-found faith prompted him to turn to another new form of music – the oratorio. Handel invented the English style of oratorio, which helped him to recover the standing that he had enjoyed before. It is a mix of masque and anthem. The best-known – and an undoubted masterpiece – is *Messiah*, written in 1741. It had its première in Dublin where Handel was at the time. In the opinion of the Dublin *News Letter*, 'it far surpasses anything of that nature which has been performed in this or in any other Kingdom'. People everywhere would agree with the Irish music critic today. It is still one of the most performed works in the English repertoire. It was always a sell-out in its day, with the sponsors often urging women 'to come without their hoops and men without their swords' so as to make as much room as possible for the huge audiences it attracted.

Handel did not abandon other forms of composition. In 1749 he wrote *Music for Royal Fireworks* to commemorate the Treaty of Aix la Chappelle concluding the War of the Austrian Succession the year before. There was a hugely successful rehearsal in Vauxhall Gardens on 21 April with an audience of over 12,000 and, it was reported, a three-hour traffic jam of carriages afterwards. The actual firework display a week later in Green Park was disappointing. It was 'mean', according to Horace Walpole, who added, 'What contributed to the awkwardness of the whole was a pavilion catching fire, and being burned down in the middle of the show.'

It was the oratorio, though, that became the great legacy of Handel's later years. In all, he wrote twenty before total blindness in 1751 prevented him from composing more. His blindness did not stop him playing the organ at performances of his oratorios to great emotional acclaim. Charles Burney, that industrious chronicler of London's musical life, wrote, 'To see him led to the organ and then conducted towards the audience to make his accustomed obeisance, was a sight so truly afflicting and deplorable to persons of sensibility, as greatly diminished their pleasure in hearing him perform.'

Handel died on 14 April 1759 in his house at number 25 Brook Street. He had bought the then brand-new house in 1723. It has been restored and is now home to the Handel House Museum. There the visitor can see a replica of his canopied four-poster, dressed in crimson narateen. There is double-manual harpsichord built to the composer's specifications. This was where he wrote *Messiah*, and told the public through the press that this and other works were to be had 'From the author, in his house in Brook-Street, Hanover Square'. He was seventy-four when he died. Three days later the *Public Advertiser* printed these verses

> He's gone; the soul of harmony is fled!
> And warbling Angels hover round him dead
> Never, no, never since the tide of time
> Did music know a genius so sublime.

Universally mourned by the British who had long accepted him as a true Englishman, the great composer was buried in Westminster Abbey. Rebecca was nine when Handel died. The man had dominated English music making for half a century. For an upwardly mobile family like the Scotts, determined to rise in the world, it is extremely likely that she may have attended a performance of *Messiah*. She almost certainly would have studied and played some of his music in her early lessons.

The year after Handel's death George III came to the throne – the first of the Hanoverian royal family who had actually been born in

England and for whom English was a language he spoke as well as German. The young King's education had included music, to which he was passionately devoted. Princess Sophia Charlotte of Mecklenburg-Strelitz, whom he married in September 1761, was an equally keen musician. Just before she left for England her music master had been a member of the now legendary Bach family. In those days the Bach name did not have the resonance that it has in our century. Johann Sebastian Bach was an obscure Kapellmeister in Leipzig whose passion for counterpoint made his music sound very old-fashioned. The Bach genes, though, had music deeply imbedded in them and two of his sons had very successful and important musical careers. One of them, Johann Christian, the youngest son and the eleventh child of the second marriage of the great and manifestly uxorious Johann Sebastian, became the young Princess's music master while she was still living in Mecklenburg-Strelitz. This young man had the sweetest of natures and was soon on very good terms with the rather shy Princess. She invited him to come to London to continue as her music master. He kept the job for life. Bach was the second great German in England whose example would give much encouragement to young Schroeter.

Johann Christian Bach arrived in London in the summer of 1762. He was twenty-seven years old. He was as different in style, taste and personality from the great Handel as it is possible to be. Whereas Handel was larger than life, a 'charming brute', as one contemporary called him, the 'London' Bach, as Johann Christian became known, seems to have had a much more placid nature. His friends loved him and cared for him – and he had many. Handel and Bach, though, had similar backgrounds in Italian opera. Johann Christian went to Italy when he was nineteen, and had a very successful operatic career in Naples and Turin. He became a Catholic and was appointed organist at Milan Cathedral. Like Handel, he made his mark in London with a very successful opera, *Orione*, which was put on at the King's Theatre in February 1763. Charles Burney was as enthusiastic as any critic at the time and wrote, 'Every judge of music perceived the emanations of genius throughout the whole performance . . . .' Bach's next operas, though, flopped. Burney remarked of his *Adriano in Siria*, 'Everyone seemed to come out of the theatre disappointed.'

Bach, like Handel, was a complete musician and like his predecessor was keen to supply the public with what it wanted. And what the public wanted as much as anything was instrumental music with an Italian feel. The often overlooked English composers of the century, Arne, Boyce, Avison and Stanley, produced a large amount of fine music. But there was frequently a prejudice against them. One young soloist went so far as to ask the public to come and hear him play, even though he was a native Englishman. Just before Bach arrived in London William Boyce, who had studied with Pepusch, had published his eight symphonies. While passionate about opera, Bach was, like most musicians of the day, able to turn his hand to anything. The new management at the Opera House, under Giovanni (later Sir John) Gallini, avoided asking anything from Bach. So Bach concentrated on writing instrumental music. Already in 1763 he had published his first set of harpsichord concertos dedicated to the Queen. This was music in a lighter style and Charles Burney remarked, 'In general his compositions for the piano forte are such as ladies can execute with little trouble.' No wonder Bach was soon acquiring a large clutch of willing young ladies from good families who wanted to learn the piano so as to shine in society. His most prestigious pupil was the Queen and most weeks he would spend an evening with the royal family providing a piano accompaniment for the King, who played the flute. Such relationships opened the doors of the highest society to the young 'Saxon professor' as he styled himself.

Bach was not content to be just a composer, performer and teacher. He was as aware as anyone that real financial success came from being an impresario as well. With no opera commissions, Bach teamed up with another German musician to promote a series of subscription concerts. He was Karl Friedrich Abel. Abel's father had been a chamber musician and violinist at Cöthen Chapelle when Sebastian Bach was in residence as Kapellmeister. He had also studied at the Thomas Schule in Leipzig during Bach's time. The two men, despite the fact that Abel was ten years older, had known each other since childhood. Karl Friedrich had arrived in London just three weeks before the great Handel died in 1759. From his opening concert he quickly became an established viola da gamba player in much demand. The pair announced their first concert in the *Public Advertiser* as follows:

FOR THE BENEFIT OF MR BACH AND MR ABEL:

Great Room in Spring Gardens, near St James's Park.

This day, February 29
A new Serenata in two Acts Composed by Mr Bach. To which will be added several new Pieces of Instrumental music by Mr Abel. To begin exactly at Half an Hour after Six. Tickets at Half-a-Guinea each to be had at Mr Bach and Mr Abel's Lodgings in Meard's Street, St Anne's Soho.

This was the first of what was to become one of the great musical attractions of the next twenty years in London – the Bach–Abel concerts. They seem to have been an instant hit with the usually fickle public. Indeed, when the Mozart family arrived the same year, they made a point of calling at Meard's Street and it was largely thanks to their intervention that the 'little wizard' was invited to play for the King at the palace on 19 May. Wolfgang amazed everyone in the audience that evening. What he did was to play at sight whatever piece of music by Handel, Bach and Abel was placed in front of him. Bach loved the little boy and became a kind of surrogate father. He was the sort of father that young Wolfgang would have wanted, rather than the complex, grumbling disciplinarian who was his real parent. Neither ever forgot their time together, though after Mozart left London they would only meet once more.

Bach's and Abel's concerts were soon so successful that they decided to move from Meard's Street to much better apartments in King's Square Court, now Carlisle Street, Soho Square. This was a very elegant area frequented by the best of society. They accepted an invitation to move to the imposing Carlisle House, which stood on the corner with Sutton Street. A certain Mrs Teresa Cornelys had acquired the lease. She was an actor's daughter who had been born in Venice in 1723. She had first arrived in London in the 1740s as a singer. She was not a very successful one. According to Charles Burney, 'she had such a masculine and violent manner of singing, that few female symptoms were perceptible'. She travelled first to Vienna, then to Amsterdam, where she married a man called Cornelis de Rigerboo. She also had a short affair with Casanova and had a child by him. She was, as they say, a lady with a past. She came back to London some time in 1760 to sing at the Little Haymarket Theatre as 'Mrs Cornelles'. In December that year the *Public Advertiser* told the 'Nobility and Gentry, Subscribers to the Society in Soho Square' that its 'third and fourth meetings would be held on Thursdays 1 and 15 January 1761 at Seven O'clock'. One contemporary poet wrote, probably as a piece of paid puffery for the newspapers, as follows:

> Where Carlisle House attracts the light and gay,
> And countless tapers emulate the day,
> There youth and beauty chase the hours along,
> And aid time's flight by revelry and song;
> There masques and dancers bound on footsteps light
> To jocund strains that echo through the night
> Till morning's rosy beam darts full on all
> Who leave, though loath, this gorgeous festival.

Before long Mrs Cornelys asked Bach and Abel to organise their concerts at her house. In 1765 they were soon providing some of the best music in town in a sumptuous setting – a salon hung with blue and yellow satin. Encouraged by her success, Mrs Cornelys wanted to open up another venue in the City in 1766, but her move was strongly opposed by the merchants, who always viewed with suspicion the rather more frivolous approach to music and concerts by the West End of the town. Rebecca's father was still alive at the time, and living and working in the City, and he was more than likely a member of one of the many all-male musical societies that met frequently in City taverns. He would no doubt have shared the views of his fellow City merchants about the likes of Mrs Cornelys setting foot in the Square Mile. It also would mean that Rebecca would have been very unlikely to have been allowed anywhere near such a place as Carlisle House to dance the night away.

Bach's bank account at Drummonds showed that the money was rolling in. Once again he and Abel decided on another move, this time to King's Square Court. This address was well known to the literary and artistic worlds – because Bach and Abel, like another of their neighbours, their friend Domenico Angelo, were prodigious entertainers. If they had kept a visitors' book the curious would have seen the names of Garrick, Sheridan, Wilkes, Horn Tooke, Joshua Reynolds, Gainsborough, Bartolozzi, Zoffany as well as louche characters like the Chevalier D'eon.

Bach's career was reaching its peak. By 1768 he and Abel decided to relocate their concerts at Almack's. Almack's was created by a former Scottish manservant whose real name was Macall. He devised a meeting-place that quickly became very popular with the gentry. Bach at this time was beginning to favour the pianoforte over the harpsichord and his interest stimulated harpsichord makers to experiment. One of the most successful was the Swiss-born Burkat Shudi who had arrived in London at the age of sixteen. When he died in 1773 the firm passed to his partner and son-in-law, the Scottish born John Broadwood. The beginning of what was to become the unstoppable rise of the piano as a concert instrument can be dated to this decade. The earliest public use of the piano is a theatre bill for 16 May 1767, which says that at a 'Benefit', 'Miss Brickler will sing a favourite song from *Judith*, accompanied by Mr Dibdin on a new instrument called a piano forte'. Dibdin's career would have been a warning to any young musician. He wrote forty operas, hundreds of songs and sea shanties. But he died destitute and friendless in 1814 aged nearly seventy.

This was the year that saw another German musician arrive in London. He was thirty-five-year-old Johann Christian Fischer, an oboist. Almost at once he became a leading wind player at the Bach–Abel concerts, making his debut with them, according to the *Public Advertiser*, 'For the benefit of Mr Fischer. At the large Room, Thatch'd House, St James' Street, this day June the 2nd will be performed a grand concert of vocal and instrumental music . . . tickets may be had of Mr Fischer at Mr Stidman's, Peruke Maker in Frith Street, Soho.' The notice also said that Mr Bach would perform on the pianoforte. It was here in 1772 that Johann Samuel Schroeter made his debut, under the auspices of Bach and Abel.

The Bach–Abel concerts continued on their successful path until 1775, the year of Rebecca's marriage, when the two musicians joined forces with Giovanni (now Sir John) Gallini to develop a site on the east side of Hanover Square. The first concert was scheduled for 25 January 1775 but, as they had to tell the readers of the *Public Advertiser*, they were 'obliged to postpone their First Concert to Wednesday the first of February, on account of some unexpected Disappointments of part of the Furniture and Ornaments of their new room'. There is a wonderful letter by Mrs Gertrude Harris, the wife of James Harris the Member of Parliament for Christchurch, who was there for the first night. 'It was the opening of his new room,' she told her son at Oxford,

> which by all accounts is by much the most elegant room in town; it is larger than that at Almack's. The statue of Apollo is placed just behind the orchestra but it is thought too large and clumsy. There are ten other figures or pictures, bigger than life. They are painted by some of our most eminent artists: such as West, Gainsborough, Cipriani, &c. These pictures are all transparent and are lighted behind; and that light is sufficient to illuminate the room without lustres or any candles appearing. The ceiling is domed, and beautifully painted with alto-relievos in all the piers. The pictures are chiefly fanciful; a Comic Muse, painted by Gainsborough, is most highly spoken of. 'Tis a great stroke of Bach's to entertain the town so very elegantly.

This, then, was the world that Rebecca was about to join through her marriage. She would spend much of her time within the German community, but she would mingle with Italians and all the other nationalities that flocked to London, then unquestionably the centre of the musical universe. She would move among the elegant, like Bach and the members of the royal band, she would meet overbearing opera singers. She would have to become adept in the business side of music, mixing with the middlemen, the shopkeepers who sold tickets, the engravers who designed them. She would have to live with the ups and down of a musical career. She would learn to worry about what the public wanted. Rebecca would also meet that curious musical phenomenon of the age – the soprano castrati who were a great attraction in London. In 1774 Venanzio Rauzzini, one of the greatest, came to Britain, to sing at the King's Theatre. Since the times of Pepys, castrati had been a fixture of the musical stage. Pepys, an amateur musician, thought they sang well but, not surprisingly given his love of women, preferred the female voice. Handel, the professional, rated castrati highly. Not everyone shared his opinion. When Nicolini, who had appeared in Handel's first great opera, *Rinaldo*, left England an anonymous writer raged, 'Away with this object of pleasure and shame for our nation. May Great Britain no longer be corrupted by frivolous trilling. Let such a race of singers return to that country where lust and dissolute behaviour prevail. Great Britain wishes to assert her liberty.' Rebecca would no doubt have heard similar sentiments among her father's Scottish friends, had they ever deigned to discuss such a subject in mixed company. As she ran up Bedford Row that July morning towards Schroeter's coach, little would she have realised how very different her new world would be from the one she had known for the first twenty-four years of her life.

CHAPTER THREE

T*he* Music Master

Johann Samuel Schroeter, just like Rebecca, was up betimes on his wedding day. Like her, he was dressed by six. In his rooms in Duke Street the nervous bridegroom probably and rightly felt much more foreboding than his bride-to-be about their plans. As a man of the world he appreciated better than she what was in store for them. As a foreigner in chauvinist Britain, he knew what it was to be an outsider. He understood the pain of social rejection. There is no doubt whatsoever that Rebecca passionately loved him. She had often told him she 'would have no other'. In view of her background, her fortune and her family's social ambitions, he realised that he was a 'bad match'; so he had to compensate personally for what he lacked in social standing. It was an affront to his dignity that they were to be married in secret. But that was what Rebecca wanted and Schroeter, who loved her, was ready to do as she wished. They knew they risked losing Rebecca's significant dowry, so a short-term deception on their part would, he now believed, not necessarily be to their disadvantage in the longer term.

Not for one moment did Schroeter consider that he might be marrying above his station. His was an honourable name and in the German principalities his was a respectable calling. On the Continent, life for musicians was well ordered and closely regulated, but they had an established place in the pecking order. The local court or the larger cities kept musical establishments which provided good, usually well-paid employment. There were annoyances and frustrations to be sure. Johann Sebastian Bach had constant battles with the town council in Leipzig; one of his sons, Carl Philipp Emanuel, did not enjoy his time at the court of King Frederick in Berlin, and decided to leave and take up the job of director of church music in Hamburg. For those who never achieved any fame, it was a life of drudgery writing music to order in some obscure court far from the pleasures and excitements of the great musical centres such as Paris, Rome, Naples or Vienna. Yet they did not starve, nor were they made to feel insecure. The great Joseph Haydn served his princely masters for over thirty years. In England, unless he achieved fame on a level with Handel or Bach, Johann Samuel Schroeter would always be made to feel that he was an outsider and an inferior being. As a mere music teacher he knew and had had to accept that he was considered a person of suspect morals, and was seen by many as of the servant class. Moreover, in London music was a cut-throat profession. There were too many talented musicians stepping eagerly off every cross-Channel boat determined to make their names and reap the financial harvest that English fame would bring. New talent with new ideas kept coming up, and the careers of many good musicians could suddenly nosedive. The London public was fickle.

Schroeter was well prepared. He was born into a family of professional musicians in 1750, or 1751, which makes him about the same age as Rebecca. His birth certificate has never been found, testimony to the peripatetic life his family led. Whereas Rebecca had spent the first thirteen years in one place, and the following eleven years in another, the Schroeter family seem to have been among the most itinerant of Continental musicians. Johann Samuel's father, Johann Friedrich, was an oboist in the service of Augustus III, Elector of Saxony and King of Poland. Johann's older sister, Corona, was a fine singer. She was also famous for her beauty. She certainly captured Goethe's heart when they met in Leipzig and he invited her to Weimar where she became a star performer in the court theatre group run so enthusiastically by the Duchess Amalia. There are some portraits of Corona and, if there is any family likeness, her brother must have been a very handsome man. In a biography of the Duchess Amalia[1]

[1] Frances, Gerard, *A Grand Duchess and her Court*, P. Dutton & Co., 1902.

we are told that 'Corona's beauty lay principally in her Junoesque figure and wonderful grace ... she sang exquisitely ... on stage her walk and every motion was full of grace'. The few hints that we have about her brother's performances suggest that he shared many of these attributes. Of his other siblings we know little. Heinrich was a composer and violinist; his youngest sister, Marie Henriette, was a singer. Johann Samuel was also a singer until his voice broke. It is said he gave his first piano recital in 1767.

Johann Friedrich Schroeter, who was born in 1724, promoted his four children as 'child prodigies' à la Mozart. He was a teacher of the old school, believing that if you spared the rod the child would never learn. There is a report, thought to be written by Dr Burney, that Schroeter's father beat his eldest son, who was the most talented, and starved him to force him to practise. 'The discipline of Germany is almost as severe in musical as in military movements and the elder Schroeter was a martinet of very terrific abilities. By virtue of hunger and hard blows he compelled his son to practise for several years without intermission eight hours a day.'[2] This report says, too, that young Johann had some lessons from C. P. E. Bach when the family were in Berlin. Johann Samuel also took lessons from Johann Adam Hiller, a recognised master in the art of singing and a very respected musical figure in Leipzig, where he founded a singing school, was musical director of two churches and conductor of the Gewandhaus concerts. Corona took singing lessons from Hiller as well. Whatever criticism we may have of the father's methods, he at least made sure that his children had some of the best training available, introducing them to important figures in German music.

Like many other musicians, Schroeter's father decided that the life of itinerant performers in Continental Europe would never yield enough income. So he bowed to the inevitable and set his sights on London, the undisputed mecca of music. The family landed in England early in 1772. They knew it was a huge gamble. Even the

[2] *The European Magazine and London Review,* 1788, vol. xiv.

undoubted genius of Wolfgang Amadeus Mozart had not secured enough wealthy patrons when he and his father had visited England less than a decade before. The Mozart children had even been invited to play before the King and Queen, yet still they struggled really to make their mark. They stayed eighteen months in London before going back home to Salzburg.

The main challenge for any visitor to London at the time was the high cost of living. London was by far the largest and richest metropolis in Europe. It was spreading out in all directions swallowing up small villages on its edges. From all over the country hopefuls went there to find work and make a future for themselves. Too often the peasants ended up in drudgery living in desperate slums. There was noise, and filth, and danger in the streets. It was also an unhealthy place to live – the Mozarts had to postpone a number of concerts because one or other of the family had bad colds. Those who could afford it left town in the summer to regain their health in the clean fresh air of the English countryside. There was rudimentary plumbing in the houses, many thrown up by property speculators making money out of an almost constant building boom. If it was tough for the natives, it was even harder for the foreign visitor. Continental Europe was still a collection of relatively compact towns and cities. Mozart's home town of Salzburg was a small city state, where the Prince-Archbishop Hieronymous Colloredo controlled a narrow system of patronage. He decided which musicians were welcome and which were not. It is this man who literally had Mozart kicked out of his palace because the self-aware young upstart refused to accept his lowly position in the household. Later Mozart recalled, 'There was no stimulus for my talent. When I played, or when any of my compositions were performed, it was just as if the audience were all tables and chairs.' It was because of such indifference that eighteenth-century composers studied hard what kind of musical sound had what kind of effect on an audience. Haydn and Mozart in their letters often talk about how the audience reacted. Haydn, especially, was keen on little musical jokes, sudden pauses, and in one celebrated case a drum roll to wake up the gentlemen in the concert hall who arrived late after a good dinner and a bottle or two of port, and had gone soundly to sleep.

In London the choice of patron was huge. The audiences were becoming increasingly discerning and therefore demanding. Even so, the visitor needed some good advice about whom he should flatter and whom he should avoid. Private concerts were a good source of income where the fashionable gathered to hear amateurs and professionals. Fanny Burney writes in her diary that 'on Thursday morning we went to a delightful concert at Mr Harris's. The sweet Rauzzini was there and sung four duets with Miss Louisa Harris.' Today we can only try to imagine the special sound of the castrato voice. It has been described as a woman's voice, but with male lungs. The top-class castrato could hold notes for a minute or more, we are told. Young Louisa Harris must have seemed a very small voice in comparison. There is no way of knowing how much Rauzzini must have held his own voice in check, so that his young singing partner was not swamped. Fanny Burney tells us that they sang four duets together. The Harris family, though, were paying, so Rauzzini did as he was bid. Mixing professionals with amateurs was sometimes called 'stiffening', in that the talent of the professional hid the wayward abilities of the enthusiastic amateur. It was not something the professionals really enjoyed. They much preferred showing off their talent to their admirers alone without having to hold back and match the hesitant notes of the society belle. Nevertheless it was a source of income. Leopold Mozart, with his eye always on the main chance, wrote in 1764, 'During the coming months I shall have to use every effort to win over the aristocracy and this will take a lot of galloping round and hard work. But if I achieve the object which I have set myself, I shall haul in a fine fish or rather a good catch of guineas.'

The high cost of living meant that unless a person began to make money quickly, the price of food and lodgings would soon run away with his savings. As London spread out, so carriages were needed to call on the houses of the fashionable. And clothes would be needed, because the musician had to make a good impression. The wealth of the aristocracy, plus the new fortunes being made by merchants, such as Rebecca's family, meant that performing fees for a musician in demand were unimaginable to most foreign visitors. If the musician could break in, he not only recovered his investment but made a handsome profit as well. Many tried, but relatively few died wealthy. The same inflexible rule applied to home-grown talent as well. In 1772, when the Schroeters arrived in Britain, the career of the colourful Mrs Teresa Cornelys came to a sudden halt. She was declared bankrupt and twenty years later she would die destitute in Fleet Prison. She was a prime example of how even the most successful promoter could fall victim to the whims of the 'mode' overnight. Where once she had been able to command attendance at her sumptuous Soho Square house, her former patrons began increasingly to frequent the Pantheon, a much more magnificent and purpose-built concert venue that had been opened in Oxford Street. Monday night concerts there during the season soon became the fixed attraction for the cream of society.

By the late 1760s Johann Christian Bach and Friedrich Abel had severed their connection with Mrs Cornelys. They now organised their concerts, on Wednesday evenings, in another venue. Bach would be in charge one week and Abel the next. Organising weekly concerts during the winter months created a huge demand for new talent, as well as regular employment for those musicians who found favour with the ever expanding audience for music. Without the right connections the Schroeters would have found it all but impossible to break into London's musical world. Happily Schroeter *père* had already met Bach and Abel, and he managed to persuade them to give the newly arrived family a chance to win over the critical and often very partisan London audience. Under their auspices, Johann Samuel and Corona made their London debut on Saturday, 2 May 1772 at the Thatched House Tavern. It was not a bad venue to be given for one's first concert. It was in St James's Street, in the middle of town. It was well known and had a wide and quite wealthy clientele. Until the Hanover Square Rooms were built for Bach and Abel it was one of the best places to play. Bach and Abel set about promoting their new attractions with advertisements in the London press. The

Gazetteer and New Daily Advertiser proclaimed the 'grand concert of vocal and instrumental music was under the direction of Messrs Bach and Abel'. Apart from Schroeter's father, young brother and older sister, the bill also featured Johann Baptist Wendling, a leading flautist from Mannheim. Mannheim boasted an orchestra famous for its sound. One critic said of the members of the band, 'they are all generals'. What was especially admired were the huge crescendi and delicate diminuendi. Audiences were said to be in awe of the great rising of sound and then moved almost to tears when the music slipped away to silence. According to musical writers of the time, no other band could quite reproduce such dramatic or delicate sounds. Famous Mannheim players like Wendling, therefore, were in great demand as visiting star attractions in European concert halls. Completing the bill was Johann Christian Fischer, the oboist. All these names were to play a crucial part in the musical life of the English capital over the next few years – and the fact that the Schroeter family was invited to make music with them would have seemed a very good omen.

Five days after the Schroeters' debut concert at the Thatched House Tavern, Bach and Wendling left for Mannheim where Bach planned to produce an opera for Elector Karl Theodore. Abel went off to Paris – a typical set of travels in the lives of leading musicians of the day. Schroeter was left somewhat to his own devices in those first few months. It had not been the most successful of concerts – hardly noticed by the newspapers and not that well attended. But it helped in two ways. If the German community in London looked out for its own, so too did the Scottish community. Like the Germans they had come in search of fortune and not a little fame. It was Scottish immigrant William Macall, who had established Almack's, one of the leading clubs of the age, who owned the Thatched House Tavern. It was probably through Macall that Schroeter met the music publisher William Napier, another Scottish immigrant, who was taken enough by Schroeter's talent both as a performer and as a composer to offer to publish some of his music. Napier was a recent arrival, too, in town. He had set up his shop at 474 The Strand, at the corner with Leicester Court. As so often happened in those days, it was a case of one newcomer taking a risk on another newcomer. The hope was that both might prosper. But it was quite a risk Napier was taking. Schroeter was not in the words of one writer 'marketable'. He was newly arrived in England and knew relatively few people – save in the German community. One wonders whether he could speak English, or whether he had a thick accent such as Handel and Bach both retained after many years living and working in the English capital.

The young pianist was chronically short of money, living hand to mouth in an expensive foreign city, and needed all the help he could get. He approached Count von Brühl, the Hanoverian ambassador, for help. Johann's father had served as a military musician in Brühl's regiment. It was a case of *noblesse oblige*, and the ambassador pulled a few strings and Johann was appointed organist in the German chapel. Playing church music was not the quickest way to gain public notice, but it did pay a few guineas.

To augment his income Schroeter, like so many musicians, was forced to give lessons. At least, now that he was a published composer, he had a small reputation to help him. One of the first pupils to study with him was Charlotte Albert who later married Christopher Papendieck, a court oboist in the employ of Queen Charlotte. Schroeter, she tells us, charged the standard half a guinea per lesson. Writing half a century later, her memories suggest she was obviously smitten by the musician. He was, needless to say, a presentable young man – well dressed, well mannered and suitably obsequious when the occasion demanded. Against him was his youth. In some of the advice books to the gentry it was recommended to employ much older and usually married men to teach the young – it was a lot safer that way. Marketable or not, Schroeter managed to gain a few pupils – and it was probably through Napier's Scottish connections that he was employed by the Scott family.

The Scots, like the Germans in London, were clannish, but not exclusively so. They helped each other whenever they could, but they also recognised that a successful career meant getting on well with everyone within one's social sphere. William Napier, his publisher, was Scottish and would be known by many of his compatriots. The piano maker John Broadwood was also Scottish. Then there is the sociable banker James Coutts who invited a wide range of people to his table: Boswell writes in his diary of a jovial dinner with Coutts where there was 'good Scottish company'. Coutts, with his links between the worlds of commerce and the arts, could well have provided the final push that made Schroeter seem the right man for the job with the Scott family. All we know is the cautious Scott would not have accepted Johann Samuel as a tutor unless he came highly recommended.

Appointing a music master for one's wife, daughter or sister was a very chancy business in those days. The young woman's reputation was paramount. There must not be a whiff of scandal. One of the first considerations was a man's standing as a musician; the better known the musician, the better for one's reputation. Naturally, being better known put up the cost of the lessons. More important by far than musical skill was that he had to be a man you could trust. After all, he would be in a position of some intimacy with the female members of the family. These were innocent women, it was believed, sheltered from the harsh realities of the outside world. It was a very real concern – and one that had been in existence for a good many years. There are so many stories[3] of young women allegedly seduced by their music teachers, as shown in popular prints, books and plays.

A fairly typical – albeit fictional – tale is that concerning Mr Woodcock in a play called *Tunbridge Wells*. Mr Woodcock worries that his daughter is becoming what he calls a 'town lady'. 'First she's sent to dancing school, where she's led about the room by a smooth faced fellow. Squeezed by the hand and debauched before she comes into her teens. I'll be sworn dancing masters, singing masters and such followers of the women make greater havoc among maiden-heads in London, than the Germans did among the fine fiddles at the battle of

---

[3] Richard Leppart, in his excellent study of music and class in Britain (*Music and Image*, Cambridge University Press).

Cremona.' It is a wonder that any young woman ever had a music teacher, given their reputation as seducers of the flower of England's girlhood.

Schroeter must have had something about him that both attracted students and reassured their parents. Everyone who wrote about his playing remarked on its special quality and style. William Napier certainly thought that he was worth signing up. Within five days of the concert Napier was offering six sonatas for the harpsichord or pianoforte, with accompaniments, composed by Schroeter. The price was 10s 6d, or half a guinea. Significantly, one of the works was 'most humbly dedicated' to 'Miss Scott' and is dated 1772, according to the British Library. And Napier even took space in the *Public Advertiser* to let the public know the name of his new 'star' musician. Perhaps Rebecca had been at that concert with Frances Coutts or other friends and decided that the languid, rather romantic-sounding Schroeter was the man she wanted for her teacher.

Meanwhile J. C. Bach's trip to Mannheim did not turn out as he had expected, no job was offered and he was thwarted in a love affair – so he was back in London early in 1773 and began to organise his next series of concerts. He had not forgotten the young pianist who had featured in the last concert of the previous year's season. It was through Bach that Schroeter had met the Papendieck family. Charlotte Papendieck is well known to historians of the period for her memoirs of court and private life in the second half of the eighteenth century. Mrs Papendieck's jottings are not always as accurate as the fastidious researcher would like – but they are full of gossip and personal reflections of the men and manners of the period. The problem with them is that they were scribbled down in barely legible handwriting some fifty years after the events: an old woman, looking back through rose-tinted glasses at the triumphs and excitements of her youth. After Charlotte Albert married Christopher Papendieck, she and her husband had become close to Bach, not least because he was Master of the Queen's Music. Bach was often at their house, improvising on the piano, even giving the occasional lesson.

Papendieck, Abel, Cramer, Fischer and Bach all played in the

Queen's Band. And they were kept pretty busy because the Queen gave unofficial concerts on Tuesdays and Thursdays. Anywhere between 200 and 300 people were invited to hear the music and play cards. Often visiting musicians could be co-opted – and Schroeter must have been invited to play from time to time. Bach's preference for the pianoforte and his standing in the musical public's affection had by now made this relatively new instrument one of the most popular of the age. Schroeter's manifest abilities on the instrument are what attracted Bach's attention and he quickly recognised in young Schroeter a future master of the pianoforte. The ease with which he played, the way he seemed gently to caress the keys, combined to produce sounds and performances that stunned his audiences.

The piano's more expressive sound qualities, and the possibilities it offered to composers to explore new sonorities, soon attracted the attention of the younger generation of musicians. Schroeter certainly made his mark: the all too brief references to him talk of a handsome young man who made the act of playing so natural that the melodies seemed to arrive fully formed from his imagination while he was at the keyboard. At the time it was called the 'singing allegro' style of playing. However, good as he was, he would also soon face some fierce competition from the newer generation. There was, by now, a young man who would take over from him as the public's favourite. He was Muzio Clementi who was about the same age as Schroeter. Born in Rome, at the age of fourteen he was bought from his father by a rich Englishman, Peter Beckford, and taken to live in Dorset as the in-house musician. He finally got his freedom in 1774 when he moved to London and became conductor at the King's Theatre. Ominously for Schroeter, his skill at the piano was already beginning to attract audiences.

For the moment Schroeter's star was rising. In 1774 Napier published his Opus 3 – six concertos for the pianoforte with an accompaniment for two violins and a bass. Paul Angerer and the Concilium Musicum Wien[4] have recorded them on authentic instruments,

[4] The CD is number 3–1242–2 on an Austrian label, Koch. Issued in 1994.

including an early fortepiano of the type that Schroeter would have recognised. Angerer talks about its 'clear silvery tone, which still resembles the harpsichord'. There is a faster version of just one of Schroeter's concertos Opus 3, number 3, played by Murray Perahia on the Sony Label. It's two minutes shorter than Angerer's version. The slower Angerer treatment seems to match the few descriptions of Schroeter's languid style of playing. W. T. Parke, the principal oboist at the Theatre Royal, Covent Garden, wrote in his *Musical Memoirs* that Schroeter's 'execution was neat ... he played in so graceful and quiet a manner, that his fingers were scarcely seen to move'. The great Dr Burney used the word 'natural' to describe his playing. The concertos in Opus 3 certainly impressed one young contemporary. He was none other than Wolfgang Amadeus Mozart. At the time young Mozart was largely seen as a virtuoso player rather than the genius of a composer that he is considered today. He thought the music 'beautiful', a rare compliment from him to another composer. Opus 3 was published in Paris in 1775, the year of Schroeter's marriage and had quite a widespread circulation. The music is to be found, for example, among the papers of Lord Nelson's great love, Emma Hamilton, after her death.

Bach had a good eye for talent and was obviously right about his young German compatriot. 'Schroeter', Charlotte Papendieck recalled, 'was brought forward as the new performer on the pianoforte.' Bach, Mrs Papendieck went on, 'perceived [Schroeter's] excellence, and assisted him as a friend, for his heart was too good to know the littleness of envy. He gave Schroeter advice from his experience of the country, and was also of great use to him in the theory of his profession. He loved him almost as a son, and deploring that his disposition was such as must, in the end work to his bane.'

Johann Samuel Schroeter – John, as his English contemporaries called him – is a most elusive figure. There is no portrait; there are only a few examples of his handwriting. The first is his signature on his marriage certificate; the last a very shaky signature when, near death, he signed his will. There are no letters. No one quotes a memorable phrase he used. There are only scanty clues as to what he was really like. His obituary in the *Gentleman's Magazine* described him as a man 'distinguished for good sense, varied information and mild unassuming manners'. So far extensive research has failed to track down any portrait or silhouette purporting to be Schroeter. Only the likeness of his sister Corona gives any idea as to family features. She was considered beautiful and the writer Schiller, like Goethe, seems to have fallen a little in love with her. 'Even into her fifties', he wrote, 'she retained her looks.'

It is to Schroeter's music that one must turn to get any idea of the object of Rebecca's passion. The musicologist Konrad Wolff wrote one of the very few learned essays on Schroeter.[5] Wolff deduces quite a lot from Schroeter's music.

For an artist as honest, as intelligent, and as gifted as he was – his music testifies to all that – it must indeed have been tragedy to realise that despite the vitality, seriousness, directness, crispness and sensuousness of his scores, he was excluded from the great happenings in music, and his efforts were doomed to remain outside the main stream in these epoch making years. Hence the 'languor' mentioned by Burney as distinguishing both his music and his looks, and hence the depressiveness which paradoxically enough, now constitutes the most appealing, individual and human element in Johann Samuel Schroeter's music.

He was the type of man who, perhaps, would appeal to a romantically inclined young heiress. If this 'languor' was so dominant a feature, had she made the entire running? Like Rebecca, he had few friends and no family near to whom he could turn for advice as he contemplated his life up to meeting Rebecca and his future with her. If her family now refused the dowry, he had barely enough to live on his own, let alone keep a young wife who was used to the best that money could buy. If word got out that he had run off with an heiress, he might even lose the few teaching jobs he had. His only friends

[5] The *Musical Quarterly,* vol. 44, 1958.

were other foreign musicians – not best placed to offer advice or counsel about marriage with an English lady. Even a good friend, William Lindeman, who was one of the two licensed curates at the German chapel and had agreed to be a witness at the wedding, was not sure whether he, as a man of the cloth, really approved of secret marriages.

Furthermore, Schroeter could not embark on the marriage without some considerable practical effort on his part. As the groom he had to make all the arrangements. He may have agreed them with Rebecca, but he had to fix the time and place to be married. More important, he had to apply for a common licence. He had posted a bond for £200 when he applied for the special licence the previous day at the Faculty Office in Knight Rider Street near St Paul's. Whether he had walked there from Duke Street in Westminster, or gone by chair, the trip would have taken a couple of hours out of his day alone, plus the time while the clerk laboriously wrote out the licence by hand in good copperplate. All official matters proceeded at the speed of the clerk's handwriting. He had to make what was called an 'allegation', a sworn statement that what he said was true. He also named the church where the ceremony was to be performed – St Martin-in-the-Fields, Rebecca's parish church while she lived with her sister in London. There is a copy of his allegation in the records kept at Lambeth Palace. Schroeter signed in a rather childish hand – as if he was still learning the letters of the alphabet. Applying for a common licence was the accepted way for couples to wed who did not want any publicity and wished to do it quickly. The licence allowed them to marry without any banns being read in church over three previous weeks. He would hand the licence to the curate, John Justamond, when he arrived at St Martin-in-the-Fields. The £200 bond that Schroeter had signed was a surety that he was telling the truth. He states that both he and Rebecca were at least twenty-four years of age and therefore free to marry – and it was a sizeable sum indeed in those days. It would have been a very irresponsible young man who lied with that kind of debt hanging over him. Uncertain of English law, he no doubt hoped and prayed that nothing would cause him to have to honour the bond. He would probably have ended up in debtors' prison.

So was it love of Rebecca or love of her money that found him waiting for a coach to take him to his wedding early upon Saturday morning? Perhaps it was a judicious mixture of the two. Love was something women talked and dreamed of, and hoped to marry for. Men saw the world as a pretty unforgiving place, if a person had no wealth or position to shield them from the economic pressures of life. There is no reason, of course, why a couple could not have both love and money. To quote that aristocratic cynic, Lord Chesterfield, whose advice to his son was, 'If you marry for money . . . let the woman at least be such a one that you can live decently and amicably with, otherwise it is robbery.'

Yet young Johann Samuel Schroeter seemed to be at the beginning of a fine career in music and was marrying into a rich family. The day before at the Faculty Office in Knight Rider Street he had sworn that 'he, this deponent not knowing or believing any lawful let or impediment by reason of any pre-contract, consanguinity, affinity, or any other lawful means whatsoever to hinder the said intended marriage prayed a licence to solemnise the said marriage in the church of St Martin-in-the-Fields aforesaid'. And he had signed himself 'John Samuel Schroeter of the Parish of St Martin-in-the-Fields in the County of Middlesex, Musick Master'. The licence is still filed away in the Library of Lambeth Palace to this day.

CHAPTER FOUR
A Secret Wedding

The distance between Bedford Row and St Martin-in-the-Fields is not much more than a mile as the crow flies. Unfortunately, the young couple had to travel on the ground, where the narrow and congested streets of Hanoverian London made such a journey tortuous, even dangerous. On Friday a steady downpour had thoroughly soaked the capital. Nearly an inch of rain had fallen, muddying the streets, and causing minor flooding as the rudimentary and often choked watercourses struggled to cope. That Saturday morning it looked as if more rain was in the offing. Even if the weather had been fine and dry, it would be difficult to know exactly how long such a trip could take. One of the biggest hazards to life and limb was losing a wheel, turning over the carriage and everyone with it. Often the way was simply blocked. For example, a crowd might have gathered to watch a fierce altercation between two burly characters whose job was to carry sedan chairs. These chairmen, as they were called, were notoriously pugnacious, loudly claiming the right of way in some tight street. Unless you were a wealthy person of quality who had footmen forcibly to clear the way ahead, it could take an hour or more to cover the distance between Bedford Row and the church. As a precaution, the young lovers had left early to give themselves plenty of time.

Even at that hour London was already awake, noisy and bustling, as coaches, chairs, wagons, horses and people jostled for space. The hardy street vendors were crying their wares, adding to the din of the early morning commotion. London was one of the noisiest cities on earth. It was also one of the dirtiest. Human and animal waste was everywhere, with dogs and cats scavenging for what they could. There were potholes to contend with. With solid wheels and little in the way of suspension, it meant a bone-shaking ride, before Rebecca and Johann were finally deposited at St Martin-in-the-Fields. Despite its name, the church no longer looked out over fields. It was surrounded on all sides by buildings but it would be another sixty years before the modern Trafalgar Square was created, complete with Admiral Nelson's column. The church front was opposite what was then called the King's Mews, at the bottom of St Martin's Lane.

In 1775 the church was just fifty years old. Appropriately enough, given Rebecca's background, a fellow Scot, James Gibb, had designed it. The building stood on the site of a former Tudor church, which had indeed once been surrounded by fields. It was already an important church. One of the first churchwardens had been King George I and the royal family still had their own box. St Martin's has not changed much down the centuries. Rebecca would still recognise it today – from the elaborately decorated ceiling to the ornate, high-sided pews. Lit only by candles in the early morning, it would have seemed a solemn place for such a happy event. The solid walls, with the high windows and the inner doors, all combined to deaden the noise in the streets outside. Given such a central location in the heart of London, St Martin's is not the sort of church one would normally associate with a secret wedding.

The licensed curate on marriage duty that Saturday morning was John Justamond, a graduate of Clare College, Cambridge and a man of Huguenot descent who could well understand the feelings of a foreigner such as Schroeter. The Huguenots were Protestants. But they were still seen as foreigners in the fiercely sectarian England of the time, even though they had settled in the country over a century before. The first task after the curate arrived at the church was to enter the names of the couples to be married that day in the register. Justamond had a very neat hand. His script is beautifully proportioned and easy on the eye. He had read mathematics for his first degree and his brother, Obadiah, was a scientist who translated a number of technical works from the French. The family obviously shared a common trait for precision and neatness of expression. The first entry for 15 July reads 'John Samuel Schroeter of this Parish and Rebecca Scott of the Parish of St Andrews Holborn were married in this Church by LAB this fifteenth day of July 1775 by me ...' Then he added, 'This marriage was then solemnised between us in the presence of us ...' The necessary spaces were left blank to be filled in later. There was one other couple to be married that morning: John Saywell and Mary Dyke, who were also in a hurry to marry. They too, according to the record, were to be married by licence of the Archbishop like the Schroeters.

As they went into the church, Rebecca and Schroeter came across a cleaning lady. She was busy sweeping the pews of the dust and the mud brought in by visitors and worshippers alike, despite the double set of doors. It was an endless task, for no sooner had she finished one part of the church than she went back and began all over again. The job paid a pittance, but at least she was warm and dry. She also acted as an unpaid guide to visitors. The old lady pointed them in the direction of the vestry where the Reverend Justamond was waiting for them.

Back at the house in Bedford Row Fanny, the maid, had raised the alarm and told the Master that Miss Rebecca had left the house early in the morning and got into a gentleman's coach. The maid told her master she had recognised the man – he was Miss Rebecca's music teacher. Charles Murray, who had been asleep, dressed as quickly as he could. He had all the servants assembled. He asked each of them in turn if they knew why Miss Rebecca would be leaving the house this early. Some may have guessed immediately that she had run away to be married. They all denied any knowledge. To be suspected of involvement in a family scandal of course risked instant dismissal without references, which would make it all but impossible to find similar work again. The presence of servants about the house was taken for granted and usually ignored by their employers. Servants always paid close attention to what their betters were up to. It helped them do the job and gave them something to gossip about. They missed very little and were adept at reading the signs of, say, an illicit love affair. Servants tended not to trumpet the news. Some, though, might manage to win a few bribes from their betters to keep their secrets. In the end, Charles Murray was given little choice but to conclude that it must be an elopement. He was *in loco parentis* and he now had to face the worrying possibility that he might be seen as in some way colluding with Rebecca. Worse was the fact that his in-laws might well see him as an accessory to the deed. Rebecca was under his roof and he was, as the man of the house. It was as important to his reputation and position in the family as care for Rebecca that he should pursue the couple and stop a marriage that could have a dramatic impact on all their lives.

Murray could have deduced that, if it was a secret marriage Rebecca was embarked upon, it was by special licence, since no banns had been read anywhere. In gossipy London such news would have travelled very fast and over three weeks someone would have passed on the information. He knew that Schroeter lived in Duke Street in the parish of St Martin's, so it would be very likely that it would be that church to which the couple had gone. Rebecca would not be known there. Whereas Bedford Row was in the parish of St Andrew Holborn where she would have worshipped every Sunday with the Murrays and where she would have been recognised immediately by the curate had she gone there to be married. When Murray later told the story of what happened next he was partial in the extreme. He says Schroeter was 'a foreigner' who had 'deluded' a 'young lady of fashion', his social superior whom he had 'carried off' against her family's wishes. Murray says Rebecca's family had been among 'the first to employ him' and did not deserve such treatment.

The events of 15 July can be reconstructed quite accurately because the whole affair led to a protracted legal battle being fought out in the Court of Chancery. Over a period of three years, legal clerks copied out the sworn evidence given by the main protagonists. After stripping out the legal verbiage, this is what is known of the sequence of events from the moment Rebecca left her brother-in-law's house in Bedford Row and went by carriage with Schroeter to St Martin-in-the-Fields. After questioning the servants Murray ordered his coach and hastened after them. At the church he met a cleaning woman and demanded to know whether a 'young lady of fashion' had arrived with a foreigner 'intending to marry'. The cleaner showed him the chapel where the weddings took place. Murray rushed in and demanded that the ceremony stop immediately. He informed the Reverend Justamond that Rebecca and Schroeter could not be married, because Rebecca was under age. Justamond would have found this claim difficult to believe. At the age of twenty-four Rebecca would obviously have looked of an age to marry. There was not only the evidence of his eyes; he had Schroeter's sworn allegation to that fact. Murray was obviously an important person and seemingly not the kind of man who would deliberately tell an untruth in God's Holy Church. Justamond nevertheless asked for proof of age. Murray, playing for time, said he needed to fetch the requisite document that would prove his assertion. Despite a vehement rebuttal by Rebecca and Johann that Murray's claims were untrue, the startled curate agreed to delay the wedding from eight until eleven o'clock. In the seven years that he had been a curate in St Martin's, nothing like this had ever happened before.

Rebecca and Johann did not want the delay, but they knew that the proof that Murray claimed to be able to produce did not exist. Murray decided too much was at stake for him to shoulder all the responsibility of stopping the marriage and sent for John Pringle, a family friend, who lived round the corner in St Martin's Lane. Pringle arrived at the church within the hour. He and Murray between them managed to persuade the couple that a delay was in everyone's interests. The second couple waiting for Mr Justamond to marry them that morning, John Saywell and Mary Dyke, must have watched in amazement as these events unfolded. They might well have believed they were in the theatre not a church. Finally, after some heated exchanges, Rebecca and Johann agreed to leave the church and go to her brother's house in Wimpole Street. Rebecca insisted on one condition: that she and her husband-to-be must stay together.

Meanwhile another emissary arrived at number 25 Wimpole Street to inform Robert Scott what had been happening. Rebecca's brother was beside himself with anger. He sent for his mother to be brought from Blackheath eight miles away. Throughout the day the clan began to gather to try en masse to persuade Rebecca to give up any idea of marrying 'the foreigner'. Robert's plan seems to have been to divide the couple, so that he could rule his sister the better. So a second lie emerged in this family fight. Rebecca and Johann Samuel only agreed to go to her brother's house if they could stay together. Once there, Robert reneged and Schroeter was told to leave. For the rest of the day Rebecca kept to her room, determined to marry Schroeter whatever they might say or do.

On Sunday there was a huge family gathering. Rebecca must have felt as if she were the accused in the Star Chamber. The family were both judges and jury. There was Rebecca's mother, Elizabeth, her sister and brother-in-law, and an aunt, Sarah Manson, her mother's sister. Apart from close family Robert Scott had called in Thomas Cheap, the former consul in Madeira and a partner in business to both the Scotts and the Murrays. It was a powerful coalition in opposition to the marriage. Robert must have believed that his young sister – a well-brought-up young woman who was expected to be obedient and dutiful – would not be able to hold out for very long. At any one time an isolated Rebecca could have faced half a dozen implacable opponents. Robert had underestimated his sister's courage and determination. As a man of his time, he no doubt believed that his word was law within his family. Rebecca repulsed all attacks and stood fast. There were tears, there were raised voices and there was violent argument. The servants, listening at the doors, would have had much to gossip about with their friends when they saw them. And they, too, probably took sides.

The Scott family found Schroeter completely and utterly unaccept-able as a future relative by marriage. When Rebecca repeated time and again that she would marry Mr Schroeter and would not budge, the family became desperate. Her mother even suggested that her daughter could love Schroeter, but that she did not need to marry him. 'Why will you not live single?' she was asked. For a God-fearing and respectable family this was a most unusual offer indeed. It seems tantamount to encouraging their wayward daughter to have an affair. The family obviously thought this 'love' she claimed to have for Schroeter would pass. Given that a woman's reputation was so crucial to her position in society, if such a relationship became public knowledge, and it was realised that the family had condoned it, the damage to everyone's reputation would have been huge.

A love affair, they must have persuaded themselves, meant that she could still marry if the right kind of suitor for a woman of her rank made his appearance. Rebecca, they believed passionately, should be marrying 'a man whose birth, education and employment gave him rank as gentleman'. Rebecca was not interested in all that. She argued that Schroeter was a fine man and esteemed in his profession. The family tried another tack. Schroeter, they said, using another potent argument, was a Catholic. This was yet another lie. Rebecca dismissed the suggestion and repeated her determination to marry him. When the meanness of his profession, his alleged Catholic faith, his German nationality and his low birth did not shift her, the family deployed the ultimate weapon in their armoury – money. Time and again they pointed out that they, as executors, must give consent; otherwise she would forfeit her dowry. Rebecca said she did not care about that. All she cared about was Schroeter: She declared, like a heroine from a romantic novel, 'I love no man on earth so much as Mr Schroeter.' When British chauvinism allied to religious intolerance and threats about future poverty all failed to persuade Rebecca to give him up, the desperate family fell back on bribes. They offered to buy Schroeter off with £500 and, should he marry someone else, promised to help him set up home. He scornfully rejected the offer out of hand.

Schroeter, to his credit, did not leave Rebecca to face the foe alone. In a show of equal determination he went back to Wimpole Street again on Sunday afternoon. Although the servants had been instructed to refuse him entry, he managed to get past a footman and went to a downstairs parlour. Rebecca, hearing of his arrival, immediately ran downstairs to join him. When brother Robert was told that they were together his temper got the better of him. He rushed into the room, pulled Rebecca from Schroeter's protective arms and physically carried his sister away. Shaken, maybe bruised by the force of the physical attack, Rebecca still refused to submit. If anything, the assault made her even more determined.

The family's despair is understandable. Having worked hard to rise in the world and to become fully assimilated into English polite society – along the way losing their Scottish accents together with their Scottish acres – here was the youngest daughter throwing it all away because of some sentimental reason she called 'love'. The family's extreme anxiety about the marriage pushed them to involve outsiders. They prided themselves on knowing the world. They understood profit and loss. They could calculate commercial risk to the last farthing. But 'love', whatever that was, was an unknown quantity. To the end the family believed rational argument allied to the power of money would carry the day.

They sent Charles Murray to see Schroeter again. Murray was a man used to difficult diplomacy – having got used to dealing with prickly Portuguese government officials on Madeira. His experience there could hardly have prepared him for the events of this kind of mission. Schroeter was still with his music publisher William Napier at his shop in the Strand. Murray offered money, but Schroeter would not listen. Murray tried to involve Napier in the argument, but the publisher wisely refused. Meanwhile Robert sent for Rebecca's close friend, Frances Coutts, herself a future heiress, but she was not at home. The arguments seemed finally to have run their course. Neither side had shifted at all. Finally exhausted, drained by all the emotional turmoil of the weekend, the family agreed that they would not physically prevent Rebecca from leaving the house on Monday morning, knowing that she was to be married. Rebecca obstinately stood her ground through all of this. The more the family elders ganged up, the more they protested, the more it served to strengthen the determination of the young woman to go through with her plans. Rebecca's resistance became heroic. As she had read often in her favourite romantic novels, all true heroines have remarkable strength of will – otherwise how could they have survived the cruel world and come through to peace and happiness with the man they truly loved and who truly loved them?

Monday morning was bright and sunny as Rebecca stole away from her brother's house in Wimpole Street. Did the rest of the family see her go, or had she already been dismissed as a member? The turmoil of that weekend has left its own small mark in the Marriage Register of St Martin-in-the-Fields. There are two entries. The first, dated 15 July 1775, reads, 'John Samuel Schroeter of this Parish and Rebecca Scott of the Parish of St Andrew Holborn were married in this church by LAB this fifteenth day of July 1775 [name of curate left blank]. This marriage was then solemnised between us.' However, there are no signatures, neither from the two witnesses, nor the young couple, nor Mr Justamond. There are just three straight ruled lines through the entry; put there by the bemused curate as he watched the unhappy couple and their agitated relatives depart the church. Justamond probably expected never to see them again, even though Rebecca and Johann insisted that they would be back on Monday.

It was no doubt with some misgiving that the curate wrote out the marriage entry again on the 17th. They would be the last of four couples to be married that morning. When their turn came the Reverend Justamond might well have kept a close eye on the church door while Rebecca and Johann stood before him. Rebecca and John (as Justamond had named him in the entry) were finally married and their two witnesses – William Lindeman and Charles Booth – testified to the fact. Just to keep the record straight, the Reverend Justamond added under the cancelled entry for the previous Saturday, 'See folio 164 17 July 1775 when this marriage was solemnised.' Rebecca had won.

CHAPTER FIVE

The Tartan of Commerce

The wealthy middle-class world that Rebecca abandoned in July 1775 was an ordered though not always a contented one. The vast amounts of money earned in international trade by merchant families like the Scotts and the Murrays did not guarantee the social standing they craved. The *ton*, as fashionable society was called, looked down on them. One's class, then as now, was an English obsession. Any obvious attempt to achieve social status was mocked persistently in the literature and the satiric prints of the day. In her best-selling book, *Evelina or The history of a young woman's entry into the world* Fanny Burney introduces her readers to a classic of the type – the Brangton family. The book, which was published in 1778, describes a type of family that Rebecca would have known well. Mr Brangton, Fanny tells her readers, 'does not seem to want common understanding, though he is very contracted and prejudiced: he has spent his whole life in the city, and, I believe, feels a great contempt for all those who reside elsewhere'. She could well have been writing of Rebecca's late father, Robert Scott, or his son, Rebecca's brother.

Of Mr Brangton's daughter, Polly, Fanny Burney says, 'she is by no means ugly, but looks proud, ill tempered and conceited. She hates the city, though without knowing why; for it is easy to discover she has lived no where else.' Rebecca would have been proud, of that there is little doubt. She wanted to be considered a woman of the modern era, a woman of some importance. After all, she had to believe that her decision to marry was the right one, despite everyone in her closest family telling her it was not only wrong but potentially disastrous. If not outright conceited, Rebecca was certainly stubborn, which is another form of conceit. Whether she was ill-tempered there is no way of knowing, though stubbornness leads to frustration and frustration might lead to ill temper. What is certain is that Rebecca, like the fictional Polly, would certainly have had an equally restricted experience of life.

The men in her family were merchant traders and that fact more than any other explains the continuing ordeal they put Rebecca through over the next few years. Her early life was spent in one of the mean and narrow streets in the City of London – where trade and commerce ruled. She was born in Mark Lane, near the Tower. A person had to be tough to survive in the Square Mile. It was a noisome, dirty, crowded and unhealthy place. The smell of unwashed bodies and the open sewers, mingling with the odour of cooking food, assaulted the nose. The grating of metalled wheels on the cobbles, the street vendors' cries, arguments and shouted conversations created an incessant din from before first light until way after dark. It was hard to hear oneself think. Nor did the eyes escape – watering from the acrid smoke that belched from thousands of chimney pots. The City was overcrowded and a breeding ground for disease. Despite all this, it was a place where fortunes could be made by determined men who were not averse to risk and hard work.

Rebecca's father, Robert Scott, was such a man. After the Act of Union in 1707 ambitious Scots needed no longer to stay in the backwater that was their birthplace. Economically backward, Scotland, however, could boast a much better education system than England. The Scottish Church might be dour and harsh in its beliefs, but it made sure that its parishioners were well educated. Inevitably, Scotland's intelligent and well-educated young men were driven by ambition to look beyond Hadrian's Wall for a more secure and comfortable life. 'The noblest prospect in Scotland which a Scotchman ever sees', said Dr Johnson, 'is the high road that leads him to England.' The Union made them Britons and although many of them resented rule from London they took full advantage of the economic opportunities that it provided. London was the place to be. Scotland, though, was a fine training ground. Most Scots first acquired the skills needed to survive in the risky world of international trade in bustling Glasgow where there was, after 1707, a thriving tobacco trade. The individual learned the value of kinship, which was always the first consideration when going into business. He learned how to judge people. Were they sober and hard-working? Were they honest? Could they be trusted? He learned how to keep books, maintain records, to compose proper business letters. A man with ambition in those days had to know a great deal about the world and its ways, about men and matters, about ships and seafaring, and about money and book-keeping.

Some time in the 1720s, when he felt sufficiently equipped for business, Robert Scott set out on the road south, following in the footsteps of hundreds of his fellow nationals. Another Scot, Tobias Smollet, in his book *The Adventures of Roderick Random*, described his eponymous hero's journey south and the people he meets and the adventures he has on the two- to three-week journey. Throughout he encounters the anti-Scottish bias of the English. The further south he journeys, the worse the chauvinism. By the time Random and his travelling companion Strap (a barber's journeyman) reach London, they have been arrested, attacked by a highwayman, drunk too much and often not eaten enough. In London, they lose everything to a card-sharp. Random seeks a job in the Navy as an assistant surgeon. When he goes for his surgeon's ticket he is interrogated by an English surgeon in Barber-Surgeons Hall in Monkwell Street. Random is asked, '"Where was you born?"' To which question I answered "in Scotland". "In Scotland," said he, "I know that very well – we have scarce any other countrymen to examine here – you Scotchmen have overspread us of late as the locusts did in Egypt." '

Scott went not to London but even further south, to the island of Madeira. With him were his brother John, and his oldest friend and distant kinsman John Pringle. Once on the island they prospered mightily. Scott and Company became one of the biggest trading firms there by the middle of the century. According to some recently discovered port records, cited by Professor John Hancock in his book

Citizens of the World,[6] Robert Scott and his associates were responsible for some 800 different ships entering or departing Madeira between 1727 and 1771. One of their most lucrative ventures was shipping Madeira wine to Jamaica, then sugar from Jamaica back to Britain. They soon moved into tobacco from Virginia and slaves from Africa.

In 1737 Robert Scott moved back to London and left his partners in charge on the island. One of his first decisions was to marry. For a rising merchant this was a critical decision. Love rarely came into the equation. The partnership was too important to be based on such a notion. Without much hesitation Robert Scott chose John Pringle's sister Elizabeth. It was a typical move by a man of his class. There were many advantages in such a match, the most important of which was that it cemented a business relationship by effectively making the partners kinsmen as well. Equally typical was that it was a late marriage by today's standards: Scott was around forty years old and, since he knew his bride well, he was confident that she would make a good wife and mother. It must have taken a lot of adjustment for them both when they moved from balmy Madeira back to grimy London.

Once back in London, Scott's priority was to establish his own counting house. The name of the business was Pringle and Scott, reflecting both the marriage and the partnership. The 1730s saw the beginning of Britain's rise to commercial dominance around the world. Trade was following the flag. In India, Africa and the Americas new markets were all opening up. The merchants tended to deal in raw materials, foodstuffs, wines, hardware and even luxury goods. In fact, these merchants tended to ship whatever was asked of them. The one random factor that none of them could control was the danger of putting to sea – mutiny, piracy and the weather were the

[6] Cambridge University Press, 1995. This chapter would be threadbare without Professor Hancock's very detailed research into the Scottish merchants of the City of London and the lucrative trade between Europe, Africa and America, which quickly made them the equivalent of modern-day millionaires.

three great enemies of commercial enterprise. Success meant having ships full of cargo outward bound and on the return voyage.

The counting house was the centre of all merchant operations. Today we would call it the corporate headquarters. In those days the owner lived over the shop, so it was both workplace and home. It was also home to his unmarried clerks and his servants. Since Robert Scott was already a quite rich man, he could well have chosen a double-fronted house. These all followed a familiar pattern. The façade would be quite plain and would begin at the edge of the pavement – if a pavement existed in the early years. The buildings were tall and narrow, but would go back at least twice their width. There would be cellars below ground. The ground floor was where business was conducted. The front room facing out on to the street was the public room. This is where business visitors would arrive. Behind that room was the clerks' room – with massive desks and filing cabinets, and three or four young clerks. In a smaller room at the back the partners had their 'closet' or office. It usually had a fireplace and was the inner sanctum were the business visitors would be ushered in to pay their debts, receive credit, and to haggle over price and delivery dates. On the first floor were the dining room and kitchens, and usually a small library. The Scottish habit of self-improvement stayed with them all their lives. The men who were involved in these trades were great believers in education – one house belonging to an associate had nearly 400 books in the library. The family or the clerks were encouraged to learn and to read. On the third floor were the main bedrooms for the family. Finally, up in the attics were the unmarried clerks and the family servants. They would have simple beds sleeping up to four to a room.

There was little division between the staff, the servants or the family. It really was a communal life in all senses, with very little private space. Robert Scott's counting house was in Mark Lane, near the Tower, and it was here that his three children were all born. First was Rebecca's sister Elizabeth, then her brother Robert. Rebecca, the youngest, was baptised round the corner at St Olave's in Hart Street on 13 May 1751. This typical little City parish church is where Pepys and his wife worshipped and are buried. Somewhat changed, it still stands today – though the surrounding area has long since fallen prey to modern office blocks.

Rebecca spent the first thirteen years of her life in the bustling counting house. At any one time there could have been over a dozen people in residence, with her mother and father, brother, sister, plus the clerks and the servants – and no doubt a steady stream of visitors from around the globe. Robert Scott knew Benjamin Franklin when he was in London and he could well have dined here on the first floor. How much she saw of her father is difficult to measure. Like all men of affairs at the time, he would be mainly preoccupied with his business. It is doubtful he was involved that deeply in her life and upbringing – that would be her mother's responsibility. Her father's business affairs, extending to Africa, to Madeira and the Americas, would have more than filled his waking hours. Scott was always on the lookout for new business opportunities.

Scott moved into the slave trade with great success[7] and he became one of its most fervent supporters; he bought the maximum shares in the South Seas Company; he helped set up and managed a company of merchants trading to Africa to replace the bankrupt Royal African Company. He formed a partnership with an even more successful man of trade, Richard Oswald; and Scott frequently appeared before the Board of Trade to advise on questions of African policy in which he had made himself an expert. He took on more partners. For example, the new consul in Madeira, Thomas Cheap, joined Scott's group. The processes of administration, communication and transportation were slow. All the handwritten inventories, accounts and records were kept in leather-bound letter books, daybooks and registers. It could take eight weeks or more to get to America, a couple of weeks to Madeira, maybe two weeks more to go on to Africa. It was a century when sailing was still a very hit and miss affair, because one could not always be sure exactly where a ship was in the ocean.

Yet Scott seems to have handled all the challenges with great

[7] Professor John Hancock, *Citizens of the World.*

aplomb. He created a slave business on Banff Island. Then he helped make Madeira into the key staging post and a provisioning port for the slave trade to America. In America he had partners and correspondents who filled his ships for the return passage. As a Scottish immigrant, he also had to be aware of the politics of the time. He made sure that everyone knew he supported the King during the '45 uprising (a necessary precaution for a Scotsman doing business in England). He was active in City affairs too. He was a City alderman for eight years. And he was appointed Sheriff in 1750 – which marks him out as a prominent figure in City affairs.

Loyalty was the most common trait of these men and Robert Scott was not a man to desert a friend. He came to wider public notice when he joined with others and tried to secure a royal pardon for Admiral Byng, who was court-martialled for losing Minorca to the French and was subsequently executed by a firing squad of marines on his own poop deck. Byng had been stationed in Madeira for a number of years and knew the family well.

Money, of course, makes money and Scott was also a part-time banker to his friends. For example, in 1751, the year that Rebecca was born, he lent £5000 to one of his associates. That was a not inconsiderable sum in those days. A few years later he lent twice that sum to another associate.

Robert Scott was, then, a man of parts. But as a fairly typical but successful businessman, was he also a nice man and a loving father? There is a curious memoir lurking in the vaults of the British Library that talks about his brother John. If Robert was anything like him he could be both stern and unbending, uneasy in the company of women, yet generous when he wanted. This document is called *The Memoirs of Janetta* and it was written by Mrs Janetta Norweb and printed for her in 1812. She claims her father's name was Scott, 'at the time of my birth a wealthy merchant resident in Madeira. I was at that time his only child and the sole information I ever obtained to my mother was, that when my eyes opened upon this busy scene, hers closed forever.' No one seems to know how much of this is truth or fiction – but many of the details ring true. When Janetta was a year old, she says she was sent under the care of Admiral Byng, now her guardian, to stay in England. Once in England she was put in the care of Byng's sisters, the Honourable Mrs Stukely and Lady Masters, both widows without children. Janetta says her earliest recollection of Scott is that 'she rather feared than loved him; he was extremely violent in his temper and too haughty in his manners to conciliate the affection of a child; the chief portion of my regard towards him was obtained by many costly presents'. When Scott came back to England he informed Janetta's guardians that he wanted his daughter to begin her education in 'one of the principal schools in the metropolis or its neighbourhood'. Janetta was sent to Mrs Tomlinson's School together with Lady Caroline Stuart. Lady Caroline was the daughter of Lord Bute, the controversial tutor to the Prince of Wales, later George III. It is not inconceivable that Rebecca went to the same school as her alleged cousin.

Janetta prattles on about her life as a young lady of fashion, how she met Uncle Walter who had recently married the widow of a Captain Sutherland. Walter, it seems, had taken a house at Mile End Green. We do not know whether she met her cousins Rebecca or Elizabeth. She is vague about dates, but she was about five years older than Rebecca so it would have been surprising had she not met her uncle's children. As obviously well brought-up and docile daughters, they cannot have impressed her much so they weren't worth mentioning. When she was fourteen, around 1760 (Rebecca would have been nine), Janetta met her father again and was, she recalls, 'received with all the formal hauteur of an Eastern Monarch'.

This Scott, she does not give his first name, gave a ball for Janetta. She was delighted because 'dancing was my favourite amusement; and my heart beat high with anticipated delight'. Her father left the details of the ball to his wife and Admiral Byng's sisters, while he went off to a levee at St James's Palace, looking, recalled Janetta, superb being 'habited in green with a profusion of gold lace, embroidery and a diamond sword knot'. Among the guests at the ball were the Hon. Mrs Stukely, Lady Masters, Lord Minto, Sir James Lowther, Sir George Pocock, Lady Bute and her two daughters. Janetta wore a pink silk dress trimmed with a silver fringe and tassels. And she wore what her father had called 'some baubles' when he had given them to her for the ball – a pair of diamond earrings.

Janetta also recalls going to a concert to hear Giusto Tenducci, the Italian castrato. She talks of giving concerts at home to the great pleasure of her father and her uncle. Almost certainly Rebecca's family moved in similar circles – she might have attended Mrs Tomlinson's like her cousin; she may have gone to the ball or a ball like it when she was fourteen or fifteen. Robert Scott, an ardent royalist, would certainly have known Bute. His friends included the bankers Coutts.

If Rebecca had the kind of education that Janetta speaks of – or something very similar – she would almost certainly have lost any trace she might have had of a Scottish accent. Her father would be only too aware of the disadvantages of being a Scot in London in this century. Despite the Act of Union in 1707, Scotsmen were openly mocked for their way of dress, their accent and their manners. Boswell, a social climber, was more than aware of the image of his countrymen and he ensured that his children were educated for the most part in England. His son went to Eton. So did Robert Scott's son and heir. Time and again in his diary Boswell proudly notes his younger daughter Betsy's 'English', as he called her way of speaking. He placed her in Miss Hockley's boarding school at Blacklands House in Chelsea. His oldest daughter Veronica was taught by a respectable widow, Mrs Buchanan, for, as Boswell wrote to her, he wanted her to be 'more confirmed in her English manners'. And another insight into the education of Scotsmen's daughters was Boswell's wish for Euphemia that 'she learns the habits of submission and application which are so necessary to make her a useful and agreeable woman'. This was seen as the whole point of educating women – to make them useful and biddable. Scott and his wife would have thought long and hard about educating their daughters. They would be very unlikely to be in the vanguard of those who argued that women were capable of higher things if given the education. Scott was obviously very conservative by nature and a social conformer – so it is unlikely that either daughter would have had anything other than a polite education, with music, some French, some lessons in speech and manners. There is a temptation to believe that he saw his daughters as useful commodities in his ambitions to better himself and his family.

In 1764 the Scott family made the move that all their class made when their fortune was secure. They quit the crowded counting house in Mark Lane, near the Tower. They left behind the dirt, the smell, the clamour and the crowding of the City, and moved to the healthy air and rural calm of Blackheath overlooking Greenwich Park. The house Robert Scott leased from the Crown still stands today and is known as McCartney House. Age has been kind to it and, though there have been a number of additions to the original house, one can see what its attractions would be to a successful City merchant. In Scott's day it was simply known as Crooms Hill. The lease became vacant in 1764 with the death of Henrietta Wolfe, widowed mother of General Wolfe who died at the moment of victory on the Heights of Abraham outside Quebec. His embalmed body was brought back to Crooms Hill in November 1759 and lay in state for three days before it was buried at the local parish church of St Alphege's in Greenwich.

In Scott's day the house was about seventy feet long and about thirty-five feet wide. It had views overlooking Greenwich Park at the rear and London beyond – a view that both Pepys and Evelyn had admired in their time over a century before. In a trade directory of the time we are told that Greenwich 'may be said to be one of the genteelest as well as pleasantest in England. The inhabitants, many of them persons of note and fashion, who have served abroad in the fleets or the armies and here, pass the remainder of their days in ease and delight. Indeed, all around it are scattered the villas of the nobility, gentry and capital merchants.'

The next-door neighbours in this charming and exclusive enclave included the celebrated and snobbish Lord Chesterfield, whose letters to his son and godson about how to succeed in life became a best-seller after his death in 1773. His house, called the Ranger's House, was later to become home to Princess Caroline, the unhappy wife of the Prince Regent. The Scott family must have acquired a copy of Lord Chesterfield's letters when they came out in 1773 – maybe to see whether they were mentioned in them. So Rebecca probably read Chesterfield's advice about marriage. Her brother would certainly have agreed with it. 'Do not be in haste to marry,' Chesterfield told Philip Stanhope in this undated letter. 'There are but two objects in marriage, love or money. If you marry for love, you will certainly have some very happy days, and probably some very uneasy ones. If for money, you will have no happy days and probably no uneasy ones; in either case, let her be of an unblemished and unsuspected character, and of a rank not indecently below your own.' It was for these thoughts, as much as for anything, that Dr Johnson dismissed the letters as teaching 'the morals of a whore, and the manners of a dancing master'.

Rebecca was to spend a dozen years in Blackheath with its world of rich, respectable and famous inhabitants. One wonders how much she had been prepared for the dramatic change in her style of living. There were no more clerks and counting house rules. No more noise, bustle and dirt. She must quickly have relished the much more leisured and comfortable, even pampered, existence that befitted a young lady of fashion. There was sadness too. Her father died in 1771 and was buried in the parish church of St Alphege, like the former tenant of McCartney House, General Wolfe. After her sister Elizabeth's wedding at the same parish church the following year, Rebecca and her mother stayed on at Crooms Hill, rattling around the now roomy place and wondering what to do. As the youngest daughter, perhaps she was already aware that she could end up as her mother's companion – a fate that befell a huge number of well-born women who never married.

Young unmarried ladies were left to fend for themselves. They filled their time as best they could. For most it was embroidery that helped the hours pass. Others did a little painting. And there was, of course, reading. Above all there were novels but also many books about how young ladies should comport themselves. Some women even wrote books, an early sign that woman's role in society could change. The most important thing in their restricted lives was friendship with other young women in similar positions. Sometimes to the modern eye the professions of love and affection in letters between young women then can be misunderstood. Innocence, though, protected them from any erotic feelings or wrong moves. Above all, most young women shared a passion for music. Musical interests were encouraged in young ladies of fashion. It was a desirable social asset. Too often for comfort, blushing daughters were called upon to play or sing at social gatherings regardless of whether they had any real talent or not. Given her interest in music, Rebecca and some of her friends must have gone to the occasional concert when in London. Among the most popular were the Bach–Abel concerts held in Hanover Square and perhaps it was there, where the London public paid enthusiastic homage to Europe's finest musicians, that Rebecca Scott first saw Johann Samuel Schroeter.

Rebecca comes across as a strong-willed and determined young woman with a clear sense of what she wanted. She seems to have been the one who took it into her head to have music lessons and presumably made all the necessary researches. She also paid for lessons out of her own funds, just as she paid her mother an annual sum to remain in the family home. However it came about, some time in 1772 just after he had set foot in England, Johann Samuel Schroeter was offered the job. It was not exactly a well-paid position and was a form of drudgery. Dr Charles Burney – although well established – often left his house before nine in the morning and, on some days, did not arrive back home until eleven at night. Schroeter must have been hard pressed at times. Later accounts suggested he was not the best teacher in the world, but the romantic possibilities were soon apparent on both sides. Johann and Rebecca were about the same age and it must have been a conducive setting for them both in what young General Wolfe had called 'the prettiest house in England'. Their mutual love of music would make conversation easy. Is it any wonder that the young couple should find each other attractive?

Richard Leppart, in his book *Music and Image*, quotes Joseph

Barretti's *An account of manners and custom in Italy*, which was published in 1769. In it Barretti describes for his English readers, in the most suggestive manner possible, the attractions of a young lady at the keyboard 'arrayed in the thinnest silk favourable to the sultry season . . . her fingers busy in search of the most delicate quavers, languishing to *mi sento morir* of one of our most feeling composers. Where is the judicious parent who would wish to see his child in so dangerous a situation?' Barretti goes on to say, 'Such is the voluptuousness and wicked turn of mind that music gives in Italy to the generality of its professors . . . that it has brought them into universal dispute.' Barretti's strictures, of course, were meant to alarm his readers. Italian, German, French – they were all foreigners and not to be trusted.

It is very doubtful that Rebecca's brother Robert, now head of the family, had heard Schroeter play. Men at that time listened to music, but with only half an ear. According to Fanny Burney, men always turned up late for concerts. They had usually had a good dinner and cracked quite a few bottles of port with their friends, with the inevitable result that they then slept through the second half. Robert went along with the idea of music lessons not only to please his sister but to provide her with the skills to marry well into the bargain.

Why Rebecca fell in love so deeply is easy to understand. The how and the when are another matter. Since she was the employer, she was in charge, so she must have given her suitor cause to believe that any advances he made would not be rejected. Schroeter may have thought only of conquest. Possibly all he wanted was a brief fling. Given the cynicism of men towards women in the eighteenth century (and some would say it was ever so) the prospect of £15,000 would have been a mighty attraction as well.

Rebecca, though, was well brought up, an affair was out of the question. Other women in the higher reaches of London society might succumb to a practised seducer but to a woman of her class such an act was unthinkable. Schroeter was certainly good-looking and charming, yet in many ways he was still a boy. He was in his early twenties and only recently freed from a domineering father. Rebecca was now twenty-four. She knew that anything less than marriage would exclude her more completely from society than an ill-advised union. Perhaps, as the youngest in the family, she was used to getting her own way. She probably calculated that she would be able to win round her brother and mother, and that her money would solve any problems she and her future husband might have. Had she read her near neighbour Lord Chesterfield's letters? Even if she had, Rebecca must have soon decided, despite His Lordship's warning, to marry for love. As a member of the Romantic generation, she would probably have dismissed the idea that there would be any days of unease. Rebecca could think of nothing but her future with Schroeter.

The courtship, if it can be called that, took place over Schroeter's regular visits to Blackheath. They probably managed to see each other, too, when Rebecca came to town. They must have gained a great deal of pleasure from the shared secrecy of such meetings. Amid their increasing intimacy they could enjoy the touching of a hand, the look in another person's eye and the unspoken language that hides nothing, least of all one's feelings from the object of one's affections. The impossibility of the match must have made their amorous exchanges even more exciting. They were young and they were challenging convention. If one cannot challenge society's rules when one is young, when could convention be challenged? Johann Samuel Schroeter was everything this twenty-four-year-old virgin had ever hoped for, dreamed about, longed for.

CHAPTER SIX

In Chancery

Love, they say, is blind. After her marriage Rebecca's eyes were very quickly opened to the new reality of her situation. On 17 July she had gone from being Johann Samuel's employer to being his wife. As a wife she had become, in law, his subordinate. She had sworn to 'love, honour and obey'. She had swapped her reassuring-sounding English name for something foreign. With her altered role had come an equally abrupt change of home. She exchanged spacious Blackheath and the clean air of the country for the smells and crush of central London. She had moved from a stylish home into Schroeter's more cramped lodgings in Duke Street. And her income had been halved. Apart from a lifetime annuity of £200 from her father, Rebecca had also enjoyed an additional annuity of £200 a year. But her father's will said she would lose one of them when she married.

When he drafted his will, Robert Scott senior fully expected his daughter to be enjoying the income from her handsome dowry. He also expected her to have made a good match, which would have assured her of a proper place in society. In fact, he had created a legacy which, given Rebecca's headstrong choice of a husband, would prove deeply divisive. Scott senior's prescriptive will would posthumously undo much of the happiness he had worked so hard to acquire for his family. All his family's rivalries, personal interests and prejudices would be played out in the unforgiving theatre of the Court of Chancery.

Charles Dickens, that unique chronicler of London places and people, conjures up the atmosphere of the High Court of Chancery in *Bleak House* with his descriptions of the Jarndyce and Jarndyce case. He paints a vivid word picture of a foggy day in November.

> Hard by Temple Bar, in Lincolns Inn Hall, at the very heart of the fog, sits the Lord High Chancellor in his High Court of Chancery. On such an afternoon some scores of members of the High Court of Chancery Bar ought to be here mistily engaged in one of the ten thousand stages of an endless cause, tripping each other up on slippery precedents, groping knee deep in technicalities, running their goat-hair and their horse hair warded heads against walls of words, and making a pretence of equity with serious faces as players might. On such an afternoon, the various solicitors in the case, some two or three of whom have inherited it from their fathers, who have made a fortune by it, ought to be ranged in line … between the registrar's red table and the silk gowns with bills, cross bills, answers, rejoinders, injunctions, affidavits, issues, reference to masters, masters' reports, mountains of costly nonsense piled before them. Well may the court be dim, with wasting candles here and there … well may the heavy stained glass windows lose their colour and admit no light into the place …

It was written just over half a century after Scott versus Schroeter, but was still a world that Rebecca would quickly have got to know and dread. In her time the Court of Chancery sat in Westminster Hall. And, a few weeks after her marriage, that was where she and her husband sought the right to win her dowry.

As a wealthy merchant, Robert would have had few scruples about involving the law. Court cases were part and parcel of doing business. What was more important, he could afford it. In contrast, the prospect must have filled Rebecca and her husband with dread. Then as now, seeking recourse to the law was always an expensive business. Chancery cases were exceptionally convoluted and drawn out. There were four terms a year, each lasting about three weeks, when the court would sit. Hilary covered the end of January, Easter term was in May, Trinity was mid June to early July and Michaelmas term fell in November. In effect, very little happened for nine months of the year.

When there was activity, everything moved at a snail's pace. Depositions were written out laboriously by hand. Everything had a cost. There were fees for the subpoena office; fees for the six clerks' office, there were fees for sworn clerks (including stamp duty), there were fees in the affidavit office, the register's office, the examiner's office and so on. Even the doorkeeper had a set fee. It worked out at ten shillings for every case heard – both sides having to pay him, win or lose. It could cost a guinea to have a document perused; and there were those dangerous animals, 'unspecified fees', which could go as high as ten guineas.

A case was launched when one of the parties to the dispute filed a bill of complaint seeking the court's guidance. The complaint would be filed with one of the six clerks' offices. An under-clerk would copy out the details. In this way he formally accepted the bill. The longer the bill, the longer it took. Everything moved at the speed of painstaking handwriting. In theory the Lord Chancellor took the final decision on advice from his staff of clerks. At this time it was Lord Bathurst, a nice enough man but not a legal giant. Indeed, it was strongly rumoured that when he was appointed to his high office in 1771, Bathurst was the most incapable of the three candidates. Essentially he was a political appointment and it is said his legal decisions have no value in the profession. Once a bill of complaint was received, the next issue was to get the defendant to reply. There were all kinds of response – a defendant could accept the truth of the complaint; he could fight it, or he could seek what was called a 'demurrer' which, while admitting the truth of the charge, sought to argue that the charges did not present any cause to which the defendant might reasonably be expected to answer. In Scott versus Schroeter and, as it later turned out, Scott versus Scott, pretty much the same evidence was given, on oath time and again. The process follows a set pattern. A number of questions or 'interrogatories' are set out and replies are then made. Each document contains much the same information as the previous one. The name and family connection are given, the deponent's address. Then follow the basic facts of the case as the 'deponent' sees them. Once all this has been gathered together and all the evidence is on file, the documents are then presented to the Lord Chancellor or the Master of the Rolls for a final adjudication. That was how the Court of Chancery liked to claim it worked. In practice documents got lost, replies were delayed, or witnesses could not be found.

Every step of the way had a price. The money went to line the pockets of the lawyers and the clerks. The legal system had no interest in speed or short cuts. For example, in the files of this case there is a short document sworn before a lawyer to the effect that Rebecca and Johann did actually reside in Duke Street – and that would have cost at least a couple of guineas. Often the point of the exercise was to delay everything as long as possible so that one side or the other would give up. A typical example is the case of the notorious property speculator, Sir Nicolas Barbon, in the late seventeenth century 'who threatened to keep Proby [his opponent] in suit in Chancery about two years, and in that time will make out and convert all the brick earth' on the premises in dispute.[8] Perhaps this was Robert Scott's intention. By delaying he would make Rebecca see the error of her ways and feel the pain of being on the wrong side of the family.

Family disputes are like any civil war. They tend to be more brutal and unforgiving than any other fight. Knowing how nasty such fights could become, Rebecca tried at first to be conciliatory. In her statement on 1 May 1776 she told the court,

Your orator and oratrix have frequently and in a friendly manner applied by themselves and their agents to the said Elizabeth Scott, the widow, and the said Robert Scott, and requested them to pay the said £15,000 and lay out and invest the same, and your orator and oratrix well hoped that the said Elizabeth Scott and Robert Scott would have complied with such . . . reasonable requests, as in

[8] Public records handbook no. 27, Chancery Equity Records and Proceedings 1600–1800 by Professor Henry Horwitz.

justice and equity they ought. But now, so it is, may it please your Lordship, they ... do refuse ... sometimes pretending they will not ...

The friendly approach did not work. Time and again Robert Scott said 'No'. So, in late September 1775 within weeks of their marriage, Rebecca and her husband applied to the court to release the funds provided for her under her father's will. It was either a very naive move or a calculated gamble to blackmail her family into handing over the money and avoid bad publicity. Perhaps Rebecca was naive, yet given her family background and the attitudes of the time, she cannot have been so blinded by love as not to know what her relatives were capable of. If it was a gamble that they would acquiesce rather than go to law, she lost.

On the face of it Robert Scott seemed to be trying to keep to the terms of his father's will. At first he talked only about the fact that he did not give his consent; therefore, under the terms of the will, the dowry was forfeit. But as the evidence was taken again and again, one gets the firm impression that he also saw an advantage in with-holding the money. The nub of Rebecca's case rested on the moment during that traumatic weekend when her brother Robert had finally said that he would allow her to marry Schroeter *if* the family could not dissuade her from the match over the weekend. The truth was that Rebecca did not change her mind. Given what Robert had in her view promised, she claimed the right to assume that the family had accepted her marriage as she headed for the church of St Martin-in-the-Fields on Monday morning.

Then the young couple played their trump card. 'If the court decides the said Johann Samuel Schroeter and his wife Rebecca did not have her family's approbation, then they will submit that the said Robert Scott, as residuary legatee should not be entitled to the £15,000 as a result of his refusing his approbation, and that the condition in her father's will should be considered as *in terrorem*.' Those last two Latin words were a lawyer's way of suggesting that the provisions in the father's will which said Rebecca would lose her dowry if she did not have the family's consent constituted a threat. A threat is unenforceable in law.

The response to the young couple's application for the money was as swift as the lumbering engine of the law allowed. Early in October Rebecca's mother Elizabeth swore a bill of complaint against Rebecca and her husband. In it she again laboriously ground through the events of the weekend of the marriage. She insisted that at no time did the couple receive her or her son's consent. Further, she alleged they said they were aware of the conditions of the father's will but would marry anyway. She sought to have them questioned as to the facts she had set out.

In their reply, on 8 October, Rebecca and Johann Schroeter claimed that after their marriage Robert's attorney, Mr Booth, told them that Scott would allow them £200 a year for as long as they lived out of England. If in time they succeeded in getting Rebecca's fortune, Mr Booth said, then they would have to repay the money given to them. The young couple's reply suggests that they had thought long and hard about how they should appear before the court. It would seem they were well advised; they told the court Robert Scott 'did use many violent and harsh expressions to dissuade her from and prevent such a marriage'. Schroeter declared that he rejected an offer of £500 from John Pringle not to marry Rebecca 'as the truth is that it was his regard for the other defendant [Rebecca] now his wife and not love of money that induced him to marry her'. Schroeter also said that he 'always behaved, as he does now and ever means to behave towards her with a proper and becoming decency, respect and regard'. The newly weds also claimed that a marriage agreement was made before the wedding by Schroeter, in which he stated that the £15,000 be invested for Rebecca's use only: 'These defendants further say that the agreement was prepared by and with the privity and advice of John Pringle, a particular friend of the family.'

There is a surprising canniness to the young people's arguments. Their insistence on marriage might have been driven by passion, but they were clearly prudent enough to consider, too, their legal options. Perhaps John Pringle, her father's business partner, had given them advice, although he denied it. In any case, in the apparently unequal struggle between Rebecca and the rest of her family, it seemed the evidence might just favour a rebellious daughter.

Rebecca's claim that she was duped by a false promise from her brother was never denied by him. Time and again the witnesses called by her brother simply repeated the facts of the weekend: the shouting, the urging, the persuasion and the tears. All this did was add weight to Rebecca's assertion that she was being coerced, that an agreement had been made '*in terrorem*'. She therefore had every right to proceed with the marriage. But perhaps the most telling point is the suggestion that her brother's main interest was getting the money, nothing else. Rebecca argued that she wanted only what was rightfully hers, but that if the court found against her, then Robert Scott should not be allowed to keep the dowry. She said that he should have no other interest save that the court found that he was right to withhold his consent to the marriage. As far as Rebecca was concerned, her brother's refusal of consent was to win the £15,000 dowry for himself. The clear implication was that he would have refused any request for marriage.

Her instincts as to her brother's motive seemed to be born out by the claim he made in July 1776 when he told the court, 'The defendant, Robert Scott humbly insists that such sum of £15,000 did upon the complainant Rebecca's marrying with out consent as in the said will sink into and become part of the residue of the said Testator's personal estate.' In other words, Robert kept the money.

Brother Robert's anger at the match, far from receding with time, actually increased. It is hard to conceive of anything more wounding than to find your own brother taking you to court. Rebecca would have felt that she had no choice but to fight the case, not only to gain what she saw as 'rightfully' belonging to her, but also because she wanted to prove once and for all that Schroeter was worthy of her. Even so, as she pressed on with her suit in Chancery, her new role in life as Schroeter's wife was underlined time and again. He was always referred to first and she was tagged on after as 'Rebecca, his wife'. Suddenly she was entering a patriarchal world with a technical language all its own. She was either a 'deponent' or an 'oratrix'. She would learn all about 'demurrers' and 'interrogatories'. She will have spent hours telling her side of the affair to total strangers, who laboriously took down all she said in legal shorthand and then transcribed it in longhand on to 'skins' or large sheets of parchment. The case can only have increased her feelings of being abandoned by her family.

Her husband was not much help to her. He knew little of the British legal system, would not have been able to brief lawyers and probably did not want to get too involved lest his enthusiasm was construed as an unhealthy interest in the money rather than anything else. Rebecca's motivation for continuing the case may not have been solely defensive. Her father's will also stipulated that not only should the money be invested for her and her husband, but after her death the income would pass to her heirs. It is one thing to deny oneself a wealthy lifestyle for the sake of love, but should a mother deny her children? There are no records of any children born to Rebecca and Johann Samuel, but in the early days of the marriage that was still very much a possibility.

Rebecca knew that she had a fight on her hands. She also knew that she was fighting from a weak position. When she had been an unmarried heiress society would have accorded her all due respect. Had her family not been in trade, she would have been counted among the gentry: she had been bred and educated as gentry and would have had its attitudes, and she would have expected the proper acknowledgement due her station in life. Overnight she had forfeited that respect. By her own volition she had decided to become the wife of a foreign musician. Now she was a disobedient daughter and sister. Society could be pitiless towards such women. Within the Scottish merchant class word would have travelled fast and many doors would have been swiftly closed to her.

Rebecca ought to have known what to expect. Her case was by no means an isolated example of a daughter letting her heart rule her head. Even some of the most successful and famous women had to put up with such pressures when they contemplated marrying foreigners. Fanny Burney, for example, who married a French refugee,

General d'Arblay, caused a short rift with her father who, at first, could not accept her choice. A few years earlier Fanny herself had behaved with equal dismay when her friend and Dr Johnson's muse, Mrs Thrale, decided to marry an Italian singer, Gabriel Piozzi. 'Poor self-deluded creature,' Fanny commented in a letter, 'how can she suffer herself noble minded as she is, to be thus duped by ungovernable passions?'

In her diary the forty-year-old widow Thrale pondered much over whether she should marry the man she undoubtedly loved. Piozzi was a Catholic and, while an amiable fellow and obviously in love with her, he had neither high birth nor social position. Moreover, the marriage prospects of her daughters and any other children would have been blighted. Hester Thrale's marriage plans ended her friendship with Samuel Johnson. That excluded her from the company of men like Reynolds and Burke. Women could be just as cruel to their sisters, for even Mrs Montagu's bluestockings shunned her. There are other examples where music was seen to undermine social status. Perhaps the most surprising is Richard Brinsley Sheridan, playwright and later politician, who eloped with the divine singer Elizabeth Linley and then insisted that she no longer perform in public after their marriage. Ironically the painter Gainsborough, a great lover of music and musicians, did all he could to prevent his daughter marrying Johann Fischer, the German oboist who had played alongside Schroeter at his debut concert at the Thatched House in 1772. That marriage was not happy and did not last.

The biggest challenge for Rebecca in this protracted Chancery case was always the immediate and practical one of the impact on her now much-reduced income. Her annuities, if she still received them, plus whatever Schroeter could earn, allowed them but a very straitened standard of living. Schroeter would have had to dress well, given the company he had to meet and entertain. In the Schroeters' case the legal fees were expenses that most young couples on at most a few hundred a year would have found difficult to fund. The lawyers' fees would soon have eaten into any reserves they had.

Rebecca was also claiming that her brother still owed £10 of her annuity – it had come to her counting every penny. Added to money worries was the personal distress they suffered. Rebecca and Johann had to cope with the fact that the whole family was against them. It would have been extremely painful to read the evidence of her mother and brother. Rebecca and her husband cannot have found any of this easy to cope with. The relationship would be unusual if the strains did not cause friction as each adjusted to the reality of their embattled situation and mutual dependence, and the consequences they were now forced to live with. Did all this lead to that lack of 'temperance' which some contemporary accounts mention when they talk about Schroeter? His friend and sponsor, J. C. Bach, was said to have 'deplored that disposition' which would 'in the end work to his bane'.

Robert's attempts to keep the dowry for himself could be seen as just plain greed on the brother's part. It was certainly a sensible strategy as far as his business affairs were concerned. He was probably under some financial pressure following the 'shot which rang around the world' that launched the American War of Independence. Soon Boston and other key New England ports would be closed. Later on, British shipping often had to run the gauntlet of French or Spanish men-of-war who came in on the side of the thirteen American states after 1778. The American colonies accounted for well-nigh half his business. Robert Scott's income will have taken a severe knock.

Elizabeth Scott, the widowed mother, was in an increasingly impossible position. She was torn between son and daughter. Her son took the hard line but she understood her youngest daughter's needs. While she still did not approve of the marriage, she seems suddenly to have come round to her daughter's point of view that the dowry should, at the very least, not go to Robert. Rebecca in one of her depositions said 'her mother well knows . . . that the said Johann Samuel Schroeter is of the first eminence in his profession and a man of general good character and universally esteemed'. Rebecca must have used all her diplomatic skills to win her mother's support. Perhaps the mother was more sympathetic to the idea of marriage for love than her son could ever have been. Mother and daughter were obviously close and, with her other daughter in Madeira, Mrs

Scott must have worried about her own future. Who would be there to care for her in old age? These concerns prompted Mrs Scott to seek the court's direction as to what she should do. She asked that, whatever its decision, she at least be reimbursed for the costs involved in going to law.

Rebecca's tactical success, though, meant that mother and son became caught up in a fight of their own. Robert could not let his mother get away with such a change of heart. He immediately sought the court's support for the line he was taking. And in his evidence sworn on 27 April 1776 he got as close to calling his sister a liar as was decently possible. He stated that 'the said Rebecca gives out and pretends that her said mother hath since her ... intermarriage ... forgiven the said Rebecca and the said Elizabeth Scott ... will lay out and invest the sum of £15,000 ... for the benefit of Schroeter and Rebecca his wife'. The phrase 'gives out and pretends' was a neat bit of legal jargon for saying Rebecca is lying. Even worse from Robert's point of view, his mother 'refuses to let him have any residue of the personal estate of his father without the direction and indemnity of the court'. If his mother does as he suggests it will be 'in prejudice of and contrary to the manifest rights of your orator'. There were now two court cases running in Chancery: Scott versus Schroeter, and Scott versus Scott. When Rebecca and her husband moved house in May, from Duke Street to Little Suffolk Street, Rebecca must have felt that she had made some progress. In nine months, her brother had been isolated and her mother won round.

Robert, on the other hand, became even more determined to win. Nonetheless he was under great pressure. He was now fighting his mother, while the family business was under threat from the deteriorating situation in the former American colonies. Worse still, the struggle to retain the colonies was turning into a proxy European war. Things may have looked bleak, but Robert decided on a bold move. In the very month that the French fleet set sail from Brest in search of English shipping his lawyer, Thomas Searle of Philpot Lane, officially requested witness statements from Charles and Elizabeth Murray in Madeira. Robert Scott was prepared to pay for a four-man commission to sail there to take evidence. They were, he claimed, 'material witnesses being privy to and present at the time when the disapprobation of the said executor to the said marriage was signified to the said Rebecca Schroeter'. It would cost a lot of money but suddenly, it seemed, the principle (or was it the dowry?) was worth it.

Robert was now the sole plaintiff in an action against his mother, sister and brother-in-law. But how could he behave otherwise? As the head of the family, he felt it was his duty to protect all that his father had worked for. As a man in the eighteenth century he would have thought it reasonable to say that his mother was old and grown sentimental, and that, like all women, she did not think of the consequences of her actions. It was his duty to protect her. Neither a sister nor a mother could be allowed to do exactly as she wished. It was typical female weakness putting the heart before the head. His legal action might be distasteful but what else could a rational man do?

Following Robert's decision to send for witness statements from Madeira, nothing more happened for eighteen months. One probable cause for the delay was that Elizabeth Murray gave birth to a son, Charles, in 1777. He was her first and, as it happened, only child. Everyone would have wanted to relieve her of any worry at the time and so it is likely that the family squabble was put to one side. The other possibility is that Rebecca herself became pregnant and was confined to bed. Death in childbirth was a very real possibility for women. One in three died this way, while nearly half of all children died in birth or did not survive very long. The stress of the case and change of circumstances would have been a major contributory fact had this indeed happened. There is, it must be said, no evidence whatsoever for this but it could explain the silence of eighteen months from a young woman who had otherwise been so voluble and determined to defend herself in Chancery.

The witness statements and the names involved in the case of Scott versus Scott suggest that, as always in Chancery cases, the dispute was as much about business as family. Consequently members of the wider family got involved, as well as business partners. Even the servants had to talk to the lawyers. It was not until 14 April 1778 that the court heard from the maid who raised the alarm. Fanny was now lodging with a widow, Mrs Smith, off Cupors Alley in Long Acre. It is almost impossible to imagine what terrors the poor woman went through with this experience. She told her story simply and well.

The crux was as follows: 'On Friday the 14th of July 1775 Rebecca, being on a visit to her sister, the wife of Charles Murray informed me that the family was going out of town and she should have some things to put up and therefore I should call her at six o'clock the next morning.' She did as she was told and at six 'went into Rebecca's room and found her already up and dressed, and soon after she went down stairs on tiptoe'. Fanny was curious and said, 'She believes that Rebecca had a hat hidden under her apron.' A hat was a sure sign that Rebecca was going out and that piqued Fanny's interest even more. When she looked out from an upstairs window, she said she saw Schroeter at the corner of the street beckoning to Rebecca. Another maid then told Fanny that Rebecca had gone out and left the street door open, and that she had met Mr Schroeter. Fanny then said that she 'immediately ran down stairs and followed them to the bottom of the street where she saw Rebecca get into a carriage and drive into Holborn'. That was when she informed the Master, Mr Murray.

It cannot be very often that one has such a full and detailed account of the moment of elopement by a third party. The rest of Fanny's evidence followed almost word for word what other witnesses said about the weekend, although she was not present. She too said she understood that no consent was given and that Rebecca knew she could forfeit her fortune. That part of her statement looks to be the most rehearsed – and in a modern court would be classed as 'hearsay'. This is probably how one should treat one fascinating new 'fact' that only she offered the court. She believed that not only was Mr Schroeter offered a substantial sum not to marry Rebecca, but also Robert Scott promised his sister another £5000 to add to her fortune if she gave him up. It is probably nothing more that below-stairs gossip – £500 or £5000 were such huge sums for servants as to be unbelievable. The statement was then read back to Fanny because she was illiterate. She made her mark in the shape of a cross – a firm downward stroke and a rather shaky horizontal line.

On 4 May it was the turn of Sarah Manson who was Elizabeth Scott's sister and Rebecca's aunt. Her husband was a shipwright and they lived in Bermondsey. Her evidence included the information that she went first to Blackheath at her sister's request, and that they travelled up to London and Robert's Wimpole Street house. John Pringle gave his evidence three weeks later on 25 May. Pringle was the only witness to have anything good to say about Schroeter. 'Until the fifteenth day of July 1775,' he recalled, 'the relations and friends of the deponent Rebecca had not, as this deponent, the least suspicion that John Samuel Schroeter had obtained or attempted to obtain the affections of the said Rebecca but as this deponent had always understood appeared to behave with proper distance and respect.' Pringle was the only witness to use the word 'elope'. That word, he recalled, was in a message he received from Murray on the Saturday morning 'requesting his immediate attendance at the Church'. Pringle made no mention of being asked to draw up any marriage agreement.

Finally the court received the evidence back from the consul and his wife in Madeira. It is interesting how much detail Murray remembered after three long years – as if he was reading from a diary that he kept. His deposition put on record for the first time the details of events and conversations crucial to deciding the rights and wrongs of the Scotts' bitter and long-drawn-out dispute, and with it the future and reputation of Rebecca Schroeter and her husband. He gave a clear picture of what Schroeter was doing while his fiancée was being pressured by her family in Wimpole Street. With all the authority that His Britannic Majesty's consul could muster, Murray assured the court that what he said was accurate and true.

Charles Murray, H.M. Consul on Madeira, aged 35 and over, says he has known Robert Scott, Elizabeth Scott, and Rebecca Schroeter for seven years and more, and he knew Johann Samuel Schroeter

for about six or seven months before his marriage to Elizabeth
Scott. He says Robert Scott and Mrs Scott gave no consent or
approbation to Rebecca's marriage. From the time of her father's
death (c. May 20th 1771) Rebecca had lived at her mother's house
at Black Heath. Murray knew Robert Scott (senior) having been
long connected with him in trade.

Murray then related the details of how he was woken by his maid,
Fanny, how he rushed to the church and how he stopped the ceremony. Murray said that Rebecca agreed to go to her brother's house
as long as she was not detained there by force. He added that he did
not go with her, because he was sure she was very angry with him
for stopping the ceremony. He said that had he tried to reason with
her, she would not have listened to him because of her anger. He
painted a picture of a strong-willed young woman not averse to
making her position plain if she were of a mind to.

On Sunday, 16 July Mr and Mrs Murray decided to face up to
Rebecca and after church they went to Robert Scott's house to join the
rest of the family. There were 'strenuous arguments and solicitations'
used, Murray told the court's commissioners. Rebecca's mother was
in tears for most of the day. Murray said that mother and brother
repeatedly told Rebecca that she would disentitle herself if she went
ahead. Rebecca replied that she and Schroeter were fully aware of the
consequences as they had a copy of her father's will. The fact that
they had gone to the trouble of copying the will only reinforces the
idea that Rebecca and Schroeter had made some calculations as to
what they would need to say when the news of their marriage became
public.

Murray said that Schroeter came to the house before dinner, which
would have been around four in the afternoon. Although he had been
forbidden entrance, a servant took him to a parlour below stairs.
Murray went down to try to persuade him not to marry Rebecca.
When Rebecca found out Schroeter was in the house she rushed
down to see him, but was carried out physically by her angry brother.
Robert picked her up bodily and carried her from the room and from

the man she loved. Schroeter remained there alone. Then Robert Scott returned with his mother to confront Schroeter. They begged him not to marry Rebecca. Robert said Rebecca would forfeit her fortune if she married him and assured Schroeter he would not get a farthing. Schroeter refused to stop the marriage.

He was asked to leave the house. Murray took Schroeter away in his carriage. Schroeter asked the consul to set him down at Mr Napier's music shop in the Strand. On the way, Murray again begged Schroeter to give up Rebecca. Schroeter rejected Murray's demands with some vehemence. Schroeter, as Murray put it, 'persisted that he would marry Rebecca'. Murray told Schroeter that he believed the Scotts were 'a family that deserved a more grateful return from him having been among the first who gave him employment in England as a music master'. Murray urged Schroeter to accept a large sum of money or annuity for life not to marry Rebecca. Schroeter was adamant.

Later that evening Murray called at Napier's shop a second time to try to persuade Schroeter to give up. Napier was present during their conversations. When Murray appealed to Napier to ask Schroeter not to marry, Napier, as he phrased it, 'declined to offer any advice'. Murray went over the will and conditions again, and for a second time promised that if Schroeter should later marry any other woman than Rebecca, in addition to any money from Robert Scott, he, Murray, would give him £500 to buy a set of china for any wife he took apart from Rebecca. Schroeter refused to agree to this. Finally Murray begged Schroeter to defer any marriage for a few months and not to see Rebecca during that time. Schroeter said that a separation would not make any difference because 'he could not offer to desert her if after that time Rebecca still wants to marry'. Schroeter, Murray observed, 'seemed to lay a great stress on the impropriety of deserting a lady who was willing to marry him'.

Rebecca must have been very heartened to read this account. Schroeter had behaved, as she would expect the man she loved to behave, with complete loyalty. Murray still did not give up trying to win over Schroeter. He said that if Rebecca changed her mind,

Schroeter would still be given the money. Schroeter would not agree. He maintained that if after two or three months Rebecca still wanted to marry him, the Scotts must give their consent and Rebecca should have her fortune. Murray told Schroeter that he believed this would be impossible. The family would never give its consent to the match. All through it seems Schroeter acted as a decent man who would not desert the woman he loved.

According to Murray, at this same time Rebecca's brother and mother were telling Rebecca that 'they would give their permission for her marriage to any person she would at any time name, whose birth, education, or employment gave him rank as a gentleman if she does not marry Schroeter'. Rebecca 'answered thereto that she loved no man on earth so much as Johann Samuel Schroeter and that she would not marry any other man'. Clearly, both Rebecca and Johann Samuel were determined to stay together regardless of what offers were made or what pressures put upon them.

On Monday, 8 July 1778 it was the turn of Rebecca's sister, Elizabeth, to add what she could to her husband's testimony. She told the witness takers 'she did know the defendant Schroeter as a music master for two years or thereabouts before his marriage with Rebecca'. He had been hired 'to instruct both Elizabeth and Rebecca in music – she did not know that Schroeter intended paying his addresses to Rebecca, or that she admired him'. Given the strength of the couple's feelings for each other, which was now evident, it is remarkable that they managed to evade the attention of Rebecca's sister. Elizabeth seems to have been curiously unmoved either by the handsome German or her young sister's deepening interest in him. But Schroeter received little or no more attention from the family than any other of their servants. While that might have helped the couple's subterfuge, it should also have served as a warning to Rebecca as to the likely reaction when the family found out. Rebecca must have known very well the risk she ran, but was, in the words of modern psychologists, 'in denial'.

As is often the case with merchant families, it is difficult to distinguish where family ends and business begins. The Public Records

Office at Kew is full of records of such family disputes. The British were a litigious people in the eighteenth century. Witness statements made in these cases were, to all intents and purposes, public documents. For the price of four pence, a copy would be produced by a clerk. Since everyone involved could get hold of such a copy, each and every deponent had to be very careful not to give needless offence; witnesses therefore tended to be 'economical with the truth'. The danger for the business, as for the family, was that a whiff of scandal could, at worst, rapidly ruin carefully established reputations, or at best make one a laughing stock. The newspapers at the time relished gossip, especially if it involved love affairs, secret marriages and large sums of money. If the dispute became public, the Scott family would have wanted, at all events, to make sure that Rebecca, and Rebecca alone, was the guilty party. The rest of the family were doing their duty by the late Robert Scott senior.

Public attitudes being what they were in this period, it made it exceptionally difficult for Rebecca to win her case, even though the balance of the evidence seemed to be in her favour. She was inevitably cast as the errant, wilful daughter and sister. In that context it would have been understood that her brother Robert was protecting the family fortune, both for his own generation and for the future. While the case continued, Rebecca stood her ground as best she could. Like many women of the period, she recognised that the legal cards would always be stacked in the male's favour.

The battle between the siblings had drifted on for over three years. After the commission from London had taken depositions from Charles and Elizabeth Murray in Madeira, the case seems to have been dropped. No more documents have been found in the archives.

So what happened? In the end the Scott family may have done some deal with the young couple because the case was simply costing too much in time and money. The dispute was obviously harming the family's reputation. Calling Pringle, Manson and the maid Fanny in 1778, and sending a commission to Madeira to hear from Murray and his wife seem to have been a final attempt by Robert Scott to come up with some convincing facts that would persuade the court in his favour. The only possible conclusion was that the parties came to some private accommodation. When this happened, which was often, the court did not require that the agreement be communicated to it.

If Robert's intention had been primarily to protect the family fortune, in part he succeeded, because when he died in 1808 his estate was valued at around £400,000. That was an immense fortune. In his will he left 'Rebecca £500 per annum over and above what I give her now'. The phrase 'over and above what I give her now' implies that she was already receiving money from him and it seems to have been a comfortable sum. When the details of his will were filed at the Stamp Office in London the value of the legacy for Rebecca Schroeter is given as £1218 12s 6d. Stamp duty was levied at 2½ per cent – around £30. Those figures suggest he had been paying her at least £700 a year up until his death – that was a tidy amount and may have reflected what had happened to the disputed dowry. It is possible that, while he retained the capital, he agreed to pay his sister an annuity. A 5 per cent return would give her around £750 a year, which would have afforded her a comfortable lifestyle when added to her other annuity from her father of £200. A couple could live well on such an income.

Then there was what Schroeter earned. It is said in most of the obituaries of Schroeter that the family paid him £500 a year not to play in public. If that is true, it shows that the Scott family shared the prejudices of the time that having a lowly musician for an in-law was a step too far. When Schroeter began to enjoy royal favour, perhaps they no longer enforced such an agreement, because he did not seem to limit his public performances much at all. After he died in 1788, virtually penniless, Robert went on paying the £500 to his now widowed sister. He could not, despite their differences in the past, allow his sister to live in poverty. Was it conscience money for all the harsh words he had once used about her? In the end perhaps Rebecca and her husband felt that, while not winning the case, they had not lost.

There were many families like the Scotts in the eighteenth century who had daughters who challenged convention. There is the chilling tale of Sarah Lennox, the wilful woman whose early life was charmed. As a small child she was a favourite at the court of George III; as a beautiful young woman she was wooed by the Prince of Wales. Society was convinced that she would be the next queen of England. That did not happen and she married a Member of Parliament. Her husband turned out to be a bore, so she ran off with the impecunious Lord William Gordon in 1769. This made her a social outcast. The whole Lennox family turned their back on her. When she left Lord William, she promised the family that she would live quietly, dress in a sober fashion and see no one. The family slowly relented. But they hid her away in a small house on a distant estate where she spent almost five years atoning for her 'sin'. Slowly she managed to get back into society. In the end she even made a good marriage. Redemption was always possible, but the road back was hard. Sarah's story made all the scandal sheets.

At least Rebecca was spared that kind of dubious fame. How she escaped public attention is a mystery. The public looked on court cases as a form of theatre. The drama did not always spring from the dry debates of the lawyers. On one occasion a man called Parson Nixon, nursing some private grievance, exploded a charge of gunpowder in the Chancery Court while Lord Hardwicke was sitting.

Who took the first step to end the legal battle may never be known. Perhaps the combined arguments of mother and daughter managed to persuade Robert junior that after three long years consorting with lawyers Rebecca had paid the price of her ill-advised marriage. Throughout those years the couple's life had been consumed by the distressing proceedings in a musty, dimly lit hall, notable, in the words of a Scottish physician, for 'the clouds of stinking breathes and perspirations, not to mention the ordure of so many diseased animals'. Rebecca could never have imagined that her marriage would lead to such a place. ·

CHAPTER SEVEN

The Celebrated Mr Schroeter

The case in the High Court of Chancery may or may not have been officially settled. The outcome, whatever it was, could hardly have been to the Schroeters' complete satisfaction. Rebecca, though, could at least derive some pleasure from the fact that her husband managed to keep his career going despite her family's opposition. Regardless of the war in America and the worrying news from the Continent, the economic boom continued in Britain. London, the biggest city in the world, was determined to enjoy itself. Society was in a state of flux, with old money accommodating itself with new. The new money imitated the style of the old aristocracy. The men had their clubs, the women their friends and an equally busy social life of visits made and visits received. Looking back, the capital seems never to have stopped its hedonistic ways from dawn to dawn. Music was the most commonly shared passion. It was the best of times to be a talented young musician.

In his *Recollections on musical life in the 18th century* R. J. S. Stevens recalled that at the Anacreontic Society 1777, 'I have frequently heard Clementi . . . on the harpsichord and Schroeter on the piano forte'. Merchants and bankers who frequented the London Coffee House on Ludgate Hill had founded the Anacreontic Society in 1766. It steadily grew in reputation. A typical evening consisted of a grand concert in which, according to William Parke in his musical memoirs, 'the flower of the musical profession assisted as honorary members'. A few years later the society's president was a certain Mr Hankey – who could well be the same man to whom Schroeter had dedicated one of his compositions. While there must have been many in the City who would have known of Schroeter's ill-advised marriage, the bankers and merchants were happy enough to invite him to play for them. Since the Anacreontic Society was a private club, technically Schroeter was not breaking the agreement with the Scott family (if, indeed, he had such an agreement) not to perform in public.

Like any naive eighteenth-century bride, Rebecca would soon have been disabused of any romantic notions she may have had about matrimony. The first three years of the Schroeters' marriage with the pressure of the court case would have strained anybody's relationship – but people were more prepared to endure in that century than now. It was just one of the crosses she had to bear. Marriage in Georgian England rarely turned out to be the perfect happiness that women had hoped for and dreamed about, and which the novels of the time could lead them to expect. If the diaries and letters of disillusioned women are to be believed – and there is no reason not to believe them – the man very quickly resumed the selfish habits of his bachelor days, following his own inclinations and keeping company with his friends. He would spend his time in the coffee house, paying visits, dining out and even drinking late into the night if he was of a mind to. A wife had little to say in the matter. She was left to fend for herself. If she was lucky she would have the support at least of the womenfolk in the family and her friends – but Rebecca, through her actions, had left herself to a great extent isolated in her new role.

She might also quickly have discovered some disagreeable habits in her husband, which she had not noticed before. There is circumstantial evidence that Johann Samuel was an enthusiastic drinker. According to one report, his final illness 'materially impaired his constitution, which the habits of his life prevented guarding by the most exact temperance'. Among his friends and supporters was Johann Christian Bach, who was like a father to him. Bach was a sociable man, much given to entertaining his friends. Henry Angelo, the memoirist, talks of 'delightful evenings' with Bach and Abel. It was the age of good living and hospitality, and Schroeter would be sure to be invited to Bach's and Abel's house in Queen Street, off

Golden Square. There was danger in such conviviality. Abel and his close friend the painter Thomas Gainsborough were both heavy drinkers. Often the latter would pass out on his way home and would be put into a coach by some friendly passer-by the next morning. Abel, towards the end of his career, could be so drunk that he had to be helped to his chair and handed his instrument before he could play. The drink, though, did not harm his talent and some thought his music was better when he was inebriated. Finally the drink did for him. Towards the end of his all too short life Bach too seems to have over-indulged.

Yet there must have been some good times for Rebecca. Society was less rigidly divided between the male world and that of women. Increasingly the sexes mingled in company. Rebecca was young, pretty and very sociable. She and her husband would have been an interesting couple to invite to one's home. Gainsborough's chalk sketch of an informal group of people playing music shows a woman seated at the pianoforte, a woman in the background watching, and two other men playing violin and base viol. Rebecca was an accomplished pianist so it would be surprising if Mr and Mrs Schroeter were not at some of these friendly evenings.

While Rebecca was ambitious for her husband to succeed and so prove to her family that she was right to choose him, Schroeter, by all accounts, was an easygoing man. In fact, he seems to have been rather lazy. According to Charlotte Papendieck, 'He did little or no good to his fraternity in music. He played when called upon, but took no interest to forward or assist any individual, and left no immediate scholar.' Perhaps the laziness or lack of ambition stemmed from the fact that he and his wife were comfortably provided for. Johann Baptist Cramer, another musician, recalled that at the age of eleven, 'I received a few very useful lessons from the late and rightly famous player Mr Schroeter.' As Cramer explained, 'This eminent musician . . . did not, unfortunately for his pupil, possess the energetic character of a teacher.'[9]

[9] The musicologist Konrad Wolf, in the *Musical Quarterly* in 1958.

Perhaps the hardest blow of all for Rebecca was that marriage in the end did not mean that she spent more time with her husband. In fact, she probably saw less of him. Professional musicians had little time to relax if they were to earn their living. In this, at least, Schroeter was helped by his connections with J. C. Bach who was received, according to Mrs Papendieck, 'in the higher circles of society as a visitor, as a result of his teaching'. The fact that Schroeter might have agreed not to perform in public did not mean that he was unable to earn his living. The *ton* began to become more involved in private concerts, sometimes in direct competition with the public concerts held at the Hanover Square Rooms or the Pantheon.[10] Partly this was because the growing affluence of the new middle class somewhat lowered the once exclusive tone of such gatherings. Men and women in aristocratic circles vied with each other to attract the best players to their private functions. There's an early dedication by Schroeter in 1775 – the year of his marriage – to one such society hostess, the Duchess of Ancaster, who held fashionable masquerades at her mansion in Berkeley Square. Researchers[11] have discovered others – Count Brühl, the Saxon ambassador in London, and J. C. Hankey, a Fenchurch Street banker. Because such concerts were held in private at the quality's great houses, the papers tended not to cover the event as they did the public concerts. Private concerts did not need to puff themselves as the commercial concert was forced to in order to make a profit. It is impossible to be certain where and for whom he played, but we do know that Schroeter was a star performer in the late seventies and early eighties with a way of playing that caused the ladies to swoon, because he was 'one step higher in the modern style . . .'

Playing at private concerts did not bring him very many mentions in the press. As a teacher he would have had an even lower public profile. What references there are speak highly of his technique, his

---

[10] Simon McVeigh, *Concert Life in London from Mozart to Haydn*.
[11] 'More Light on Haydn's English Widow', *Music and Letters*, February 1997, pp. 45–55.

musical taste and the impression he made on his audiences. There is no doubt, though, that he did make a name for himself. Indeed, Schroeter's fame was beginning to spread beyond the shores of his adopted homeland. Back in his native Germany the head of the theatre school in Hanover wrote, '. . . It would be unthinkable to omit to mention Mr Mozart and Mr Schroeter, two Germans of exceptional talent who are both composers, conductors and pianists: their achievements are known not only here but abroad too.' And indeed they were, because there is a letter from young Mozart to his father in Salzburg written in July 1778, just as the four-man commission were in Madeira taking evidence from the British consul, Charles Murray: 'Write and let me know if they've got Schroeter's concertos at Salzburg . . . I wanted to buy them and send them to you.' And five months later Leopold Mozart writes to his son, who is now in Munich, 'Signor Ceccarelli has just arrived, sends you his greetings yet again, says he hopes to see you soon, and sits down at the piano. At the moment he is having lessons from your sister and working on the concerto no. 1 in F by Schroeter!'

In what was to be a fairly short career, Schroeter did not publish many works. Perhaps this is more evidence of his laziness, or a lack of ambition. Then again it could be that his drinking was beginning to take its toll on his creativity. When compared with the productivity of his mentor J. C. Bach, for example, Schroeter's output was very limited. His most famous work, Opus 3, was first published in 1774. The publisher was William Napier, the man who wisely refused to get involved in the Scott family's affairs. In 1775 Le Menu & Boyers in Paris also published the Opus 3 concertos. It is more than likely that J. C. Bach drew Mozart's attention to his young protégé when he and Mozart met in Paris in July 1778. As Mozart told his father, 'You cannot imagine how happy we are to see each other again. . . . There is no question but he is an honest man who treats people fairly.' Young Schroeter was extremely lucky to have such a man to be his friend and mentor.

Schroeter was not completely without ambition. While Bach was in Paris, talking about Schroeter, his absence in London provided a huge opportunity for Rebecca's husband. Heinz Gartner in his life of J. C. Bach[12] believes 'Christian made an error in judgement when he left London voluntarily, opening up the field to his competitors, though he may not have thought of them as such . . . in the concert hall the young pianist Schroeter dominated the scene. During Bach's absence, many of his pupils changed over to Schroeter.' Mrs Schroeter must have been very pleased at the progress he was making. He was now quite well established. There is a brief notice of Schroeter in 1780 playing his famous third piano concerto at a King's Theatre Concert. According to his greatest fan, 'He played the middle movement with such sweetness and grace that was perfectly enchanting, and the house was in rapture for minutes.' Had there been some kind of agreement about not playing in public, Schroeter was now prepared to ignore it. Perhaps the family was beginning to relent a little.

Bach was now in decline, both in health and in fortune. He was not yet fifty and during his last years he 'rarely wrote save under spirituous excitement'. Is this yet another clue to the drinking habits of his young protégé Schroeter? Bach had an unhappy last few months. His housekeeper was discovered to have been fiddling the books and he was virtually bankrupt. Only his friends kept him supplied with food and other necessaries. His health was failing. He wrote his will in November 1781 and died on New Year's Day 1782. Neither Schroeter, Abel nor Gainsborough attended the funeral – in fact, only four people turned up, none of them musicians. The next edition of the *Gentleman's Magazine* carried the following notice under 'Obituary, Promotions and Civil and Ecclesiastical Preferments', 'January 1st Signor Christian Bach, musick master to the Queen. Mr Schroeter, performer on the piano forte succeeds Mr Bach in the above appointment at Buckingham-House.' This appointment must have brought some pride and a measure of happiness to Rebecca. They had been married for seven years, and it had been a long haul to survive and even prosper modestly. Given the peripatetic lifestyle

---

[12] *John Christian Bach, Mozart's Friend and Mentor* (trans. Reinhard G. Pauly, Amadeus Press), p. 328.

of the musician, it must have been a lonely life. Schroeter would be away from the family home quite a lot, doing the rounds. There were twice-weekly concerts organised by the Queen at which he would be expected to attend. And Her Majesty held unofficial concerts as well. Rebecca would no doubt have worked hard to support her husband with dinners for his friends. It is impossible to say whether she would have been invited to the grand affairs and private concerts where he played.

What emerges is a picture of a young heiress who married for love coming face to face with the lonely reality of married life. But she had finally settled with the family and she was back on good terms with her mother, who now spoke of her husband as 'greatly esteemed in his profession'. The Queen's Music Master had at least some status in society and it was recognition that the man Rebecca had been willing to sacrifice so much for was worthy of her.

Schroeter, though, was beginning to find some stiff competition for public affection in the person of a young Italian, who would become the acknowledged pianist of his generation and known to history as the father of modern piano technique. Mutius Philippus Vincentius Franciscus Xaverius Clementi was known to posterity simply as Muzio Clementi. The son of a silversmith, he was born in Rome in 1752, which makes him about the same age as Schroeter. He came to London in the year Schroeter married Rebecca and was appointed director of the band at the King's Theatre in the Haymarket. Everyone who heard Clementi play marvelled at his technique. In 1781 after a piano 'duel' with Mozart in Vienna, his opponent cruelly dismissed him as a 'mere mechanicus'. Clementi's life almost had a parallel with Schroeter's in that he eloped with an eighteen-year-old heiress he had met in Lyons. The irate father appealed to the authorities for help and Clementi decided that he could never win. He did not go through with his marriage plans. His sponsors, the Beckford family, the richest by far in England at the time, gave him an entrée that Schroeter could not match.

In the 1780s Clementi would become the most sought-after piano teacher in London, and he also decided to go into the music business by setting up a publishing company and piano-making concern. Schroeter, meanwhile, continued to make his living as a virtuoso pianist and teacher, but he does not seem to have had quite the same determination to survive and prosper as his rival. It is only speculation, but if he were indeed financed by a stipend from Rebecca's family he did not need to work too hard. Furthermore, by not actively seeking to be invited to perform at every opportunity, Schroeter tacitly kept to the bargain that he would not perform in public. The extent of his private work, away from the public gaze in fine houses, may also have kept him more than busy enough.

A couple of months after Schroeter 'inherited' the Mastership of the Queen's Music, yet another German musician arrived in London to make his mark. His name was Johann Peter Salomon. Schroeter's position at court, as well as his nationality, would make it certain that the newcomer would seek him out. By a curious coincidence Salomon was born in Bonn in 1745 in the same house, number 515 Bonngasse, where Beethoven would arrive in the world twenty-five years later. Salomon had already built quite a reputation for himself as a composer and soloist on the Continent, employed by Prince Heinrich of Prussia, among others. He made his debut at the Covent Garden Theatre on 23 March 1781 and the next day the *Morning Herald* reported, 'He does not play in the most graceful style, it must be confessed, but his tone and execution are such as cannot fail to secure him a number of admirers in the musical world.' He was to figure largely in Rebecca's life over the next few decades.

Meanwhile the rest of Rebecca's family continued to prosper. In 1782 her brother, the implacable Robert, married Emma Assheton Smith at Lyndhurst in Hampshire. It is almost certain that Rebecca would have been among the guests, now that the dispute over the money was in the past. Given her husband's new commitments in London as the Queen's Music Master, and his popularity in private concerts that took place almost every night of the week, she may well have gone alone. Her brother's wedding must have been a bitter-sweet occasion for Rebecca, whether she made the trip into the country or not. Given her closeness to her mother, which would remain until her mother's death, the two ladies probably journeyed into Hampshire together. Robert had married into a well-connected family. Its members included landed gentry and one or two titles. That knowledge would only have served to underline the different path Rebecca had chosen for herself with her marriage to Schroeter. While meeting new relations she would have encountered many members of her own family and, with the passage of time, some of the wounds must have healed – especially since her mother, at least, seems to have forgiven her. Being introduced as Mistress Schroeter, wife of the Queen's Music Master, did sound really rather presentable.

Her brother had begun selling the family estates in Scotland. By doing what many of his class and background did he severed all connections with his father's homeland to become a true English gentleman. He was planning to buy an estate of over 200 acres at Danesfield in Buckinghamshire for the substantial sum of £24,000. As Robert prospered and rose in the world, Rebecca could content herself with a relatively agreeable life in London. She now moved in what was politely termed 'court circles'. In the 1782 Royal Calendar listed under the Queen's Chamber Band is her husband 'Mr Schroeter', together with 'Signor Abel, Mr Simpson, Mr Nicolai and Mr L. Papendieck'. Mrs Papendieck, who talks so often and in such glowing terms of Schroeter, never mentions his wife, save the reference to running away with a rich heiress. So she was aware of the story – how could she not have been, given her friendship with the pianist? It would be surprising if she and Rebecca did not know each other and possibly were even friends. After all, their husbands were not only in the same profession but played in the same band.

It is to Mrs Papendieck that we are indebted for a description of Salomon's concert in 1783, at which Johann Samuel was among the main performers. She creates a wonderful sense of the occasion.

On Friday, February 14, was the concert for the new Musical Fund, which always took place as early as possible, in order to introduce to the public the foreigners engaged for the season. Salomon was this year the great star. He called upon us, and when Mr. Papendiek returned his visit, he was fortunate enough to find him at home, and cordial friendship seemed at once to rivet them. .... Salomon was to play first, and the desk was brought on as it still continues to be. Then he appeared, introduced Carl Friedrich Abel, Johann Christian Fischer and Mr Papendieck following. Salomon was not handsome nor of an imposing figure, but the animation of his countenance, and the great elegance of his manner, soon caught the public eye.

Having bowed, he so placed the desk that not the smallest particle of his violin was hidden, and the 'Tutti' of his favourite concerto, by Kreutzer, commenced rather mezzo piano, and increased to a crescendo that drew down volumes of applause. Now came the solo: a repetition of the melody an octave higher, which he played with an effect perfectly sublime. It was in the minor key, and the cadence he introduced was a long shake, with the melody played under – something new, which put Fischer almost into fits. The adagio movement he performed in such a manner that Fischer was heard to say, 'I will play it no more; he has outdone me.' Then the rondo followed in the same key as the first movement, and Salomon introduced one short variation that struck upon the ear in such a manner that it was difficult to keep quiet.

Having finished, he returned his instrument to the attendant, but retained the bow which assisted his graceful bow. Abel, who had been permitted to sit, now rose, and they went off arm in arm. Such a debut has scarcely ever been experienced. We were jumping from our seats. Schroeter played in the first act, and made a most successful debut also. His graceful and sweet manner of touching the pianoforte found its way to the approbation of the public.

By the 1780s it was now very acceptable for women to attend such concerts, so it would have been surprising if Rebecca was not in the audience, being loyal and supportive as ever, cheering her husband on. She would have met Salomon as well afterwards. That same year, says Mrs Papendieck, Schroeter often breakfasted with us, and 'Salomon would often call to plan some entertainment'. H. C.

Robbins Landon the great Haydn scholar, described Salomon as 'an eighteenth-century Gentleman who was a clever and sensitive impresario'. He was also scrupulously honest. Soon he was launching his Hanover Square concerts, the true successors to the celebrated Bach–Abel concerts in the same venue. In his day he was rightly famous and highly thought of. He is buried in Westminster Abbey, although he is known largely as 'The man who brought Haydn to London'.

In 1786 Schroeter was given another royal appointment. He was asked to join the Prince of Wales's musical staff at Carlton House. The young Prince's extravagance and his awesome appetite for food and women were already the talk of the town. The still handsome young heir to the throne may have been extremely decadent in his personal life, but there is no denying his artistic taste, or his musical abilities. Prince George instituted a series of morning concerts where he expected silence from the audience while he joined in the music making with professional musicians like Schroeter.

Breakfast with the Papendiecks, morning concerts with the Prince, private performances in the evening made for a heavy work schedule, and kept Schroeter away from his home more and more. His career, though, was beginning to take off. The young couple had been married for over ten years and felt it was time to move to a new address in James Street, Buckingham Gate, close to Buckingham House, the King's London residence. The lease was in Schroeter's name.

While Rebecca and Johann seemed to be doing well, her brother was doing even better. Robert decided to mark his marriage to Emma Assheton Smith by commissioning Sir Joshua Reynolds to paint his wife's portrait. Today that portrait hangs in Waddesdon Manor in Buckinghamshire, having been bought by the Rothschild family for their collection of eighteenth-century portraits. Emma Scott is wearing a white dress with a blue sash and her hair is powdered. She has on a broad hat set at a rather rakish angle. It's an unusual and, in the words of one art critic, 'utterly unsculptural'[13] portrait by

---

[13] Desmond Shaw Taylor.

Reynolds. The artist recorded eleven appointments with Mrs Scott between 12 April and 1 June in 1786. The portrait cost Robert 100 guineas. The style worn by Rebecca's sister-in-law was probably how Rebecca would have looked at the time. Given her life in court circles, she would still be interested in the latest fashions. Going to her husband's concerts, and her connections with the court no matter how tenuous, would have demanded that she paid great attention to what she wore. With the court case long settled and family relationships repaired, Rebecca may even have gone along to Sir Joshua's studio to keep her sister-in-law company on occasion.

Just as life was seeming to go well – two royal appointments, a new house in a better part of town – illness struck. Johann Samuel began to display symptoms of what might now be diagnosed as a cancer of the throat. The illness seems almost to have stopped him from speaking. The *Gentleman's Magazine* said that he had lost his voice by a severe cold and could only make himself understood in a whisper. He 'languished', as the saying was, and on 31 October 1788 he made his will, leaving everything that he possessed to his 'dear beloved wife'. The well-informed Charles Burney, in Rees's *Cyclopaedia*, says he 'died of a consumption'.

If, indeed, it was some form of throat cancer it must have been a terrible time for Rebecca in those last few months. The perennial treatment, prescribed regardless of the illness, was bleeding. It inevitably made a person even weaker and less able to combat his or her malady. The only medicine that doctors could prescribe to relieve pain was laudanum. This form of opium was addictive and, if a patient recovered, he or she often continued to take the drug. Any pharmacist would prepare a draft. Rebecca would have had the responsibility of nursing him to the end. In the new house they had rented, as his career seemed to be moving forward, suddenly she was left with a very sick man who could hardly speak. The kind and caring Rebecca's patience would have been stretched to the limit, with long nights by his bedside and the daily tedium of the doctor's largely useless visits. They had been married just over thirteen years when he succumbed at last. She was not yet forty and already a widow. She must have derived some comfort, perhaps, from the kind words printed about her late husband – and some relief that the story of their marriage was told in but a garbled version – she was never identified by name by any of the papers or magazines that reported the death of the 'celebrated' Mr Schroeter.

Knowing a little more about him, and much more about Rebecca, it is instructive to read the longest obituary printed in the *European Magazine*. The indefatigable Dr Charles Burney is probably the author. He knew Schroeter and was the acknowledged expert on the musical life of Britain. The original format, emphasis and spelling have been retained.

In a musical age like the present, the biography of a Musician becomes an object of more general curiosity than the life of a philosopher; and the death of an eminent Professor is lamented as a national misfortune. To gratify our musical readers, a correspondent has favoured us with the following authentic particulars of the late celebrated Schroeter. –

JOHN SAMUEL SCHROETER was a native of Saxony. He came to London about fourteen years ago with his father, a musician of no great eminence, but who bestowed many pains in giving his son a complete musical education. The discipline of Germany is almost as severe in *Musical* as in *Military movements*; and the elder Schroeter was a *Martinet* of very terrific abilities. By virtue of *Hunger* and *Hard Blows* he compelled his son to practice for several years without intermission eight hours a day; and to this may be imputed the remarkable facility with which he executed the most difficult music at sight. But while he applied thus diligently to the practice, he did not neglect the theory of the science, the rudiments of which he acquired under the famous Emanuel Bach, which he afterwards cultivated and improved from studying the works of that great master in *Score*.

For some time after his arrival in London, the splendid talents of young Schroeter were either unknown or neglected. He occasionally played the organ at a German chapel in the city, a situation which by no means accorded with his genius, as he was not there permitted to indulge his fancy in any musical flights beyond the formal rules of the cathedral school. It was at this time that he composed his first set of lessons for the Piano Forte, which he offered to several of the music-sellers of London on their own terms, but in vain. His name was not then *Marketable*, and few of the vendors of music know any thing more of the art. The late J. C. Bach at last recommended him to Napier, music-seller in the Strand, who soon distinguished his merit as a composer, and purchased the copy-right of his work at a liberal price.

Being now announced to the musical world as a composer, Schroeter began to acquire some celebrity in the profession, which procured him several scholars in the fashionable circles. Upon the publication of his first set of concertos, his reputation was such that he took the lead as a performer in all the musical entertainments of the Nobility at which he assisted.

Soon after this period he married a lady who was his pupil, by whom he was entitled to a very considerable fortune; but her friends taking violent offence at the match, and threatening poor Schroeter with the terrors of the Court of Chancery, which he then conceived to be more dreadful than the *Inquisition*, he gave up his claim to her fortune, in consideration of receiving an annuity of 500 pounds. Clogged with a very unreasonable condition, 'that he was to relinquish his profession so far as never to perform at any public concert'. This, which more ambitious men would have spurned at, Schroeter, who had much indolence of disposition, as well as carelessness of fame, agreed to, and for some years he retired from town, and resided chiefly in the country. But talents like his could not be long buried in oblivion. The Prince of Wales heard him play at a private concert, and expressed the highest admiration of his performance. His Royal Highness's household was then about to be established, and without any solicitation Schroeter was appointed one of his band of music, with a liberal salary. His last set of sonatas, which have a very elegant accompaniment for a violin and violoncello, were composed at the desire of the Prince, to whom it was dedicated, and his Royal Highness frequently accompanied Schroeter in his favourite work.

The grand Piano Forte was Schroeter's favourite instrument. His stile of playing was distinguished by that peculiar elegance and delicacy, which a chaste and correct taste improved by science, alone can acquire. Though he possessed the most complete dominion of his instrument, he seldom indulged in those capricious difficulties and *Harlequin* tricks, by which many of our modern performers catch the applause of the vulgar. His mode of fingering was so peculiarly easy and elegant, that it was even pleasing to *See* him perform. In his *Cadence* he often gave rein to the luxuriance of his genius, and astonished the professor as well as the *Amateur*, with the novelty, the beauty, and the endless variety of his modulations. His manner of playing an *Adagio* was unrivalled, except perhaps by the *Viola de Gamba* of *Abel* in his better days, when inspired by a flask of generous *Burgundy*. He seldom could be prevailed on to touch a harpsichord, but he was extremely fond of playing the violin, on which he was an elegant performer; his tone was thin, but his manner of touching it was masterly, and he delighted in attempting to surmount the difficulties of that instrument, more than in his most finished performances on the Piano Forte.

As a composer he certainly ranks very high; his melodies are in general exquisitely beautiful, and his harmonies are rich, and often display the originality of his genius. He excelled more in the *Cantabile* than in any other species of movements, though some of his *Allegros* possess much spirit and beauty. Had he applied to that department of the science, his talents were eminently formed for the composition of vocal music, and some time before his last illness he had determined to *Set* one of Metastasio's Operas, which it is to be regretted he did not live to accomplish. About three years ago he was seized with a severe cold, which affected his lungs, and at last terminated in his death, an event which the musical world will long regret.

Whoever wrote the piece obviously had some respect for Schroeter.

And the length of the article suggests that perhaps history has undervalued the impact which he had had on his contemporaries. Today he is usually a footnote in musical primers. He was probably around thirty-eight when he died; no one has found any kind of birth certificate. He is generally thought to have been born between 1750 and 1752. He was buried on 11 November in the St George's, Hanover Square burying ground. Did he go to his grave as alone as his mentor Bach, accompanied by just four people? Women did not attend funerals. Did her frail mother join Rebecca at her London home that day? Or did all her family desert her when she needed them? There is only his burial number 1183. All that remains of his tombstone is what is recorded in a manufacturer's handbook: 'Died November 1st 1788 Age (defaced)'.

In fact, history seems to have conspired to remove as many traces of him as possible. Even though the newspaper mentions are few and far between he was always referred to as the 'celebrated' Schroeter; he seems to have worked fairly consistently in the private sphere and two members of the royal family thought highly enough of him to take him on to their payroll. His music is being recorded over 200 years later. Schroeter was in all probability more of a success than the skimpy records suggest. His last few years, though, were sad, as his health declined and his voice gave out. Rebecca would share the agony of the decline. We know his last thoughts were of his wife as he dictated his will the day before he died.

He left her very little. Rebecca did not bother to prove his will until twenty-seven years later when it was estimated to be worth only £300. It seems a paltry sum for all the effort he had been making in his career. Perhaps he had been spending money as fast as he earned it, in entertaining and on his wardrobe. It does not suggest that the subsidy from the Scott family was paid to him, but rather to Rebecca, because on his death she took over the lease of the house in James Street. Schroeter's will is brief and to the point: 'I give, by this my will, everything by me possessed, both real and personal to my Dear Beloved Wife, Rebecca Schroeter, whom I also make my sole executrix . . .'

The signatures on the will and on his marriage entry in St Martin-in-the-Fields are the only tangible relics that remain of the once 'celebrated Mr Schroeter', whose delightful melodies had charmed so many people during the brief span of his career, and whose delicate and sure touch on the keys of the fortepiano entranced those who saw him play. The final signature is so sad to see and visibly makes the point of how far he had succumbed to his last illness. He was hardly able to hold the pen as he laboriously wrote 'J. S. Schroeter'. It seems obvious that he was barely conscious, if one compares this final signature with the firm hand displayed in the register of marriages in St Martin-in-the-Fields thirteen years earlier. This last physical act must have taken great effort. One of the witnesses – neighbours of the Schroeters in James Street – had to guide his hand. It was the last thing he ever did.

There is no trace in the records of Rebecca Schroeter between her husband's death in November 1788 and June 1791. The period of mourning would have lasted at least a year. She would have ordered black clothes for herself and for her servants. Her background and perceived rank in society would have meant that she would need new clothes; only the poor saved money by having a set of workaday clothes dyed. There would be letters to write to tell Schroeter's friends of his death. She may well have written to his sister Corona in Weimar, and his father who was then living in Hanau. No such letters have been traced. Convention demanded that she led a very restricted life for a suitable period. At least relations with her family had been re-established – she visited her ailing mother in Blackheath on a regular basis. Her brother Robert continued to pay her an annuity, so that her standard of living did not fall when she was widowed – the fact that she could afford to take over the lease of James Street is testimony to that.

Widowhood, once the grieving was past, had at least some advantages for a woman in the eighteenth century. A widow had a respected place in society. Widows regained control of their lives and their assets. As a member of a rich merchant family, Rebecca would still have been a catch. It was up to her whether she sought another husband or remained a widow. At the age of forty she was still a young and beautiful woman.

CHAPTER EIGHT
The Kapellmeister of Esterháza

As the grieving Rebecca regained control of her life, the one event she could not have anticipated was that within eighteen months she would meet a man who would become very important to her and, for a time, the centre of her life. Once again he would be a famous foreign musician. The reason that such a prospect would have seemed far-fetched was that the man in question, Franz Joseph Haydn, had never left his native Austria. Rebecca certainly knew his music. Anyone who professed to love music knew the works of the famous Kapellmeister of Esterháza. Attending any of the public concerts in the past decade, she would have heard his 'modern' symphonies and quartets. Frequenting the musical world she would have known that London audiences craved to see and hear the great man in person.

By 1788, the year of Schroeter's death, Franz Joseph Haydn had become the most famous Kapellmeister in Europe while all the time in the service of one employer, the Princes of Esterházy, the richest and most powerful of the great Austro-Hungarian aristocratic families. It was a remarkable achievement. When he was born in 1732 it would have been a very brave soothsayer who would have foretold such a rise in the world. Haydn was born in obscurity in a tiny village called Rohrau, not far from the little walled town of Hainberg on the Danube. His father was the village wheelwright and his mother had been an under-cook for the local overlord, Count Harrach. The village's prosperity depended on its vineyards. Life was very hard and the muddy river Leitha occasionally flooded the village. The Haydns were a devout Catholic family, decent, hardworking and even musical.

His mother survived twelve pregnancies, though six of her children died very young. Joseph was the eldest of the remaining six. Haydn showed early musical talent and went first into the village choir, then later, aged eight, into the choir school at St Stephen's Cathedral in Vienna. When his voice broke, ten years later, he was expelled from the cathedral school and from then on he had to make his own way in a largely hostile world.

Haydn was never a child prodigy like Mozart. It was sheer hard work and study, and a resolute determination to learn his craft, that drove him until now, forty years on, his was the name that music lovers uttered with respect and even awe. Famous though he had become, the fifty-eight-year-old composer had never travelled further than Vienna, where he went during his princely employer's winter sojourns in the city. For the previous thirty years he had spent most of his life in a remote part of Bohemia. From the outside the beauty of Esterháza rivalled Versailles in its glittering grandeur. Behind the walls, life for even a talented servant like Haydn was unremitting. Haydn signed a contract with the Esterházy family when he accepted the job, which involved fourteen tasks. What was expected of him was truly mind-boggling. He was responsible for maintaining the instruments, keeping the musicians trained and in order, looking after manuscripts, writing music to order for twice-weekly concerts, almost weekly operas, not to mention other occasional works for his prince's name-day, or the name-day for other members of the family. And he was expected to wear the livery of a servant, a clean white shirt and to have his hair powdered.

At the time there was many a court musician like Haydn turning out small operas, quartets, sonatas, songs and other musical divertimenti at the whim of their aristocratic masters. Some, like Bach's elder son Carl Philipp Emanuel, became well known and influential. Others, probably the majority, languished in obscurity and penury unheard and unappreciated. Haydn found certain advantages in his remoteness. As he later recalled, because he was far from the centre of things, 'I could experiment, observe what heightened the effect and what weakened it, and so could improve, expand, take risks. I was cut off from the world, there was no one near me to torment me or make me doubt myself, so I had to become original.' Not only had he become 'original', over thirty years he had, without leaving his workplace, become the most famous and respected musician of his generation. His indulgent princely employers did not limit his work to their own family. Publishers rushed from all over Europe – including Britain – to secure his compositions for their shops.

From the British point of view Haydn mania began in the 1770s. At the start of the 80s a publisher, William Forster, asked the British ambassador in Vienna to help him secure the rights to Haydn's works for his newly established publishing venture. Within six years Forster published a staggering 129 works by Haydn, including eighty-two symphonies. When Lord Abingdon set up the Professional Concerts in London in 1783, he tried to get Haydn to take over their direction. Time and again there were rumours that Haydn had agreed to come to London; time and again the public were disappointed.

In 1787, a year before Schroeter's death, the opera impresario Sir John Gallini was trying to entice Haydn out of Bohemia – and the composer himself seemed to be agreeable. Haydn wrote to Forster that he expected to see him before the end of the year. Another English publisher, John Bland, even travelled to Esterháza to meet Haydn in person. Karl Geiringer tells the story that the two men met while the composer was shaving with a very blunt razor. Haydn is said to have remarked to Bland, 'I would give my best quartet for a good razor.' Bland dashed back to his inn and returned with his own excellent set of razors. Haydn kept his promise and the *Razor* quartet is indeed one of his best. Most of the musicologists who tell this story always add that it is in all probability apocryphal, the product of Bland's imagination. But it fits the popular image of Haydn. The British were not alone in hoping to entice the Kapellmeister of Ester- háza abroad. There was international competition, with the French and the Italians among the most persistent. All the time Haydn felt that he must honour his contract with the Esterházy family. He had been their music master for nearly thirty years and, although he was beginning to find life in what he called his 'desert' more and more onerous ('too many annoyances,' he wrote in a letter to a friend), he was determined to keep his promise to serve his prince. Haydn had once drafted a short autobiographical sketch, which ended with this phrase: 'Kapellmeister to his Highness Prince Esterházy, in whose service I hope to live and die'.

The more one knows of Haydn, the more one likes him. Fame does not seem to have changed him. He remained, according to his first biographer Albert Dies, a kind, simple man, 'whose eyes beamed with benevolence'. His other contemporary biographer Griesinger says Haydn never forgot his humble origins. 'I have had intercourse with emperors, kings and many a great personage and I have been told by them a great many flattering things. For all that, I do not care to be on intimate terms with such persons and prefer to keep to people of my own station.'

When Prince Nikolaus died in 1790 everything changed. His successor, Prince Anton, did not have much appreciation for music. Consequently he decided to dispense with the court musicians. The new Prince was mainly interested in church music, and kept on just a few members of the wind band. Only Haydn remained in his employ – even Anton recognised that Haydn's fame and reputation added to the name of Esterházy. Haydn was not only asked to stay, but given a pay rise. In return he promised to retain the title Kapellmeister to the Esterházy family. The late Prince Nikolaus also bequeathed him a generous pension so Haydn, for the first time in his life, felt free to set foot on a bigger stage. Now that he was relieved of the onerous daily routine in Esterháza, Haydn came to Vienna and took lodgings with his friend Johann Nepomuk Hamberger on the Wasserkunstbastei. Hamberger was a typical friend of Haydn. He was a minor Austrian government official but a lover of music. Another friend was Franz Bernhard von Kees – also a bureaucrat, but blessed by musicologists down the years because he kept a record of all Haydn's symphonies.

Once in Vienna, Haydn began an active social life. He plunged into a round of musical evenings with friends such as Hamberger and von Kees. Karl Geiringer says Haydn's friends belonged mostly to the lower aristocracy or to the wealthy middle classes. These were the people who liked to play or hear music in their homes, people just like Rebecca Schroeter, whom he would meet when he came to London. The Irish singer Michael Kelly recalled one typical gathering at the Vienna home of Nancy Storace, the young opera singer who created the role of Susanna in Mozart's *Le Nozze di Figaro*. She was soon to go to London where she would become a great success. According to Kelly one evening the musicians included, apart from Haydn, another famous Kapellmeister, Karl von Dittersdorf, Mozart and Johann Baptist Vanhall. He was one of the first independent musicians who wrote over 700 instrumental works. Musical talent of that order must have entranced the other guests, who included a famous Italian opera composer, Giovanni Paisiello, and a poet, the Abbate Casti. 'After the music feast was over,' Kelly recalled, 'we sat down to an excellent supper and became joyous and lively in the extreme.'

Haydn and Mozart, who each had such respect for the other's genius, were often together learning and listening to each other. When they could they made music together – and one cannot begin to imagine how that must have affected those who were privileged to be in the room when the old master and the young genius played. Mozart saw Haydn as his father in music, perhaps Haydn saw Mozart as the son he would have liked to father. Haydn not only appreciated Mozart's talent but also tried, whenever he could, to boost Mozart's reputation. He even turned down the offer to write an opera to be performed in Prague. He said, were the opera for a private performance he might accept, but having heard what Mozart had achieved, he realised his own talent was far beneath it. What emerges out of all the recollections of Haydn is a picture of a man unaffected by his fame, generous to a fault and a father to all the younger musicians who worked for him, or with whom he came into contact.

Life was not just about musical evenings. This brief period in Vienna gave Haydn, though he would not have realised it at the time, a foretaste of what was to come. Once the word was out that Haydn might be able, with his prince's permission, to move from Esterháza to work elsewhere, would-be employers rushed to secure his services. King Ferdinand of Naples made him an offer, which the Kapellmeister was very inclined to accept. Then another proposal came from Prince Anton Grassalkovicz, which would have kept Haydn in Austria. While he was trying to decide which of those two to accept, a man suddenly appeared at his door in Wasserkunstbastei and announced, 'I am Salomon of London and have come to fetch you. Tomorrow we will arrange an accord.' Salomon had been in Cologne when he heard the news of the death of Prince Nikolaus Esterházy. He took the next coach to Vienna and went straight to Haydn's lodging to make his dramatic entrance. Financially it was a contract that very few musicians would have refused. It was a very generous deal indeed. Haydn would get £300 for a new opera to be written for the King's Theatre; the same sum for six symphonies; £200 for the copyright of them, another £220 for twenty newer though smaller works and a guaranteed £200 for a benefit concert. In all, he was offered the mighty sum of £1200 for his labours. Haydn's productivity was never in question, but to modern musicians the thought of writing an opera, six symphonies and twenty smaller works, as well as conducting and performing all the said works, is mind-boggling. All his life Haydn had been used to write to order and, like the great Johann Sebastian Bach, probably saw himself as a craftsman doing no more than plying his trade. Composers then worked within a medium largely bound by convention, rather than today's attempts to be strikingly different. Haydn's genius was to keep expanding the possibilities of the accepted conventions, so that his string quartets and his later symphonies became the standard by which all others were judged.

Haydn had been very tempted by the offer from King Ferdinand of Naples, but something about Salomon seems to have persuaded him that London was the better choice. It was not just the money that tempted him, though £1200 was a sum that must have seemed beyond the dreams of the son of a village wheelwright. While he was a shrewd businessman, as his letters to his many publishers testify, he was not avaricious, but he knew his worth and always expected a fair return for his labour.

Karl Geiringer[14] seems to have it exactly right when he gives this reason for Haydn's decision to go to London. Haydn, he writes, was confronted by a crucial problem. For many years he had cherished the dream of travelling to the classical land of opera. Again and again he had suggested such a trip to his patron, always to be put off with some excuse or other. Now, however, when the decision rested entirely with him, Italy seemed much less glamorous. Geiringer noted that Haydn's 'interest in composing operas had waned considerably, partly because of the supremacy of Mozart's masterpieces. More to the point, Haydn felt keenly that instrumental music was his particular language. In this field England, with its large, excellently trained orchestras, was definitely the leader. Moreover, there was the question of personal freedom, which had become extremely important to Haydn.' When Mozart heard Haydn's decision he is said to have exclaimed, 'Oh Papa, you have had no education for the wide world and you speak no languages.' Haydn answered, 'But my language is understood all over the world.'

Joseph Haydn left Vienna on 16 December 1791. He and Johann Peter Salomon took seventeen days to cross Europe and sail to England via Calais and Dover. A modern biographer[15] speculates that 'Salomon must have enjoyed the ... journey with Haydn. ... There are few things more pleasant for a seasoned traveller than a companion to whom travel itself is a new experience, and who in addition possesses that lively and fascinating interest in everything and everybody reflected in the odd assortment of facts ... "Anectods"[16] (as he pronounced the word) and statistics collected by the composer in his travel notebooks.' It is because of those notebooks that we can read the twenty-two letters that a certain Mrs Schroeter wrote him while he was in London. But all that was in the future. Haydn left behind him in Austria three women who had become important in his life,

[14] *Haydn: A Creative Life in Music*, University of California paperback, third revised edition, p. 95.
[15] Rosemary Hughes.
[16] Haydn's spelling of English words was often phonetic – which allows us to imagine his own accent.

though each for different reasons. One was his wife, whom he hated; another was his mistress, who was becoming a financial burden; and a third was a respectable married woman whom he worshipped but could only ever be his friend.

Albert Dies, the composer's first biographer, tackled Haydn about his relations with women during his twenty-third visit to the old man.

Because I found Haydn in such a good humour for speaking of women, I threw out in jest some searching questions. He frankly admitted that he had welcomed the sight of pretty women, but he could not understand how it came about that he was loved in his life by so many a pretty woman.

'My good looks', he added, 'cannot have led them into it.'

'You have', said I, 'a certain genial something about you, in face and figure, that people like to see and to which they must be good.'

'They can see in me that I mean well towards everybody.'

'That must have placed you open to many an advance?'

'Oh, many! But I was prudent!'

Women were important to Haydn – he got on well with them and they in turn liked him. If anything, he was a romantic. To understand both his future relationship with Mrs Schroeter and how important it was, you need to know something of the women in his life.

CHAPTER NINE
The Romantic Dr Haydn

Rebecca Schroeter was seven when, in 1758, Joseph Haydn landed his first real full-time job as a musician, with his appointment as musical director and *Kammercompositeur* to a Bohemian count, Karl Joseph Franz von Morzin. The count's wife, Wilhelmina, was a noted beauty and a great lover of music. One of young Haydn's jobs was to accompany the Countess, an accomplished singer, on the clavier. Haydn's other early biographer, Georg August Griesinger, tells the story – which he heard from Haydn himself – of what would seem to be the composer's initial real experience of the charms of the opposite sex. Once, while she was leaning over him to look more closely at the music score on the piano, her neckerchief suddenly unfolded. The proximity of the Countess's partially exposed bosom stopped Haydn in his tracks. 'It was', he said, 'the first time I had ever seen such a sight; it embarrassed me, my playing faltered, my fingers stopped on the keys.' The Countess reprimanded him, as much for stopping playing as blushing at the sight he had seen. Haydn stuttered the reply, 'But your grace who would not be upset here?' Haydn was twenty-six at the time, and the story has fuelled speculation that this devout, hardworking and driven young Catholic was still very innocent in the ways of the world – possibly still a virgin.

If this blushing innocence seems at odds with the reputation that the eighteenth century has for licentiousness, one should remember that it was the higher social classes, or the very poor, who were the most lax. In between, most decent young women needed to save themselves for marriage – otherwise they became 'fallen women' and were driven out of polite society, and could often end up as common prostitutes. All young men were urged 'for the sake of their health', as the euphemism went, to avoid loose women. The health issue was the danger of catching some sexually transmitted disease – the 'pox' in popular parlance, gonorrhoea or, worse, syphilis. James Boswell is the best example we have of the dangers of contracting such a disease. He caught the pox at least nineteen times according to his diary, after consorting with street girls – or 'fire-ships' as they were called. In the end it was the pox that killed him. Even more important than the health issue, as far as young Haydn was concerned, would have been the expense of such liaisons. As Lord Chesterfield wrote to his son, who was on the Grand Tour in 1750, 'I will by no means pay for whores, and their never failing consequences, Surgeons . . . A young fellow must have as little sense as address to venture, or more properly sacrifice his health and ruin his fortune with such sort of creatures.' Apart from a lack of money keeping him on the path of virtue, Haydn's work schedule in trying to make enough money to feed and house himself left him virtually no time for such things – beginning early in the morning musical duties at a local church, with lessons, joining singing parties in the evening and then composing and study-ing late into the night.

Yet, even so, he had already fallen in love. The young woman in question, as so often happened, was one of his pupils. But here, too, it is extremely unlikely that the relationship went any further than professions of love on Haydn's side. She was a very devout young woman called Theresa Keller. The marriage was not to be, because in the end Theresa decided to follow her equally devout parents' wishes and become a nun with the Poor Clares. All Haydn could do was write some music – an organ concerto – for her induction ceremony. This is the first example we have of what would be many pieces of music written with a woman in mind. Although frustrated in his suit, Haydn, already showing his need for friendship and love of company, kept visiting the wigmaker Peter Keller and his family at their rooms in the Untergasse in Vienna. Keller, sensing the young musician's growing reputation and talent, began to urge Haydn to marry the elder daughter Maria Anna – who, at thirty-one, was two years older than the young composer. Details are minimal – but whether out of friendship or simply a sense of duty, Haydn finally accepted the idea.

Karl Geiringer[17] argues that the reasons for Haydn's decision to marry Maria Anna, whom he did not love, are echoed in a letter written by young Mozart to his father when he announced his coming marriage twenty-one years later. Mozart too had fallen in love with one sister, but she dumped him when her career as a singer blossomed. So he ended up with the other less talented and less attractive sister, Costanze: 'The voice of nature speaks as loud in me as in others, louder perhaps … I cannot possibly live as do most young men in these days. In the first place, I have too much religion; in the second place, I have too great a love for my neighbour, and I am too honourably minded to seduce an innocent maiden; while in the third place I have too much care for my health. … I can think of nothing more necessary to my disposition than a wife, inclined as I am to quiet domesticity more than to revelry. A bachelor, in my opinion, is only half-alive …'

The marriage took place in St Stephen's Cathedral in Vienna on 26 November 1760 – the very cathedral where young Haydn had been a chorister. A copy of the marriage contract suggests that the young couple were well provided for – the bride offered 350 florins in goods and 500 florins in cash. The bridegroom put up an even bigger sum – 1000 florins in cash. Just over a decade earlier young Haydn, at seventeen, had been unceremoniously kicked out of the choir at St Stephen's when his voice broke. He spent his first night on a park bench, shivering in the cold of a November night in 1749, without a penny to his name and only 'three poor shirts and a worn-out coat'. It is a measure of his hard work and determination, working by day and studying in a garret at night, that he should be able to put up so much cash.

If Mozart believed that a bachelor is 'half-alive', Haydn was soon

[17] *Haydn, A Creative Life in Music*, p. 37.

to find that to be married to the wrong woman can leave a man half alive as well. The marriage was a disaster. Frau Haydn was, by all accounts, bigoted, quarrelsome and jealous. She hated housework and was a spendthrift. Unfortunately for them both, she could not have children. As Haydn remarked, 'She doesn't care whether her husband is an artist or a cobbler.' And later, after they had settled in at Esterháza, members of his orchestra would remark that just for spite she'd use his manuscripts to line her pans or as curling paper.

Perhaps, though, Maria Anna should not carry all the blame for the breakdown of the marriage. Looked at from her perspective, she had to put up with a lot. It cannot have been easy for her to know that her husband had truly loved her prettier sister. There were money worries too, because she was a spendthrift, while Haydn limited her ability to spend by giving money to his poorer relatives. She was jealous of him, too. Once his career with the Esterházy family got under way he inevitably began to spend more time away from her, some of it with pretty young opera singers. For a woman like Maria Anna such facts ensured that she would soon hate the life she felt she was forced to lead with the young Kapellmeister. Haydn for his part recalled, 'We grew fond of each other, but I soon found that my wife was very irresponsible.' In later years his language was much less temperate. 'The beast' he called her on more than one occasion. And yet he was to stay married to her for forty years until her death in 1800.

Haydn admitted to Griesinger in 1807 that 'because my wife was incapable of child bearing, I was less indifferent to the charms of other women'. The American music critic Harold Schonberg[18] says this is how Haydn rationalised his extramarital affairs. Rosemary Hughes, a more recent biographer, talks of 'intermittent infidelities'. In truth there is very little proof that he was a serial adulterer. He was a devout man, secure in his religion, and also a disciplined man, for whom work and duty came first and his own pleasures third. We do know

---

[18] Harold C. Schonberg, *The Lives of the Great Composers*, third edition, p. 73.

that he loved women and women's company, and that he was very alive to female charm and beauty. We also know that he, in turn, charmed women. Another modern biographer devotes some pages to analysing Haydn's will. Karl Geiringer notes that 'various bequests to women not related to him point to the master's interest in the fair sex'. The only legatee known to history is the singer Babett, or Barbara, Pilhofer, first soprano of the Esterházy court. Otherwise there are legacies to Mesdemoiselles Anna and Josepha Dillin; the blind daughter of the choirmaster at Eisenstadt; the four daughters to the wigmaker Sommerfeld of Pressburg; and to the daughter of the bookkeeper Kandler. All, or any, of these could have been sentimental attachments.

'The most tantalising of all', notes Geiringer, 'is the provision of a thousand florins for Mademoiselle Catharine Cseckh, waiting woman to Princess Grassalkovics. The Princess was the daughter of Prince Nikolaus the Magnificent, and it seems possible that she employed a girl from her father's estate who might have known Haydn well.' That was a big sum of money and would seem to go beyond the bounds of friendship. It leads Geiringer to ask, 'Was she the predecessor of Luigia Polzelli?' The world will never know, of course, unless some priceless cache of letters is suddenly found in some remote place. On the other hand Haydn scholars know a great deal about La Polzelli. She was certainly his mistress and for a time someone he truly seems to have loved.

On 26 March 1779 the Polzelli couple were engaged in the Esterháza Capelle. Antonio Polzelli was a violinist and Luigia was employed as singer in the opera company. They had a two-year-old son with them called Pietro. Luigia was described at the time as having a small narrow face, olive skin and dark eyes, chestnut hair and eyebrows. She had a graceful figure and was of medium size. Antonio was already an old man but his wife, who had been born in Naples, was not quite nineteen. The couple's musical talents did not appeal to the Prince and he dismissed them both from his service at the end of December 1780. Haydn always expected his musicians to perform well, and he worked them hard and was prepared to punish them by withholding favours if they broke the rules. Yet even though Antonio was no longer able to fulfil his duties in the orchestra because of illness, and Luigia's voice was small and weak, Haydn managed to persuade his master to keep them on. The evidence for his love and care for her comes not from letters or eyewitness accounts of them together (none exists as far as one can discover). The clues are in Haydn's musical output. These were the years of opera at Esterháza and, while Luigia's voice was so small and weak that she could just about manage the role of maid, opera after opera has a specially written aria for her – which matched her small voice and made more of her talent than would have seemed possible. In 1783 Luigia did not perform because she was pregnant. On 22 April she was delivered of a second son, Aloysius Antonio Nikolaus. Since everyone knew of the relationship between the opera singer and the Kapellmeister, the general assumption was that Antonio was Haydn's son. Haydn's letters to Luigia never suggest such a thing. Either he did not want to admit such a fact, even in private, in case his wife or someone else intercepted his correspondence, or the rumours were groundless. Nevertheless, Antonio's granddaughter in the 1870s claimed Haydn as a forebear. Haydn certainly took a close interest in both sons, but if anything preferred the elder son, Pietro, who died aged only nineteen from tuberculosis.

What we know of the relationship between the Kapellmeister and the opera singer is all drawn from the letters they exchanged in the 1790s, long after any passion they may have felt for each other had abated. Polzelli does not come out well in this correspondence. She was constantly asking him for money and help of one sort or another. Haydn paid lip service to still loving her, but it was obvious that her demands grated. Polzelli went so far as to extract a promise from Haydn that he would marry her when they were both free. But when her husband Antonio died she married someone else. Still, she extracted a promise that Haydn would look after her in his will, an act of manipulation that comes across as characteristically calculating, mercenary and hard-hearted. Once again Haydn was disappointed in love.

In 1789, ten years after Polzelli's arrival in Esterháza, another woman appeared in Haydn's life. Her name was Maria Anna von Genzinger. She was born into the minor Austrian aristocracy in 1750, so was a year older than Rebecca. Her husband, Peter Leopold von Genzinger, was a popular 'Ladies' Doctor', whom the Empress Maria Theresa had raised to the nobility in 1780; in 1792 he became Rector of the Vienna Hochschule. For many years before that he had been Physician in Ordinary to Prince Nikolaus Esterházy. It was in this capacity that Haydn would have met him and become friendly with him. Genzinger married Maria Anna in 1772 and she subsequently bore him five children, three boys and two girls. Obviously what attracted Haydn was her musical talent. She was able to read full orchestral scores and transcribe them for the pianoforte. More than that, Haydn was flattered that such a beautiful young woman should find his music so stimulating.

Their correspondence began with a letter to Haydn, back in Esterháza after a visit to Vienna, where he had been a guest at one of the Sunday soirées the Genzingers gave for their friends, to which the capital's musical elite, including Mozart, were always invited. In the course of the next half-dozen letters it becomes apparent that Haydn was very much attracted to the charming and cultivated '*gnädige Frau*'. A mutual acquaintance later recalled, 'Haydn seems to have cherished not only respect for the artistic abilities of this lady, but also more tender feelings. Their contemporaries knew nothing of such an emotion being returned, however, and Frau von Genzinger's well-disposed attitude towards Haydn seems to have been based purely on friendly attention and on her respect for his artistic position.'

Maria Anna, Marianne as she was sometimes called, says Rosemary Hughes,[19] was 'a revelation to Haydn'. She was beautiful, musically very talented and a great admirer of the composer. What man would not be bowled over by such an admirer? It all started in June 1789 when the Kapellmeister received the following letter, which began his most loving friendship:

[19] Rosemary Hughes, *Haydn*, p. 60.

Most respected Herr v Haydn, with your kind permission I take the liberty of sending you a piano forte arrangement of the beautiful Andante from your so admirable composition. I made this arrangement from the score quite by myself, without the least help from my teacher; please be good enough to correct any mistakes you may find in it. I hope you are enjoying perfect health, and I wish for nothing more than to see you soon again in Vienna, so that I may demonstrate still further the esteem in which I hold you, I remain in true friendship, your obedient servant Maria Anna von Genzinger.

And she adds very properly at the foot of the page, 'My husband and children also ask me to send you their kindest regards.'

Her letter was dated 10 June. It arrived four days later and on that very day Haydn penned this reply: 'Nobly born and gracious lady in all my previous correspondence, nothing delighted me more than the surprise of seeing such a lovely handwriting, and reading so many kind expressions; but even more I admired the enclosure – the excellent arrangement of the Adagio, which is correct enough to be engraved. . . .' And he ends the letter, 'Best and kindest Frau v Genzinger I only await a hint from you as to how and in what fashion I can possibly be of service to your Grace. Meanwhile I return the adagio, with very much hope to receive from your grace some demands on my modest talents. . . .'

This letter, while warm in tone, is still formulaic in the phrases it employs, phrases which everyone used at the time. But the more Haydn stayed at the von Genzingers' Vienna home, playing music for their friends, teaching the two eldest children, Josepha ('Miss Pepi') and Franz, the more his feelings grew. Haydn had found what he had always wanted – the perfect woman and the perfect family. He was probably in love with her. Habit and self-discipline meant that he knew his place. 'My friendship and esteem for your ladyship, tender though it is, can never become culpable, because I always keep before me the reverence due to your Ladyship's lofty virtues ...' One wonders if that was written as much to remind himself of his position as to reassure her that she had nothing to fear from his attentions.

This loving but platonic friendship with Maria Anna von Genzinger only reinforced the feelings of isolation Haydn was beginning to feel after twenty years of service in Esterháza. He called it 'my desert' after one of his visits to Vienna and the von Genzingers. In a long and chatty letter after returning to his official duties after a short stay in Vienna, he reveals how dull his life had become and what he missed about his visits to the Genzingers in Vienna. 'Here in Estoras nobody asks me "do you take your chocolate with or without milk? Will you have your coffee black or with cream? What can I pass you my dear Haydn, will you have a vanilla or a pineapple ice?" ' It is a bitter-sweet letter from a lonely, emotionally starved man to a woman whom he believed perfect but unattainable. He clearly cherished the harmless frivolities of social domestic life, and noticed this most when they were absent and his life seemed suddenly unfulfilled. Such light-hearted distraction must have been a valuable balance to the essential seriousness of his musical vocation and the demands of his public reputation. The contrast between Maria Anne von Genzinger and Luigia Polzelli could not have been sharper. The grasping Polzelli was at the same time writing him letters of complaint about his absence of attention to her, her lack of money and the need for him to help her.

Do these letters explain a great deal about his decision to go to England with Johann Peter Salomon? Clearly he thought he was in love with Maria Anna, but she could never be his. Equally Polzelli was beginning to annoy him with her demands. In simple terms, he needed a break – from these women, his wife and Esterháza. Nevertheless, it was a brave decision for a man in his late fifties who had never been away from his homeland before. Travelling anywhere in the eighteenth century was a hazardous business, but in 1790 it was a particularly worrying time to be on the road. France was in the grip of the Revolution, the French King and his Austrian Queen virtual prisoners in Versailles. Armies were on the move. Haydn's main experience of life had been in a huge palace far from Vienna which was a fairy tale place built to rival Versailles – and more than succeeded in that ambition. For twenty years he had been a liveried servant at the beck and call of his princely master. Now he was to move to the biggest and richest city in Europe. But while he looked forward to the challenge he did not forget Frau von Genzinger.

She was the first person Haydn wrote to before he boarded the boat to cross the Channel and the first when he arrived in London on 1 January 1791:

Nobly born and gracious lady: I hope you will have received my last letter from Calais. I should have written you immediately on my arrival but I wanted a few days so as to be able to write about several things at once. So I can tell you that on the first inst., New Year's Day, after attending mass, I boarded a ship at 7 30 am and at five in the after noon I arrived, thank God, safe and sound At the beginning we, for the first four hours, didn't go further than one single English mile, and there are 24 between Calais and Dower [*sic*]. ... Fortunately, however, towards 11 30 o'clock a wind arose and blew so favourably that by 4 o'clock we covered 22 miles. Since the tide had begun to ebb, preventing our vessel from reaching a pier, two smaller ships came out to meet us as we were still fairly far out to sea. And into these we transferred, and thus at last, though exposed to a medium gale, we landed safely.

Later in the same letter, he tells her that his arrival in London 'caused a great sensation throughout the whole city, and I went the round of newspapers for three successive days. Everyone wants to know me. ...' 'Everyone' included an 'English widow' of forty years.

CHAPTER TEN

'Mrs Schroeter Presents Her Compliments . . .'

On Wednesday, 29 June 1791, nearly seven months after he landed in England, Haydn was handed the following note: 'Mrs Schroeter presents her compliments to Mr Haydn, and informs him that she is just returned to town, and will be happy to see him whenever it is convenient to him to give her a lesson.' Rebecca gives Haydn her address as 'No. 6 James Street, Buckingham Gate'. He jotted it down in his notebook. It would be a house he would get to know as a second home. This formal letter raises many questions about how and where Rebecca and Haydn met. Did she really need lessons? Was it just a ruse from an admirer to meet the man who interested her?

Whatever the circumstances in which they met, Mrs Schroeter must have made quite a memorable impression on Haydn in the swirl and bustle that took over his life in London. The composer was in great demand. He did not lack for the attention of society women. He was invited everywhere. The invitations started from the moment he stepped ashore on New Year's Day 1791. He told Maria Anna von Genzinger in his first letter to her a week after his arrival in London, 'I had to dine out six times up to now, and if I wanted I could dine out every day.' He tried to put some order into what threatened to become a chaotic way of life. 'I must consider first my health, and, second my work. Except for the nobility, I admit no callers until two o'clock in the afternoon . . .' For thirty years Haydn had been used to the ordered existence of Kapellmeister to the Prince of Esterházy. That was a regulated environment where everyone knew their place. London gave him freedom, prestige and more money than he could ever have expected to earn. In return, he sacrificed the peace of mind he needed when he worked. Perhaps he saw immediately in Rebecca a woman who could provide him with some kind of home life – something he had always needed.

On 18 January Haydn was invited to the Queen's Birthday celebrations at St James's Palace. Even though he had not yet been formally presented at court he was immediately recognised by the other guests. On entering the ballroom, the *St James Chronicle* reported the next day, he was greeted by the Prince of Wales with a bow, 'whereupon the eyes of the company were directed to the composer, and everyone paid their respects'. Within three weeks Haydn had made his mark with the highest in the land. He was immediately invited to play with the Prince of Wales at his next morning concerts at Carlton House – the same concerts in which Schroeter used to play.

Haydn's work load was enormous. He had contracted with Salomon to produce symphonies and other music for twelve concerts in the Hanover Square Rooms. The concerts were scheduled to take place every Friday night beginning on 11 February. He would also direct the musicians from the fortepiano. He had agreed, too, to write an opera, *L'anima del Filosofo*, for Sir John Gallini. It turned out to be a fraught commission, with contractual squabbles between the various artists and theatres. Finally it was refused a licence, which killed off the project. Haydn, however, was paid his fee for the work. It was never performed until the Italian mezzo-soprano, Cecilia Bartoli, revived it at the Royal Opera House in 2001. The critics, while praising her, found the piece a bit heavy going and agreed it was not the composer's best work. In retrospect, Haydn may have had a lucky escape. The work on the opera delayed the start of Salomon's concerts because many of the artists were also due to appear at the Hanover Square Rooms. In the end the series did not actually begin until 11 March.

Yet in between composing, performing and socialising, he still made time to give lessons. Like everything else in London, the fees people were prepared to pay were higher than anything he had ever experienced before. Haydn, who had been born into poverty and had almost starved as a young man because he had no money, had very little to show for thirty years as a Kapellmeister. He seized every chance he could to earn money, knowing that at the age of fifty-nine it was his last chance to provide for a comfortable old age. He told Georg Griesinger, one of his biographers, that he 'gave several persons lessons on the clavier, and each lesson was paid for with a guinea'. He recalled that Haydn said, 'My eyes popped out of my head at that.' One of his pupils was Lady Elizabeth Greville, daughter of the Earl of Warwick. Another was the daughter of a rich banker, Nathanial Brassey. The only other pupil known to history is Rebecca Schroeter.

Rebecca did not necessarily have to wait until the first Salomon concert in March to see Haydn perform. She could have seen him directing a band of musicians as early as 18 February at a 'Ladies' Concert' at Mrs Blair's in Portland Place. Mrs Blair was a great patroness of music in London and such was this beautiful lady's social standing and wealth that she was among the first to have Haydn play privately at her house. According to the *Morning Chronicle*, she lived on 'that superb street where as usual artificial light out glared the moon'. Haydn was applauded wherever he went in public. 'The musical world', said the *Morning Chronicle*, 'is at this moment enraptured with a Composition that Haydn has brought forth. ...' There was another concert featuring Haydn's music at the Pantheon on 24 February.

There is little reason to doubt that Rebecca was there for the first night of the Salomon concerts at the Hanover Square Rooms on 11 March. It had become socially acceptable for women to attend such concerts. In fact, there were men's tickets and women's tickets, which were not interchangeable. One bought a ticket for the season. Society demanded that she would not go alone – a woman on her own would have been considered a common prostitute. As Fanny Burney shows in her novel *Evelina*, even a respectable woman, momentarily separated from the rest of her party, could be accosted by some young dandy on the prowl. Rebecca Schroeter would either have made up her own party or been invited to join someone else's group. Her letters often talk of 'our friends' and she took a party of eighteen to Haydn's benefit concert on 3 May 1792. Charlotte Papendieck, the wife of a court musician and a former pupil of Johann Samuel Schroeter, was certainly there. Her ticket has survived. On the back is written 'Presented to Mrs Papendieck by Dr Hayden [sic] himself'.

The redoubtable Mrs Papendieck says in her memoirs that Salomon gave her aunt and family 'a free admittance to the concerts; the same to the Janssen family, the son and daughter being good musicians'. Salomon was an honest and generous man. He had been a good friend to her late husband and a colleague in the Prince of Wales Band. Salomon could well have extended the same courtesy to Rebecca. It is quite likely that Charlotte and Rebecca were in the same party. Whether she paid for herself or not, her presence there, combined with her friendship with Salomon and the Papendiecks, would certainly have given her access to Haydn after the concerts.

A subscription to the first twelve concerts would have cost Mrs Schroeter £5. A servant would have fetched a green-coloured lady's ticket from Lockhard's Bank at number 36 Pall Mall. She would also have got all the details about the arrangements. If she went by coach, she was told, she should use the side entrance, and her coachman should point his horse's head towards the square; if she went by chair she could use the door in the square. The arrangements Salomon had to make show just how much attention to detail was necessary to handle a crowd that could be up to 800 strong. There would be hundreds of carriages, hackney coaches, sedan chairs and other conveyances being used by the ton. None of them would ever have considered for a moment walking to the concert. There were not just the concert goers to cope with, but at least an equal number of their servants as well. Even the ticketing was planned with one colour for men and another for women. A woman could exchange her ticket with another woman, but not with a man. The doors were open at seven and the concert began at eight. Polite society always made a point of arriving late, so we should feel nothing but pity for the artists who appeared early in the proceedings.

For music lovers in London at the time, the choice of entertainment was very large indeed. The attraction of seeing Haydn perform his own music in person would have been irresistible. According to a newspaper, *The Diary*, the first concert was 'attended by a numerous and very elegant audience'. Mrs Papendieck, like all the women in the audience for this special musical occasion, was concerned about what she should wear. 'My dress now had to be considered,' she recalled, 'which had come down to two muslins and the printed cambrics . . . the puce satin being at its last gasp. My blue satin cloak was quite new, and trimmed with beautiful dark fur . . . Mrs Barlow said it was most elegant to wear a wrap when cold. . . . A cap to suit I purchased of her for 35 shillings, and Kead dressed my hair for 2s 6d as usual, charging the same price if he pinned on.' Rebecca would certainly not have wanted to be outshone. She will have spent as much time, and money, making sure that she was presentable in such 'elegant' company.

Rebecca knew the Hanover Square Rooms well. They were opened, in fact, in 1775, the year of her marriage. Her late husband's friends and early sponsors, John Christian Bach and Friedrich Abel, each had had a quarter share in the project. The rooms were custom built, in an imposing building on the east side of the square at the north east corner of Hanover Square. As Simon McVeigh says, 'In many ways even a public concert retained many aspects of the Aristocratic drawing room.' The actual concert hall was on the second floor – nearly eighty feet long and over thirty feet wide, it was one of the biggest in London. The beautiful half-domed ceiling was painted by Cipriani. Gainsborough's portrait of Abel graced the room and the painter even designed ten lighted transparencies for the place. In 1791 – the year Haydn was there – the room was described as 'magnificent in its decoration, with large mirrors separated by golden ornament *en baroque*'.

This is most probably where Rebecca was first presented to Haydn and made such an impression on him. Was it her knowledge of music that intrigued? Was it the recent death of her husband, a young man of great musical talent and promise, that moved him to compassion so that he spent some time with her? They must have exchanged rather more than just polite courtesies. They must have talked about piano lessons. The content of the first rather respectful letter suggests that they may have discussed the possibility of her becoming one of his pupils. The implication is that Haydn may have asked her to wait until the summer, or conversely, she had told him that she had to go out of town to visit her sick mother in Blackheath and that she would get in touch when she was back.

Certainly they will not have seen each other very often during the summer months. Rebecca would have been mostly in Blackheath caring for her mother, who was increasingly frail. For part of the following month, July, Haydn was in Oxford where he was awarded an honorary doctorate in music by the university. In August he was invited to spend the summer in Hertfordshire at the country house of a banker, Nathanial Brassey. He wrote to Maria Anna in September when he was back in London, 'I have been living in the country, amid the loveliest scenery, with a banker's family, where the atmosphere is like that of the Genzinger family . . . in the mornings I walk in the woods, alone, with my English grammar . . . Of course I had hoped to have the pleasure of seeing you sooner, but my circumstances – in short, fate – will have it that I remain in London another eight months.' Was Rebecca now part of that 'fate'?

Haydn's letters to Frau von Genzinger paint but one aspect of his personality. When he was talking to women, he could be flirtatious, amusing, and light-hearted. His letters talk mainly about his work and the people he meets in London. His London notebooks reveal other facets. They are a mixture of the sublime and the ridiculous. They show a man fascinated by detail. Haydn seemed to want to register every experience. On 5 December that year he noted, 'The fog was so thick you could have spread it on bread. In order to write I had to light the lights at 11 o'clock.' He learned that 'The city of London keeps 4000 carts for cleaning the streets and 2000 of these work every day'. Someone told him that 'in the last 31 years 38,000 houses have been built in London'. Statistics obviously had a special attraction for him: 'At the beginning of May 1792 Lord Barrymore gave a ball that cost 5000 guineas. He paid 1000 guineas for 1000 peaches, 2000 gusberes (gooseberries) 5 shillings a basket.' He was fascinated by court cases: 'The Duke of Cumberland had to pay £25,000 in an adultery case.' 'Warren Hastings trial which took place on 25th May 1792 was the ninety-second meeting in Westminster Hall ... the trial began 4 years ago. It is said Hastings has a fortune of one million pounds sterling.' And he even noted down the recipe for 'The Prince of Wales Punch 1 bottle champagne; 1 bottle of burgundy, 1 bottle of rum, 10 lemons, 2 oranges, 1½ lbs of sugar'.

If only Haydn had decided to turn all these jottings into a travel book, he could have outsold even Tobias Smollett, one of Britain's favourite travel writers. He offers a marvellous description of a lunch given for the Lord Mayor of London. The original is written in German, but his phonetic transcription of the English words echoed his marked German accent. 'The new Lord Mayor and his wife ate at the first table, then the Lord *Chanceler* and both the *scherifs*, *Duc de Lids*, *Minuster* Pitt and the other judges of the first rank. At number two table I ate with Mr Silvester, the greatest lawyer and first Alderman of London. In this room which is called *Geld* Hall, there were sixteen tables besides others in adjoining rooms; in all nearly 1200 dined with the greatest pomp. The food was very nice and well-cooked; many kinds of wine in abundance.' After dinner Haydn stayed on to savour the music and dancing. In one of the rooms 'The dance was English ... the other tables were occupied by men who, as usual, drank enormously the whole night. The most curious thing, though, is that part of the company went on dancing without hearing a single note of the music, for first at one table, then at another. Some were yelling songs and some swilling it down and drinking toasts amid terrific roars of *"Hurrey, Hurrey, Hurrey"* [sic] and waving glasses.' Haydn was always surprised at the amount the English drank.

Rebecca's piano lessons began during the winter months of 1791 when everyone was back in town. Haydn went to her house in James Street, where Schroeter's old Broadwood piano still had pride of place. He had to make time for these lessons, because he was busy preparing for Salomon's second series of subscription concerts. He continued to make public appearances at concerts and private entertainments. Lessons with Rebecca, who was always very supportive, slowly became a blessed respite in his hectic day. She was an English version of Maria Anna von Genzinger. She was about the same age. She played the piano well, and could arrange and transcribe music. She was an ardent admirer of his talent, and told him so. Haydn found in Rebecca what he had found in Maria Anna: a woman who cared for him and cared about him. The feelings of love that he had for the married Maria Anna, a happily married woman with a family, were easily transferred to Rebecca. Rebecca was a widow and unencumbered. She could make Haydn the centre of her life. He need not share her with anyone.

At the end of November Haydn was involved in the wedding celebrations of Frederick, Duke of York, the King's second son. Frederick married Princess Friederike, the eldest daughter of King Friedrich Wilhelm of Prussia. Afterwards Haydn was invited to the Prince's English country estate at Oatlands. He noted that 'the little castle . . . has a most remarkable grotto which cost £25,000 and which was 11 years in the building'. After three days the Duke sent Haydn back to London in the royal carriage. The Duchess was a great supporter of the composer throughout his London sojourn.

There cannot have been much time for Mrs Schroeter in Haydn's busy life. But she was used to the absences of a musician in demand. She understood that his work had to come first and knew she needed to be patient with a man under pressure. It was not until December that he began to concentrate almost exclusively on the next season of concerts. The 1792 series would be quite a test of his skill, because a former pupil, Ignaz Pleyel, had arrived in London and was to play for a rival concert series. As the *Public Advertiser* reported on 5 January, 'Haydn and Pleyel are to be pitted against one another this season. The supporters of each are violent partisans.' Haydn felt the pressure enormously. Naturally he turned to Rebecca for support and affection.

When he was not there, she wrote to him. 'I wish much to know how you do today,' she stated on 8 February, 'I am very sorry to lose the pleasure of seeing you this morning, but I hope you will have time to come tomorrow.' Here is a woman who was clearly on easy terms with a close and important friend. There must have been many, many more such little billets-doux because the style was so fluent and so relaxed. Did she write to other of her friends about Haydn? Did Haydn write to her and did she keep his letters? The letters raise so many questions. But they also give us quite a few answers. They reveal a lady who cared deeply about Haydn in every way; they are flirtatious, loving, supportive and anxious about his headaches; she sends him soap, copies some of his music and borrows poems from him. It is impossible not to believe that Rebecca must have come to love Haydn as much as ever she loved her husband. Given what is known of that genial, gentle and talented man, did Rebecca now find in Haydn what she had hoped for but possibly failed to find in Schroeter: hard work, commitment, success and an international reputation?

The two men, though, could not have been more different. Schroeter was suave. He had polished manners and was well travelled. Although much younger than Haydn, he would have been more of a man of the world. If Schroeter had half the personal attractions of his famous sister, the singer Corona, the young pianist would have been handsome indeed. But perhaps he was lazy. To a determined woman like Rebecca it must have been galling that the man she had sacrificed so much for did not fulfil the early promise when he was but her piano teacher. Did the drinking and his largely unassertive nature turn him into a terrible disappointment? She soon may have lost respect for a man who did not strive to achieve something in life. Perhaps he need not have succeeded, but at least he should have tried.

The new object of her affections could never have been called handsome. Not even Haydn himself thought he was attractive to look at. Albert Dies, who spent a lot of time with him face to face, described him thus:

He was of something less than medium size. The lower part of his body was too short for the upper, something often to be encountered in small persons of both sexes, but which was very obvious in Haydn's case, because he adhered to the old fashioned mode of knee breeches that reached only to the hips and not the chest. His facial features were rather regular, and his expression vivacious, fiery, but at the same time moderate, warm and inviting. . . . Haydn had a moderately strong bone structure; his muscles were not prominent. His hawk like nose (he suffered much from a nasal polyp which had no doubt enlarged this part of his anatomy) and also the other parts of his face were strongly scarred from the pox, and the nose even had pox seams so that each nostril had a different form . . .

Another contemporary biographer, Georg Griesinger, who also knew him personally, remembered, 'His forehead was broad and nicely domed, his skin brown, his eyes vivacious. . . . And from the whole of his physiognomy and bearing there radiated prudence and quiet gravity.' Nevertheless Griesinger also notes 'an innocent waggishness or what the English call humour . . .' Haydn, for his part, thought himself ugly and often remarked that it wasn't his looks that attracted women. Having fallen in love with a handsome man once, perhaps Rebecca now saw beyond the externals and looked at the inner man. Haydn was fifty-eight when he arrived in London, which made him eighteen years older than Rebecca. In Johann Samuel Schroeter Rebecca had fallen for a man exactly her age; perhaps now the older man, being more mature, was reassuring. She was not taking a risk with his talent – he had proved it beyond measure.

And what did Haydn find in Rebecca, this woman who wanted him to give her piano lessons? First and foremost was her obvious love of music. The fact that she had been married to a musician who had achieved some reputation would have reassured him that she would understand the pressures of the profession. Haydn was a great flirt. Perhaps Rebecca had a merry twinkle in her eye, despite her widowhood. Maybe it was her status as a widow that intrigued Haydn.

Unlike his beloved Maria Anna von Genzinger, Rebecca was available. He was in a foreign country for the first time in his life. The restrictions he might have felt about pursuing an affair in London would not have been apparent. Travel can be a great aphrodisiac. The only description we have of Rebecca in middle age – she was nearly forty when they met – is Haydn's. She was, he recalled, 'beautiful and kind'. It sounds an unlikely pairing: the 'ugly' composer and the 'beautiful' widow.

CHAPTER ELEVEN
'Dearest Love'

The twenty-three letters that Haydn copied so neatly into his London notebook read like any eighteenth-century epistolary novel. In the late eighteenth century private letter writing was often called 'talking upon paper'.[20] When one reads Rebecca Schroeter's letters for the first time, what can be easily imagined is the sound of her voice 'talking upon paper' to a man she loved and admired – without affectation, unforced and intimate. Seventeen of the letters cover an intense period in their relationship between the beginning of April and the end of June 1792. The last letter was written just days before Haydn returned to Vienna.[21]

The letters are full of abbreviations such as 'F', which means 'faithful' or 'Dst', which means 'dearest'. The abbreviations may have been Haydn's way of cutting down the time involved in copying them out by hand. The correspondence inevitably seems one-sided and Rebecca is constantly imploring Haydn's attention, but her familiar queries about his well-being and invitations to visit are part of a flurry of by now intimate arrangements between lovers. As there is nothing in Rebecca's own hand it is impossible to know whether the abbreviations used were Mrs Schroeter's. Since she was writing to someone whose command of the English language was not by any means perfect, it is likely that she spelt out the phrases in full. Some words

[20] Isobel Grundy in *The Oxford Illustrated History of English Literature*.
[21] The full text of the letters as copied into the notebook is in the appendix on page 206.

were underlined – was it Rebecca's emphasis or Haydn's? The abbreviations may have been part of an intimate language between them. Unless any letters from Haydn to Rebecca come to light, no one will ever know for sure. The letters are all in the same section of his notebook, so it suggests that he copied them out in one sitting. They may have been a selection of only the most loving. There may have been disagreements, tensions and worries. There is only a hint of tension in one or two of the letters. These may be the only ones Haydn had time to copy. There has been speculation that she had asked for her letters to be returned and Haydn, eager to keep a souvenir of a very special time, copied the letters before he returned them. That idea does not really stand up. There is nothing in these letters that could incriminate or embarrass. Even so, they are a love story in miniature.

Every woman who had featured in Haydn's life became involved with the composer because of music. The only relationship that failed – his marriage – was the one that was not based on music. Haydn's wife had no musical feelings or comprehension at all. She could not understand his art – so she failed to understand him. The musically talented woman who had stirred his feelings most deeply before he came to London had been Maria Anna von Genzinger. It is therefore hardly surprising that the next woman to win his heart was one who also had a passion for music, a great deal of talent and genuine care for the man. Just as his relationship with Maria Anna had begun with a letter, so too did that with Rebecca Schroeter.

Using the dates and days supplied in the Rebecca Schroeter letters, and matching them against Haydn's very busy professional schedule, it is now possible to establish just how much contact there was between them. What is more, one can make some very informed guesses about their first few months together when what seems like a genuine love affair was in its first throes. One obvious conclusion is that Rebecca very quickly established herself at the centre of Haydn's life. He went to see her as often as he could, sometimes just to meet in the mornings, sometimes for dinner alone or with friends in the afternoons. Dinner at this time was taken between four and six in the afternoon, so he had plenty of time to get to the concert, which began around seven. Haydn visited number 6 James Street, Buckingham Gate, near Buckingham House (now Palace) at the very least twice a week.

The story the letters tell demonstrates just how close the pair had become and how easy the relationship must have been between them. Haydn sometimes had to back out of a meeting owing to his professional commitments. Rebecca was patience and understanding personified. 'I was extremely sorry not to have the pleasure of seeing you today, but hope you will come tomorrow ...' she writes on Tuesday, 8 May. In another letter she says, 'I hope to see you my dear Love on Tuesday as usual to dinner.' Tuesday or dinner must have been a regular appointment. Sometimes there are regrets on Rebecca's part: 'I was very sorry to lose the pleasure of seeing you this morning, but I hope you will have time to come tomorrow [letter of 8 February 1792]'. Almost every day of the week is mentioned somewhere in the letters 'to dinner on Saturday', hope to see you tomorrow (Wednesday)', 'For dinner on Thursday', 'I shall be happy to see you on Sunday at any time convenient'. Friday night was concert night during the season of subscription concerts promoted by Johann Peter Salomon. Mrs Schroeter, we know, attended the concerts to see her 'dearest friend' perform.

There are mentions of 'our friends' and one letter suggests that Haydn gave a musical party for just such a gathering. On 17 May she writes, 'Permit me to return you a thousand thanks for this evening's entertainment.' After Salomon's last concert of the season in 1792, Rebecca comes home to James Street and, late at night, she tells him, 'I can not close my eyes to sleep till I have returned you ten thousand thanks for the inexpressible delight I have received from your ever enchanting compositions and your incomparably charming performance of them. ... [letter dated Wednesday night, 6 June 1792].' Letter writing then was rather like a telephone call now and in the style of the letters you can hear the voice of a woman who cares deeply for – loves – Haydn. She can easily be pictured, this beautiful widow, propped up in bed, writing by candlelight one of her delicious little notes of praise for his music, talking of her affection for the man before she tells him she is 'with the firmest and most perfect attachment your friend'. We have one example of Rebecca's handwriting – as she witnessed a contract on behalf of Haydn in 1797. It looks almost too good to be true, well-formed letters, firmly written. It is the handwriting of a confident woman that must always have pleased Haydn when he got yet another note handed him by his servant the next morning.

The letters give the impression that when he could come to James Street as arranged, she knew in advance. He would have sent a little note by hand. He was an enthusiastic correspondent with Maria Anna and even the troublesome mistress, Polzelli, got fairly prompt replies. The letters he wrote to Maria Anna von Genzinger, the married woman he could only worship with respect, are marvellous examples of Haydn's intimate style. They are chatty, amusing, revealing letters about the man. Even though good manners meant he had to tread a careful line with her, Haydn does not really hold back. Here's just one example, written in January 1792 – after he had begun his friendship with Rebecca.

> Kindest and most gracious Lady! I ask your forgiveness a thousand times. I own and bemoan that I should not be so remiss in fulfilling my promise, but if Your Grace could only see how I am tormented, here in London, by having to attend all sorts of private concerts, which cause me great loss of time; and by the vast amount of work which has been heaped on my shoulders, you would, my gracious Lady, have the greatest pity on me. I never in my life wrote so much in one year as I have here during this past one, but now I am almost completely exhausted, and it will do me good to be able to rest a little when I return home.

After asking her for some music he sent her before he left Vienna – the manuscripts of two symphonies – Haydn ends, 'And now, my unique and gracious lady, I trust and pray for your indulgence. Oh yes! I can see you quite clearly in front of me, and I can hear you say:

"Well, this time I shall forgive you, you wretched Haydn, but-but!"
No, no, henceforth I shall perform my duties far better. I must close
now, by saying that as always I hold you in the greatest possible
esteem, and shall ever be . . . my most gracious Frau von Genzinger's
most obedient servant.'

That letter was written in German. The language barrier stopped
him writing in English in this playful and teasing way to Rebecca.
Haydn, though, loved jokes and stories, and his notebooks are pep-
pered with them. It is not impossible that Rebecca spoke or wrote
some German – after all, she had been married to Schroeter for
thirteen years. Perhaps she had enough German to understand
Haydn's little notes to her. Possibly it was to help his English, which
he studied whenever he could, that she wrote to him in English. In
her letters Rebecca is always very solicitous about Haydn's health,
especially whether he had 'slept well'. No wonder he yearned, at
times, for the tranquillity of Esterháza.

It was not until Friday, 11 March that Haydn finally 'presided' at
the opening Hanover Square concert. Maybe this was when Mrs
Schroeter first saw the man she wanted as a piano teacher and came
to love so ardently. But given the crush in the building, it would have
been a fleeting meeting at best. Haydn, and Schroeter before him,
would have felt very much at home in Hanover Square. The square
is an interesting example of the influence of the royal family's home
country on Georgian architecture: 'If the names of the street and the
square, the dedication of the church (St George's arrived in 1720–4),
and the professions of its first inhabitants seem to unite in fervent
loyalty to the throne of Hanover, so does some of the architecture.
Nearly all the surviving original houses in George Street and its
westward return into the square are in a style evidently intended to
be German.'[22]

The Hanover Square Rooms could hold up to 800 people, exclusive
of the performers. On special occasions nearer 1000 crammed into
the oblong-shaped room. The heat generated by such a mob of people

[22] John Summerson, *Georgian London*, Penguin, p. 99.

made for an uncomfortable evening. Personal cleanliness was usually lacking. Taking a bath was often a rare event. The resulting mix of what is politely called 'body odour' must have made quite an impression. Add to the heat and smells the smoke from hundreds of candles and it is not surprising that nobody rushed to be there early. 'Gentlemen' tended to arrive late from their clubs where they had dined – usually rather too well – and would then sleep or chat through the second half. It was perfectly normal for audiences to walk around during concerts.[23] When Haydn appeared, cognoscenti crowded forward towards the front of the room; but when a minor singer was performing the audience was completely indifferent and wandered around the hall. Private concerts attracted similar complaints. Attending one such rout, Fanny Burney's heroine, Cecilia,[24] could scarcely hear the concert for other ladies talking about forthcoming dances, though 'not one of them failed, from time to time, to exclaim with great rapture "What sweet music!"'. Even the King conversed with the company during the performance of court odes, and at the Duke of Queensberry's concerts cards 'proved a powerful rival to the music'. It is hardly surprising that for serious chamber music the Prince of Wales insisted that his morning concerts were listened to in silence. He banned any conversation.

It was for these very practical reasons that Haydn always liked to introduce his new symphony at the start of the second half when the audience was at its maximum. Mrs Papendieck is a wonderful eyewitness to the concert and the playing of the first of what would be twelve great symphonies composed especially for London audiences: 'Now the anxious moment has arrived, and Salomon having called "attention" with his bow, the company rose to a person and stood through the whole of the first movement. The effect was imposingly magnificent. ... Salomon was wound up to a pitch of enthusiasm beyond himself. The public were satisfied and Haydn was very prop-

---

[23] Simon McVeigh, *Concert Life in London from Mozart to Haydn*, Cambridge University Press.
[24] Fanny Burney's eponymous heroine in her second novel.

erly taken up.' The next day the concert was hailed in the *Morning Chronicle*: 'Never, perhaps, was there a richer musical treat.'

Given Rebecca's extensive contacts in the musical world – she obviously knew Salomon, among others – it would not have been too difficult for Schroeter's widow to arrange to be presented to Herr Haydn. In those early days conversation, beyond mere social formalities, would have been a challenge to both of them. Or was she able to speak enough German learned during her marriage to Schroeter to make an instant impression on the visitor whose English was at the time quite limited? There is a letter[25] from the Reverend Christian Latrobe to Vincent Novello recalling the meeting of Haydn and his wife at this time.

When he entered the room, he found my wife alone & as she could not speak German, & he had scarcely picked up few English words, both were at a loss what to say. He bowed with foreign formality & the following short explanation took place.

H: 'Dis Mr Latrobe House?' The answer was in the affirmative.

H: 'Be you his woman?' (Meaning wife)

'I am Mrs Latrobe', was the reply.

After some pause, he looked round the room & saw his picture & explained 'Dat is me. I am Haydn!' My wife instantly knowing what a most welcome guest I was honoured with, sent for me to a house not far off, and treated him with all possible civility.

There is another possible connection between Rebecca and Haydn during this period. In May 1791 her husband's publisher, William Napier, went bankrupt. Napier was a fellow Scot and obviously well known to Rebecca, so she would have wanted to help. Music publishing was a notoriously difficult business and the fact that he had twelve children cannot have helped his finances either. Napier had not only published Schroeter's music, but had played with him in the Prince of Wales Band from time to time. It is not known exactly how

---

[25] British Museum Department of Manuscripts.

much he owed, but it must have been a substantial sum as his creditors were told to expect only two shillings in the pound. According to Dies, 'Haydn told me he had set some 50 Scotch songs. The man was so poor he could not afford to pay Haydn for them so Haydn, knowing him to be a worthy fellow, gave him the music as a present. Napier published the songs, and had so much success with them that he found his state suddenly transferred from one of penury to one of comfort.' In her second letter Rebecca sends Haydn 'the words of the song you desired' – which might well be a Scottish song for the Napier project. It seems logical to suppose that Rebecca played a part in the arrangement, interceding with Haydn on Napier's behalf. She would certainly want to be loyal to a man who had refused to take the family's side that fraught weekend in July 1775.

So somewhere, somehow they met. Somewhere, somehow the attractive widow caught the susceptible Maestro's attention long enough not only to talk about music lessons, but to give him her address as well. Haydn loved lively company. He did not seek friendship in high society but rather with those people who merited it. Back in Austria were three women with whom he was involved – his wife, his former mistress and, above all others, Maria Anna von Genzinger, whom Haydn worshipped and who had helped him experience what a real home was like. Haydn may well have sensed that Rebecca could play the same role in London as Maria Anna in Vienna. On the other hand, he did not have a huge amount of leisure time – the demands of his contract with Salomon left few spare hours to socialise during the season.

There is an abrupt change of tone between the first letter and the second, which is dated eight months later. In the first letter, of June 1791, she simply 'presents her compliments'. The relationship may well not have begun in earnest until September when both of them were back in London. By February 1792 she is writing 'My Dear Inclos'd I have sent you the words of the song you desired . . .' and ends the short letter with the words 'My thoughts and best wishes are always with you, and I am ever with the utmost sincerity My Dear, your friend . . .' Perhaps Haydn thought this was the first letter in which Rebecca put her feelings on paper, and it became a sentimental keepsake. In this letter there is also a clue as to how often they were meeting. She says she was sorry not to see him on Wednesday morning, but hopes he will have the time to come on Thursday. Already, it seems, Haydn was dropping by number 6 James Street on a fairly regular basis, and possibly when the fancy took him. Mrs Schroeter feels able to suggest any day that she wants for them to dine together secure in the knowledge that if Haydn can get away from the pressure of composing he will.

Did Mrs Schroeter, who had once before found piano lessons turning her feelings into love for the teacher, experience the same with Haydn? The letters show that she felt the power of music deeply. It is possible that she had a penchant for famous musicians. She was something like a modern-day 'fan', who falls in love, not so much with the music, but the musician. When Rebecca first fell in love she was in her early twenties, an innocent and sheltered young woman. Now she was a widow of forty, who knew her own mind, had fought hard and tenaciously for what she perceived to be hers by right, her marriage to Schroeter and her dowry. The optimist prefers to think it was a genuine love affair between two loving people who both felt at the time that they were denied the love and affection others enjoyed. Rebecca was still somewhat on the fringes of her family's circle – still paying the penalty for giving in to her feelings rather than doing her duty. Haydn was alone in a foreign city for the first time in his life; everything he knew and understood was far away.

One theme that is always constant in Rebecca's letters is her concern for his health and that he was working too hard. She obviously provided a quiet haven for him to relax in after his pressing public duties. In other words she made a home for him in the middle of the biggest, dirtiest and noisiest place in the known world. As she says on more than one occasion, 'Take great care of yourself and do not fatigue yourself with too much application to business.' How he must have missed the clean air and peace and quiet of Esterháza. In fact, just a few days after arriving in London he tells Maria Anna, I wish I could fly to Vienna, to have more quiet in which to work, for the noise the common people make as they sell their wares in the street is intolerable.'

A print by Hogarth called *The Enraged Musician* shows a composer at his window being driven mad by the noise in the street outside. There is a ballad singer, a screeching parrot, a girl with a rattle, an itinerant flute player, a milk girl calling her wares, a boy drummer, a dustman, a knife grinder, a sow gelder blowing his horn and a bawling fish peddler. There's even a little boy urinating into a coal-hole in front of the musician's window. And to cap it all, two cats are fighting on the neighbouring roof of a pewterer's shop. Hogarth's print was made in 1751. Forty years on, when Haydn was trying to compose, the situation can only have got worse, because London was nearly double the size. Almost every letter Rebecca sends him asks after his health: 'I wish to know how you do today.' And it seems mutual friends told her about Haydn's workload – was it Salomon, or Napier? In a letter dated 12 April she writes, 'I am told you was five hours at your study's yesterday. I am afraid it will hurt you ... let me prevail on you, my much loved Haydn not to keep to your studies so long at one time.'

One recalls from Haydn's personal letters to Maria Anna von Genzinger in Vienna – and he was still writing to her – that he often mentioned the way her family cared about him, made sure he got what he wanted: hot chocolate or good parmesan cheese. His conversations with Rebecca must have begun to take on the same pattern. Once again here was a beautiful and warm-hearted woman who was prepared to listen to an old man's moans, and give him tea and sympathy. The difference was that with Maria Anna in Vienna it was idealised, respectful love – a love that could never be more than deep friendship. In London with Rebecca, her letters suggest – no, 'suggest' is too weak a word – her letters confirm a physical relationship. Within a matter of weeks, Haydn had found the home life he had missed so badly in Esterháza, and which he could not fully have with Frau von Genzinger. He had discovered a real home, a loving and beautiful woman who cared.

There are two intriguing entries in his first London notebook. It could well be that he had Rebecca in mind when he noted, 'My friend, you think I love you. In truth you are not mistaken.' Or was that a phrase that Rebecca had used to him. Another entry, in German says, '*Gott im Herzen, ein gut Weibchen im Arm, jenes macht seelig, dieses gewisst warm.*' Loosely translated it means, 'God in one's heart, a good wife on one's arm, the one brings salvation, the second is warm.' If they were noted down because of his feelings for Rebecca, the thoughts suggest that Haydn had found in this English widow everything that his wife never was, everything that Polzelli had ceased to be and everything that he could never have had with Maria Anna von Genzinger.

The most significant letter – which is as close to a declaration of love as we have – is the intriguing missive Rebecca sent Haydn on 7 March.

> My D. I was extremely sorry to part with you so suddenly last Night, our conversation was particularly interesting and I had thousand affectionate things to say to you, my heart WAS and is full of TENDERNESS for you, but no language can express HALF the Love and AFFECTION I feel for you, you are DEARER TO ME EVERY DAY of my life. I am very sorry I was so dull and stupid yesterday, indeed Dearest it was nothing but my being indisposed with a cold occasion'd my stupidity. I thank you a thousand times for your concern for me, I am truly sensible of your goodness, but I assure you my D. if anything had happened to trouble me, I would have open'd my heart, & told you with the most perfect confidence. Oh how earnestly I wish to see you. I hope you will come to me tomorrow. I shall be happy to see you both in the morning and the Evening. God Bless you my love, my thoughts and best wishes ever accompany you, and I always am with the most sincere and invariable Regard my D. your truly affectionate . . .

What was this 'stupidity' she mentions, which seems to have sent Haydn away 'suddenly'? Even more intriguing was that 'our conversation was extremely interesting' and that she had 'a thousand affectionate things to say to you'. Rebecca puts it down to being 'indisposed with a cold'. Had they had a tiff because Haydn wanted to know why she felt so down and she refused to tell him? 'I assure you my D. if anything had happened to trouble me, I would have open'd my heart & told you with the most perfect confidence.' To modern eyes, perhaps he was pressing her for more than friendship and she did not feel ready to go further – at least not then – and a frustrated Haydn felt rebuffed. Was it something much less dramatic – the cold had given her a headache, or a sore throat, and she just could not keep up the 'extremely interesting' conversation? Whatever it is, his abrupt departure made her 'very sorry I was so dull and stupid yesterday'. She blames herself, as women who love often do. Perhaps it was Haydn's fault. Perhaps he had been too aroused and persistent. After all, a woman of Rebecca's class and background would have only ever made love with her late husband. By the end of the letter she is as good as begging him to come and see her soon: 'Oh how earnestly I wish to see you. I hope you will come to me tomorrow. I shall be happy to see you both in the morning and the Evening ...' And after signing herself 'your truly affectionate' she adds a postscript: 'My Dearest I cannot be happy till I see you ...'

By April everything was back on an even keel – though Rebecca had to go yet again to care for her mother in Blackheath. One wonders whether she had confided in Mrs Scott about her new love affair? It is doubtful, given the problems she had had when the family discovered her feelings for another musician. Later in April Rebecca sends Haydn some soap, a very practical gesture from a woman who wants to help her friend any way she can, even to the extent of buying household necessities. She is also confident enough in the relationship to ask him for twelve tickets to his benefit concert on 3 May. Later still that same month she leaves London again to see her mother, who is now very old and feeble.[26]

A further letter asks for six more tickets for Haydn's benefit concert, which made the Schroeter party a total of eighteen people. So yet

---

[26] Mrs Scott died in 1793 – less than a year later.

another fact we learn about Rebecca is that whatever short-term isolation her unwise marriage had caused her initially, as a widow she obviously enjoyed a good social life. It may be that her best friend Frances Coutts, now Lady Stuart, had stayed loyal and through her she had made new friends. She often speaks of 'our friends', which might mean those she had made because of her friendship with Haydn. Yet were any of these 'friends' aware of her true relationship with Haydn, or was she just seen as a good friend and nothing more? We know that she copied music for him and probably ran errands to publishers and the like. It would have been a necessary subterfuge in a gossipy town like London. Newspapers, like *Town and Country Magazine*, would have had a field day with the story.[27] Since 1769 they had been running a regular feature called 'Tête-à-Tête'. Two oval portraits of the man and the woman involved in the alleged affair headed the article. The anonymous writer would describe their meetings, their sexual and romantic histories, and even an estimate of how long the affair would last. Over the twenty-four-year life of the feature over 300 couples were lampooned. They included aristocrats, clergy, royalty, politicians as well as singers and actresses. Rebecca's family would have been horrified again had news of her affair suddenly been bruited abroad. Her stuffy brother would have been certain to cut her off without a penny.

Given that Haydn was still married, and that Rebecca was a respectable widow, the two would have been as discreet as possible in the relationship. The ever demanding Polzelli wrote in one of her letters at this time that she had heard he was having an affair and was no longer interested in her. Haydn stoutly denied it. Polzelli by this time was probably less worried by Haydn's infidelity than the possibility that he might start supporting another mistress financially and so threaten what had become more a business relationship than a love affair.

On the day of Haydn's benefit concert there was an exhibition of portraits at the Royal Academy. The exhibition included one of Haydn

---

[27] See Cindy McCreery, *Gender in 18th-century England*, Longman, pp. 207–9.

by Thomas Hardy. The original picture is now at the Royal College of Music in London. It was very likely that Rebecca would have received at least an engraving of it. The print Mrs Schroeter is likely to have owned probably came from John Bland, the publisher and printmaker at 45 Holborn, opposite Chancery Lane. Bland could well have been a member of Rebecca's circle of musical friends. He was a friend of Haydn's and sometime publisher of his music. Haydn spent his first night in London at his house, while Salomon readied his room at his own house in Great Poulteney Street. Rebecca knew full well that Haydn had but a few weeks left in England – she may also have known that he was planning to return, hence no mention of their parting for ever – she writes on 16 June, 'Every moment of your company is more and more precious to me, now that your departure is near . . .'

It would have been a bitter-sweet month for the loving pair. There are five dated letters and five undated ones written at this time, which plot their relationship. On Friday the 1st Rebecca told Haydn that she would be happy to see him at any time after one o'clock on Sunday. She also said that she hoped to see him 'on Tuesday as usual to dinner'. And she asked him whether he could make Thursday or Friday to dinner to meet a Stone family – Mr, Mrs and Miss Stone. Sunday, when she said she was free, was the day that Haydn wrote in his London notebook, 'I dined with Mons and Madame Mara, Mr Keely [*sic*] and Madame Storace at her brother's Storace.' If the evening was anything like his dinner with the Storaces in Vienna just before he left, it must have been a very lively evening. There is every chance, in this mixed company, that Rebecca would have been there as well.

The next day, 4 June, Haydn wrote in his London notebook, 'I was in Vauxhall, where the King's birthday is celebrated.' He would not have gone alone and perhaps the ever thoughtful Rebecca had got together a small group of people. Haydn was enchanted with the place where over 'thirty thousand lamps were burning . . . the grounds and its variety are perhaps unique in the world. There are 155 little dining booths. There are large alleys of trees, which form a wonderful roof above and are magnificently illuminated.' Haydn also admired

Handel's statue by Louis-François Roubiliac, which shows the great composer writing music, in his hand is part of the score of *Messiah*. On Tuesday he was in James Street 'as usual to dinner'. On Wednesday the 6th, he presided at Salomon's extra concert for the season – Madame Mara sang there. Rebecca was there too because later that night she wrote her loving letter of thanks for such a wonderful evening.

Thursday, the first of the month, was the anniversary meeting of the Charity Children in St Paul's Cathedral. Haydn was there and wrote, 'I heard 4000 charity children sing in St Paul's Church ... No music ever moved me so deeply in my life.' Later he recalled, 'I stood there and wept like a child.' He quite possibly went to dinner at Rebecca's on Friday to meet the Stone family. In fact, in her letter of the 6th she said 'come at three if you can. It would give me great pleasure, as I should be particularly glad to see you my Dear before the rest of our friends come.' There is no record of what Haydn did on Saturday, but it is not impossible that he dined at Rebecca's – a quiet evening after so much social activity. Maybe that was when he lent her some verses to copy. She thanked him in her Sunday evening letter of the 10th and hoped he could come to dinner on either Monday or Tuesday. They may have gone to the Mara benefit concert at the Haymarket Theatre on the 12th. For the next couple of days Haydn went off on a little jaunt to the races, to Ascot. Rebecca knew about the trip, and wrote to him on the evening of the 14th 'I hope you had an agreeable journey, that you have been much amused by the races.'

She said that she expected him to 'dinner on Friday', but Haydn seems instead to have gone on to meet Doctor Herschel, the astronomer, who lived at Slough. Back in London a day later than expected he received a mildly reproving letter from Rebecca: 'I was extremely sorry I had not the pleasure of seeing you today. Indeed, my dearest love it was a very great disappointment to me, as every moment of your company is more and more precious to me now that your departure is so near.' She said she hoped to see him on Saturday, the next day, or failing that Monday. Four undated letters in the notebook could well be from this time in their relationship – each talked of seeing each other, of dinners, of meetings, of the pleasure of seeing him perform his music in concert. The last dated letter was for 26 June, a Tuesday, and she said she was looking forward to seeing him on Monday, which means that Haydn would still have been in London on 2 July.

The twenty-three letters Haydn copied so neatly into his notebook run to about 2500 words. It must have taken at least an hour or two of his time. When the biographer Albert Dies made his twenty-third visit to Haydn's house in Gumpendorf on 18 June 1806 he reported, 'Haydn showed me another little book of notes. I opened it and found a couple of dozen letters in English in it. Haydn smiled. "Letters from an English widow in London, who loved me; but although she was already sixty [*sic*] years old, she was still a beautiful and amiable woman whom I might very easily have married if I had been free then." ' Dies goes on to write, 'This woman is the widow, still living, of the celebrated clavier player Schroeter, whose melodious song he emphatically praised.' How many times, one wonders did Haydn read over to himself in his heavily accented English the tender words from his 'English widow'. And how did Dies know that she was still living, unless Haydn assured him it was true? Haydn did not mention Luigia Polzelli to Albert Dies that day. He had on more than one occasion promised to marry Polzelli when he was free. Nor did he mention Marianne von Genzinger. The impression he must have wanted to give Dies was that Mrs Schroeter occupied a special place in his heart. Haydn had left London within a day or two of their last meeting. The frequency of the meetings, the intensity of the correspondence . . . can it have been anything other than a true love affair?

CHAPTER TWELVE

The Sorrows of Separation

Rebecca was one of the last people in London to see Haydn before he left for Vienna. They had seen and talked to each other almost every day in the previous months. The sad parting was lightened only by the expectation on both sides that he already planned to come back to London – maybe even to settle there. The knowledge that he was contracted to return gave Rebecca every reason to believe that her future would be a full and happy one. The relationship was like a marriage in all but name. This was somewhat unorthodox by the standards of the day. Yet society usually turned a blind eye to such arrangements. While extramarital liaisons were much more frequent in the world of music and the arts, polite society at the time was also not immune to such temptations. All that was required of the couple involved was a degree of decorum. Good manners demanded discretion, not abstinence. Rebecca knew Haydn was married, but so far that had not proved an inhibition to her feelings for him. There is no sense in that last letter of 26 June that the relationship was at an end. Far from it, Rebecca expresses her desire to spend as much time as possible with Haydn while he was in England.

Many years later when Albert Dies asked Haydn who these letters were from, having come across them in his notebooks, Haydn smiled and said 'a beautiful English widow who loved me'. Then he went on to say that he might 'very easily have married her, had I been free then'. The inference was a genuine promise of a more structured domestic arrangement in the future. Salomon's contract with Haydn meant that the composer had to come back to England. When they parted at the beginning of July, both thought that he would be back in London before the turn of the year to resume his role as the star attraction of the 1793 season of Salomon concerts due to begin some time in January.

Rebecca experienced a terrible emptiness after Haydn left. From almost daily visits she now had to readjust to a life thinking principally of herself and her own needs. It was like a second widowhood. Even her concert going lacked the special thrill of seeing her 'dearest love' seated at the pianoforte directing the orchestra ranged behind him. Her main responsibility was to care for her ailing mother who still resided in the old family home in Blackheath. Elizabeth Scott had but months to live. Without any other family responsibilities, she was expected to take on the task of nursing the old lady and making her as comfortable as possible. This could be part of the rehabilitation process after the great family rift caused by her marriage. She had also to keep her brother informed of their mother's state of health. Rebecca now depended on Robert Scott for her modest annuities. Such an arrangement brought home sharply the contrast between them.

His fortune went from strength to strength, while hers remained much as it had been since her impulsive marriage. Apart from his house in Wimpole Street, Robert now had the responsibility of his 200-acre estate at Danesfield in Buckinghamshire. While there was the family business to manage, he was now free, if he wished, to spend less time in London. As can be seen from his will a few years later, he enjoyed the role of country squire to the full. Danesfield still stands today, though largely remodelled after the family finally sold it in the early twentieth century. Nowadays it serves as a country house hotel, but it is still possible to experience what it must have been like in Robert's day – the space within the house, the surrounding countryside, the sense of wealth and achievement that drove him to acquire on such a scale.

During Haydn's absence in Vienna, Rebecca remained in her comfortable but unpretentious home at number 6 James Street, Buckingham Gate. Some of the original houses in the street are still standing. In their day they were suitable town dwellings for the middling sort, not at all the kind of house a man of means would expect to live in. As with so many physical traces of Rebecca's life, the house has long disappeared. But there is still today an enduring sense of the neighbourhood as it was in the late eighteenth century, with Green Park stretching away. In Buckingham Gate, Rebecca did her best to gather any news she could about Haydn. The travelling musicians who came and went in London on a regular basis kept her reasonably up to date and could bring a letter or two from the Maestro himself – he was a prolific letter writer. Undoubtedly she wrote to him. If she was always ready to send him a little hand-delivered note within hours of seeing him in London, it is certain that she would have wanted to know 'how you do today' when he was in Vienna or Esterháza. It was only good manners on Haydn's part to send her something by way of reply.

The surviving letters to Maria Anna von Genzinger show the gossipy tone that characterised his private letters. The only limitation in his correspondence was Haydn's somewhat stilted English with its largely phonetic spelling. We have a number of examples in his London notebooks and collected letters. The words suggest the sound of his voice when he spoke English. He always said 'dis' or 'dat'. 'I tak me the pleasure' was one of his favourite phrases. A concern of his at the time was the health of William Napier, for whom he had set so many Scottish songs. Haydn called him 'Nepire'. And he may have sent for her amusement some 'anectods'; this was obviously how he pronounced the word. His notebooks are full of curious happenings, interesting statistics and 'anectods'. For example, Haydn had been told

> when a Quaker goes to Court, he pays the door keeper to take off his hat for him, for a Quaker takes off his hat to no one. In order to pay the King's tax, an official goes to his house during the period when the tax is being collected, and in his presence robs him of as much goods as represent the tax in value. When the disguised thief leaves the door, the Quaker calls him back and asks how much

money he wants for the stolen things. The official demands just the amount of tax, and in that way the Quaker pays the tax to the King.

Rebecca's style was unchangeably warm and loving, wanting to know, as always, 'how he did' and how his health was, and that he 'was not working too hard'. In Haydn's absence from London Rebecca ran errands on his behalf, talking to Salomon and other members of the musical fraternity. Apart from letters or verbal messages carried by mutual friends, she had Haydn's music. In the drawing room on the first floor of her house she could sit and play on a small Broadwood box piano one of his sonatas, or a piano arrangement of one of his London symphonies. Knowing that he was contracted to return, she could for now resign herself to the wait. But waiting was something all women in her day were practised in. Most of their lives were spent thus.

Haydn too had some adjustments to make. Happily, there are detailed records of how he spent his time after he got back to Austria. His journey across the Continent took about three weeks and he arrived back in Vienna on 24 July. He made straight away for his old quarters at Herr Hamberger's house at number 992 Wasser-kunstbastei. After all the public attention in London, the Viennese greeted Haydn's return to Austria with silence and almost indifference. In England he had been fêted wherever he went; in Vienna he went about largely unnoticed. Those who bothered to remark his presence among them accepted that he was back for a final visit before returning to England, where he would settle for good. There were weightier matters for the Austrians to be concerned with. The Revolution in France had claimed not only the lives of hundreds of aristocrats, but the French royal family was in prison and the King and Queen would soon follow their unhappy aristocratic supporters to the guillotine. Queen Marie Antoinette of France was an Austrian Princess and the threat to her life was a threat to Austria. The grim politics of the time affected daily life in the Imperial capital of the Habsburg empire. Within days of Haydn's arrival the new Emperor,

Franz II had sent his armies to march on Paris to free the French capital from the revolutionaries who had killed so many in their purges of the aristocracy. By February the following year a British expeditionary force had landed in Holland.

Haydn in Vienna, like Rebecca in London, turned to his friends for comfort. He had bought a huge number of little gifts for them during his trip to England. On 4 August he wrote to Maria Anna von Genzinger, 'Gracious Lady, since Herr Kees has invited me for lunch today, I shall have the opportunity to give his wife the knitting needles I promised her.' Life for many people in the second half of the eighteenth century – especially those of the middling sort and the upper classes – often continued untouched by the great and seemingly earth-shattering events taking place in the capitals of the world. Despite the Terror in Paris, troops on the move in Europe, kings and princes worrying about their thrones, Haydn went on writing music, corresponding with his publishers and dining with friends. The pleasure seekers still had fun and set new fashions. An early type of waltz was invented in Vienna around this time.[28]

Haydn expected to return to London towards the end of the year. On Christmas Day 1792 Salomon 'respectfully' informed the readers of the *Morning Post* that he was planning a new series of subscription concerts in the Hanover Square Rooms 'following the highly flattering approbation with which his former concerts have been honoured'. He promised his patrons the chance to see and hear not only Haydn, but also the celebrated German soprano Madame Gertrude Mara[29] and the Italian violinist Giovanni Viotti. As a further inducement, Salomon said that he had also invited 'one of the principal opera singers from Italy, whose name he will be at liberty to announce within a few days'. Rebecca's hopes of seeing her beloved Haydn could have been no higher, but they were soon dashed.

On 11 January 1793 Salomon had to inform the gentry and nobility

[28] H. C. Robbins Landon, *Chronicle and Works Haydn in England*, pp. 208–10.
[29] Gertrude Mara, born Gertrude Elisabeth Schmeling, sang with Hiller's opera in Leipzig and knew Schroeter's sister Corona and the rest of the family.

that his concerts would be postponed until the beginning of February. Finally, he had to admit that Haydn would not be coming. The formal excuse was that he was ill. The blame was laid on the noticeable nasal polyp, which the famous surgeon Mr John Hunter had once tried to remove by force one evening in London but had been made to stop because Haydn shouted and struggled too much. Haydn himself was getting worried about the political situation both in Austria and England. The French Revolution was well under way, with news of mass executions coming almost daily. The old aristocratic world that he had known was suddenly under threat from the young hotheads. Could things go the same way in England? Certainly there were politicians, like the charismatic Charles James Fox, who had some sympathy with the revolutionary ideals coming out of France. What's more, at the age of sixty Haydn was feeling the pressure of work much more. While the political atmosphere was worrying, and long journeys becoming more hazardous, he was still feeling the effects of his heroic exertions during his first London visit.

There was something else that sapped his spirit. On 29 January Maria Anna von Genzinger died of consumption – she was forty-two years old. H. C. Robbins Landon says, 'Haydn had loved her perhaps more than he dared show in his letters. She had occupied a special place in his heart that neither la Polzelli nor even Rebecca Schroeter could replace.' It is doubtful that Polzelli was a great love of Haydn. Certainly she satisfied his sexual needs for a time and was a refuge from his nagging wife. But in the end she became a nag in her own way. Did Maria Anna von Genzinger mean more to Haydn than Rebecca Schroeter? His relationship with Rebecca was certainly more complete than that with Maria Anna could ever be. That he loved her is true, but it was a romantic, platonic love. She would always be unobtainable. She had made that clear in a letter to him. Haydn replied at once saying that he would never do anything that would embarrass her.

Rebecca, whose life was much more cloistered than her 'dear Haydn's', also suffered bereavement. Her mother Elizabeth Scott (described as a 'gentlewoman' on the death certificate) finally succumbed in Blackheath in early summer. Rebecca was left to sort out her affairs and clear the house, which was relet. On a bright summer's day, 15 June, the male members of the family attended the funeral of Rebecca's mother in the small parish church of St Alphege in Greenwich. She was buried alongside her late husband. There are no monuments to the couple to be seen in the church. Unlike their only son and their youngest daughter, Mr and Mrs Scott were modest to the end. To lighten the period of mourning for Rebecca came news from Salomon that Haydn would most certainly be back in London in the New Year.

In June Haydn wrote again to Luigia Polzelli. She was still begging him for money, despite the fact they had not seen each other for many years. Haydn told her, 'I shall stay in Vienna until the end of September, and then I intend to take a trip with your son, and perhaps, perhaps go to England again for a year; but that depends mainly on whether the battle field changes; if it doesn't I shall go somewhere else – perhaps – perhaps – I shall see you in Naples. My wife is still sick most of the time and is always in a foul humour, but I don't really care any more – after all this woe will pass one day.'

One trait that comes out clearly in Haydn's character is that he was very careful with his money. No matter how much he earned, time and again he pleaded poverty because, he said, he had so many relations to help. And it is true he did send a lot of money over the years to his relatives. One of the most troublesome was his brother-in-law Joseph Luegmayer, who was married to Anna, Haydn's sister. He was always in debt. When Haydn was asked to pay up on his behalf on one occasion, he was beside himself with anger. 'Why should I be expected to pay ...' Haydn demanded to know of the court administrator at Esterháza. 'I have fallen into the same state of insolvency as that of Luegmayer, but with the difference that he has fallen from his horse to the back of an ass, whilst I have managed to remain on the horse but without saddle or harness.' Given his peasant upbringing, he was always close with his money. There are many incidents of him asking for a free ticket to go to a concert in London pleading that as a 'poor' composer he could not afford the prices. In his notebooks there are references to the prices he had to pay while he was in England. For example, 'I had to pay 1½ guineas for having the bells rung at Oxford in connection with my doctor's degree, and ½ a guinea for the robe. The trip cost 6 guineas.'

Yet Haydn was now a man of means. Just two months later, notwithstanding all his professions of poverty to Polzelli, Haydn bought himself a small house in the Windmühl district near the suburb of Gumpendorf. It was his insufferable wife Maria Anna who had first seen the house at number 71 Kleine Steinegasse. Tactlessly she had asked him to send her some money to buy it so that, after he died, as she told him, she could live there as his widow! Haydn at first refused. He said he wanted to see the house for himself. Haydn told Dies that when 'I saw the house, I liked the still and quiet situation'. It still stands today, with the second floor that Haydn added in 1796. It is now the Haydn Museum of Vienna. Buying such a house shows that in his mind, even then, there was very little possibility that he wanted to spend the rest of his days in England.

In the *Morning Chronicle* of 10 January 1794 Salomon boldly announced that the new series would begin on 3 February. Once again the impresario was overconfident. There was still more delay. Haydn, who had been given a comfortable travelling coach by the Austrian diplomat and musical patron Baron van Swieten, had had to work hard to persuade his employer, Prince Anton Esterházy, that he should go at all. According to Dies, 'The Prince did not require Haydn to perform any duties, but he was well disposed towards him, and was of the opinion that Haydn had acquired enough fame for himself and should be satisfied with what he had, and at the age of sixty and one years should not expose himself to the dangers of a journey, and to the annoyances arising in London, out of inflamed jealousies.' Eventually, given that Haydn had signed contracts and stood to make a great deal of money, 'the Prince finally sacrificed his will for the benefit of Haydn'. Haydn would have greatly enjoyed the comforts of Baron van Swieten's luxury coach. Travelling with him was his good-hearted, faithful servant and music copyist, Johann Elssler, who served him for twenty years until the composer's death.

The two finally arrived in London on 4 February 1794. On the 10th Haydn was at the Hanover Square Rooms, seated at the pianoforte from where he directed his 'composition', as Salomon discreetly termed a symphony, which is now known as number 99. Rebecca had dutifully paid her 5 guineas for her lady's ticket and took her seat among what the *Sun* called 'a large and elegant audience'. She wholeheartedly joined the 'rapturous applause', which the *Morning Chronicle* reported the following day. The paper's correspondent said Haydn's ideas 'are as new in music as they are grand and impressive'. The overture, he went on, 'rouses and affects every emotion of the soul'. Rebecca, as emotional as any in the audience that night, went home to James Street and penned a late-night note to her 'Dearest Love', saying much the same.

CHAPTER THIRTEEN

The Lover's Return

After eighteen months the lovers were together again. During this second London visit Haydn lived in rented rooms in Bury Street. Rebecca arranged the accommodation for him. Her choice was based on the fact that Bury Street, in the heart of Westminster, is but a few minutes' walk across Green Park and up Birdcage Walk to Buckingham Gate and Rebecca's terraced house. There are no letters from Rebecca to Haydn during this time. To be precise, there are none that have been copied into a Haydn notebook. In fact, there is very little about the 'beautiful English widow' in the Haydn archive that covers the composer's second visit to London. It is known that he kept a fourth notebook but it has disappeared. One conclusion to draw is that Rebecca no longer needed to write to Haydn because she saw him much more frequently. Although she could see that he would probably never make his home permanently in England, she had no reasons, apart from heavy disappointment, to shun a man who had meant so much to her so recently. Haydn still had great need of Rebecca's constancy when so much in Vienna was uncertain and he was again far from home coping with the pressure of his commitments. His age and growing infirmities, the worsening situation in Continental Europe as the Austrian, French and British armies began the build-up to war, weighed against them. Rebecca had to begin to prepare herself for his eventual and permanent departure. The passion of their first years together might have cooled. She was, after all, in her forties and he was a venerable old gentleman of nearly sixty-two. If so, the early ardour had given way to a closer friendship that was all the more difficult to see broken by the onward march of the world and time.

Their mutual friends and, of course, music bound them together as firmly as anything. Rebecca still went to his concerts. Her assured place in Haydn's heart is clearly shown in the slow movement of one of his greatest symphonies – number 102. The moving and deeply felt adagio, some of the most expressive music Haydn ever wrote, is based on one of Rebecca's favourite themes. The symphony is sometimes called the *Miracle*, though that is a name that few in Continental Europe would use. It is only the British who call it that. But the symphony and the circumstances of its nickname allow us one last assured moment of the pair. At the end of 1794 Salomon had given up his Hanover concert series. As he told the 'Nobility and Gentry' in the *Morning Post* on 14 January, he could no longer, in the present situation of affairs abroad, 'procure any vocal performers of the first talents, but by the influence of terms which an undertaking like his could by no means authorise him to offer'. However, help was at hand. The London Opera stepped into the breach and quickly signed up Haydn to help them launch a series of nine subscription concerts. These were to be held every Monday fortnight in the Great Hall of the King's Theatre.

The first duly took place on Monday, 2 February. Besides the solo players, there was a sixty-strong orchestra. Tickets cost 4 guineas for the nine-concert series and obviously Rebecca would have sent her servant round to the banking house of Messrs Ranson, Morland and Hammersley in Pall Mall to pick up her green lady's ticket. She would have been especially keen to go, because Haydn had told her that he had based the slow movement on a theme she particularly liked. Albert Dies heard the story of what happened that night from Haydn himself many years later when he was collecting material for the composer's biography:

When Haydn appeared in the orchestra and seated himself at the pianoforte, to conduct the symphony personally, the curious audience in the parterre left their seats and pressed forward towards the orchestra, with a view to seeing Haydn better at close range. The seats in the middle of the parterre were therefore empty, and no sooner were they empty than a great chandelier plunged down, smashed and threw the numerous companies into great confusion. As soon as the first moment of shock was over, and those who had pressed forward realised the danger which they had so luckily escaped, and could find words to express the same, many persons showed their state of mind by shouting loudly 'Miracle! Miracle!' Haydn himself was much moved, and thanked merciful Providence who had allowed it to happen that he [Haydn] could, to a certain extent, be the reason or the machine, by which at least thirty persons' lives were saved. Only a few of the audience received minor bruises.

The *Morning Chronicle* the next day does not give the event quite the same prominence, but commented, 'Haydn's new Overture was played in masterly style. The last movement was encored: and notwithstanding an interruption by the accidental fall of one of the chandeliers, it was performed with no less effect.'

With Rebecca in the Great Hall that night to hear one of her favourite Haydn themes, and possibly at risk from the falling chandelier, it took a lot of professional composure on Haydn's part to be able to continue to conduct, let alone the rest of the orchestra to continue playing. For lovers of his music symphony 102 is a miracle as much for the theme itself as for the events surrounding its first performance that February night. And the adagio, always the most emotional part of a Haydn symphony, is truly impressive. He always invoked God's blessing at the very beginning of a work by writing '*In nomine Domini*' at the head of the score. On this occasion he wrote the words at the beginning of the adagio as well to signal its special significance.

During his second visit to London Haydn certainly worked at a cracking pace. If anything, he was busier than the first time. He had more friends to see and was invited everywhere. He had a punishing professional schedule, performing or conducting most nights in

London and often making the effort to watch other performers on other nights as well. While he tried to see Rebecca whenever he could, it is certain that it was not as frequently as he might have wished. He was also moving in higher circles. The royal family took him up. Rebecca would have known from her own friends at court, like the Papendiecks, that the King and the Queen wished to keep him in England. It must have raised any hopes she had that the relationship would continue.

The biographer Griesinger tells a charming story about how the royal family tried to persuade Haydn to stay in England.

'You shall have a place in Windsor in the summers,' said the Queen, 'and then,' she added with an arch look toward the King, 'we shall sometimes make music *tête-à-tête*.' 'Oh!' replied the King, 'I am not worked up over Haydn, he is a good honest German gentleman.' 'To keep that reputation', answered Haydn, 'is my greatest pride.' On repeated urging to remain in England, Haydn claimed that he was bound by gratitude to his Prince's house, and that he could not separate himself forever from his fatherland or from his wife. The King offered to send for the latter. 'She will not cross the Danube, much less the sea,' Haydn replied. Haydn later said that it was because he refused the British monarch's warm invitation the King never gave him any kind of award or payment. Of the royal family, only the Duchess of York came to his benefit concert, and she sent him fifty guineas.

The Prince of Wales also employed Haydn, who directed twenty-six *musicales* for him. The Prince was notorious for not paying his bills. Despite repeated requests, in the end Haydn sent his bill for 100 guineas via the British ambassador in Vienna to the government in London. It was then paid, and without question.

The season ended in mid June as always – and for the next two months Haydn lived quietly in the capital. During this time he was seeing a lot of Mrs Schroeter and he dedicated what were to become his most famous three piano trios to her, including the one in F sharp minor. The trios feature Rebecca's favourite theme, which he had already used in the slow movement of the symphony number 102. There was something else, which was just as personal, in the form of a lively rondo in the gypsy style. This was an echo of his homeland and his youth. It is hard to imagine anything more intimate as a musical memory to be offered as a gift. It is an echo of the happy evenings they spent together making music. Rebecca was an accomplished pianist, Haydn a good violinist. Perhaps Salomon or the Papendiecks joined in. The music is imbued with the fun and laughter of such gatherings. Haydn loved good company where there was plenty of good food and amusing guests whom he could tell some amusing 'anecdots'. It was of such musical evenings in Vienna that he had some of his happiest memories – not least of Marianne von Genzinger, his adored friend. Rebecca created similar evenings for him in London, knowing him as well as she did. Having so many English and Scottish songs set to Haydn's music must have made these evenings especially memorable. They were the most popular songs of the day, played round the family piano or in the grandest music rooms of the capital.

Saying goodbye is never easy: Haydn's last two months in London were full of bitter-sweet events. As the brutal French Revolution began to cast its long shadow over everyday life in Europe's main capitals, men and women feared that the world they had grown up in was changing for the worst. Everywhere the conversation was about politics, war and rising prices. Fewer of the great foreign artists wanted to, or could, make the journey to London. With Haydn determined to go back, and the French and Austrians moving towards war, he had no idea of what to expect as he journeyed home. He was bidding his London friends a final farewell – and they all knew it, most of all Rebecca.

One of the last press mentions of the composer was in the *Morning Herald* of 20 June. Dr Haydn, the paper reported, expected his recall to Vienna. The Emperor, it was hoped, required the presence of this celebrated harmonist, to prepare a new *Te Deum* on a general peace.

Joseph Haydn and Rebecca Schroeter both knew in their hearts that the relationship could not last for ever. He was still married, albeit in name only. He had resolved that at his age it was better to go home to die, rather than linger on, an old and increasingly frail man in a foreign country where the fate of many musicians was to live too long after their fame had deserted them. However, Rebecca may have begged him to stay, and promised to nurse him and care for him. The best Haydn could do was to tell her the truth as gently as he could. They stayed together until the last day and promised to keep in touch as best they might.

Haydn had one last duty. He signed a new contract with Salomon which would keep his name before the English public. He had a passion for order and tidiness, so it was not until everything was packed and listed that Haydn said his goodbyes. On the morning of 15 August 1795 Joseph Haydn and his servant and friend Johann Elssler set out from London on the three-week overland journey to Vienna. Rebecca Schroeter reconciled herself to being just another English widow.

CHAPTER FOURTEEN

Mrs Hunter's Poem

Just before Haydn left London to return to Vienna, he compiled a list of the works he had completed in England between January 1791 and August 1795. Setting aside the eighteen months he was back in Austria, Haydn calculated that he had written 768 sheets of music. Standing head and shoulders above everything are the undoubted masterpieces now known as his twelve London symphonies. The list of his works is truly epic and a tribute to a man in his sixties who had little to prove to himself or to the audiences who clamoured to see him. But Haydn relished his success and knew only too well that a lazy musician could easily lose the public's favour overnight. So he pushed himself hard, and all this was achieved despite a frantic social life and almost daily professional commitments rehearsing or performing.

In his private letters Haydn makes great play of being overworked, and of eye strain and headaches. He told his nagging mistress Luigia Polzelli that he was 'almost always' suffering from 'the English humour that is depressed'. In contrast, his private notebooks suggest a man who was enjoying everything that London had to offer. His complaints were just a device to win sympathy, especially from pretty women. The ever solicitous Rebecca did not mind his obsession with his aches and pains, and gave him all the support and home comforts she could to ease the demands of his professional life.

Haydn was prolific in every genre of music. The talent for writing opera, which he had developed at Esterháza, he now deployed in setting popular verses to music, which spread his fame even further. Haydn was also a generous man. At Rebecca's request he set 150 Scottish songs for her friend Napier who was facing prison for debt. The Scottish-born musician and publisher had twelve children to support, and his playing days as a violinist were over, since he had rheumatism in his hands. Haydn's songs not only got '*Nepire*', as he called him, out of debt, but made him a handsome profit as well. The *Morning Chronicle* reported, 'Nothing perhaps, can be a stronger instance of the superior genius of this great master than the facility with which he has seized the wild, but natural and affecting beauties of the Scots airs . . .' Knowing Rebecca obviously helped his understanding.

Such fulsome praise was typical of the press coverage he received and it underlines how immense Haydn's impact was on London's cultural and intellectual life. When he arrived, the town went wild with Haydn mania. He was regularly referred to as 'the Shakespeare of Music'. Charles Burney felt moved to write and publish some terrible verses in praise of Haydn:

> Haydn! Great sovereign of the tuneful art
> Thy works alone supply an ample chart
> Of all the mountains, seas and fertile plains,
> Within the compass of its wide domains . . .

Everyone was determined to show how much they appreciated his art. For example, the Anacreontic Society was meeting at the Crown and Anchor in the Strand just weeks after he had arrived. 'Before the Grand Finale the celebrated Haydn entered the room,' *The Gazetteer* reported, 'and was welcomed by the sons of Harmony with every mark of respect and attention.' The literary world paid him a very ambivalent compliment. In the March edition of the widely read *European Magazine* one correspondent submitted some verses in praise of great artists and, when he came to Haydn, deployed a rather ungainly metaphor:

> And now, to ease us of useless toil
> And fertilize our cold and barren soil
> Haydn celestial fire and compost brings . . .

History does record whether Haydn saw his music as a rare form of 'compost'.

Everyone wanted him in their homes. James Boswell, who loved the company of famous men, gave a dinner and musical party for his daughter Veronica, and Haydn and Salomon accepted his invitation to attend. Charles Burney was asked by all his friends to arrange meetings with the composer. He usually managed to oblige. For his friend Twinning he even set up a small dinner party at which Haydn and Salomon and two others played some of Haydn's string quartets.

Haydn himself recalls one evening, which summed up perfectly the passion the English felt for him:

> On the 14th of December I dined for the first time with Mr Shaw. He received me downstairs by the door and then led me upstairs to his wife, who was surrounded by her two daughters and other ladies. As I was bowing round the circle, all at once I became aware of the fact that not only the lady of the house but also her daughters and the other women each wore on their headbands *a parte* over the front a most charming curved pearl-coloured band of three fingers' breadth, with the name Haydn embroidered therein in gold; and Mr Shaw wore this name on his coat, worked into the very ends of both his collars in the finest steel beads . . .

Jostling all the rest to invite Haydn to their homes or their soirées was Mrs Anne Hunter, a poetess, whose work was known to all her friends and was even praised by her distant cousin, the Scottish philosopher David Hume.

Of all the songs Haydn set to music during his time in London, one more than all the rest seems to sum up what many of the composer's friends and female admirers must have felt as he left England.

> O Tuneful voice, I still deplore
> Those accents which, tho' heard no more,
>   Still vibrate on my heart;

In echo's cave I long to dwell,
And still would hear the sad farewell,
    When we were doom'd to part.

Bright eyes, O that the task were mine,
To guard the liquid fires that shine,
    And round your orbits play;
To watch them with a vestal's care,
And feed with smiles a light so fair.
    That it may ne'er decay.

To twenty-first-century ears it sounds too sickly sentimental to have much emotional impact. The language, too, is awkward for the modern listener. 'Deplore' in the 1790s could mean 'to grieve for'. On the other hand it catches the mood of those turbulent times. Many a woman knew that she was 'doomed' to be parted from her loved ones by current political events. Few now would understand why a vestal virgin would be needed to guard 'liquid fires'. Such classical references were de rigueur at the time. Nevertheless Haydn's melody expresses the sense of loss beautifully. Even today, when sung by a fine soprano voice underpinned by his lilting piano accompaniment, the sentiments it expresses come across so well that the actual words are no longer that important[30] to the listener. Such songs were called canzonettas, popular with the middle classes for their musical evenings with friends, when the daughter of the house would be called upon to entertain the guests. Music publishers liked to use the description 'canzonetta' because the Italian made it seem as if it had been imported directly from Italy, and therefore there was an implicit guarantee that it was of the highest quality and, most of all, fashionable.

In one of her early letters to Haydn Rebecca sends him the 'text of a poem you asked for'. It is not known to which poem she was referring, but there is circumstantial evidence that it could have been

---

[30] One of the best recordings available is by the Scottish Soprano Mhairi Lawson. Olga Tverskaya plays an early pianoforte (Opus III, Paris Label number ops 10–008).

'O tuneful voice'. In the first years of her marriage she and her husband rented a house in Little Suffolk Street, which ran parallel to the Haymarket. Among their neighbours, at number 27, was the Home family. Robert Home, from Scotland, was an army surgeon. One of his sons, Everard, went on to become a famous surgeon; another, Robert, became a painter, while his eldest daughter, Anne, generally considered the most talented of all, was an accomplished musician and poet. It is said she performed almost to professional standards on the keyboard. It was she who wrote 'O tuneful voice'. To complete the somewhat bohemian community, Angelica Kauffmann, the Swiss-born painter who was one of the founding members of the Royal Academy, lodged for a time in the Homes' house at 27 Little Suffolk Street. Angelica Kauffmann was also a talented musician. The Scottish and the musical connections would certainly have brought the Home family and the Schroeters together.

Anne was a very frequent visitor to her parents' house in Little Suffolk Street. In 1771 she had married another Scot, John Hunter, and now lived in Jermyn Street, a short walk up the Haymarket. There her husband set about creating one of the greatest collections of scientific and medical specimens in England. He was soon the most famous surgeon in Britain, and his contributions to medical knowledge and surgery are admired today. As the husband's fame – and with it his fortune – increased, his wife was able to set herself up as a society hostess. As a female intellectual, it was the most socially acceptable way of developing her interests in music and literature without compromising her reputation. These gatherings were often called conversazioni, a reference to the similar gatherings that young men had attended in Rome while they were on the Grand Tour. If women could not always travel the world, at least the world could come to their salons. Rebecca knew and took part in many such 'conversations', which were a well-established part of the social scene in London at the time. She liked to hold her own musical parties at her house in Buckingham Gate. Men at the time tended to dismiss the women who organised them as 'bluestockings'.

The emergence of the bluestockings in the second half of the century came about very much because of the changing status of women in society. Until the accession of George III women were generally considered incapable of much more than running the household and producing heirs. It was widely believed that a woman with too much learning would never attract a husband, much less keep him. Rebecca had been educated solely to provide the family with a higher social standing through a good marriage. There was an unspoken fear on the part of the men that if their wives were too well educated, the men would be made to feel inferior. In society the men and women separated after supper, with the women withdrawing to leave the men to talk of 'serious' matters, and to discuss art, literature or politics. Elizabeth Carter recalled in a letter to another learned lady, 'as if the two sexes were at war the gentlemen ranged themselves on one side of the room where they talked their own talk and left us poor ladies to twirl our shuttles and amuse each other as we could. By what little I could overhear our opposites were discoursing on old English poets, and this did not seem so much beyond a female capacity.'

The first recorded conversazione was held in the early 1750s at the house of Mrs Vesey. She was a witty Irishwoman and the wife of a wealthy member of the Irish parliament. She decided that the sexes could mix and discuss literary and other such topics as equals. In her large rooms in Bolton Street, and later in Clarges Street, she used to arrange her chairs in little semicircles. Her guests would move from one group to another as they sampled different conversations and varying styles of debate. As Fanny Burney later recalled, there was 'no ceremony, no cards and no supper'. Mrs Vesey had the magic art of putting all her company at their ease without the least appearance of design.

The origin of the name 'bluestocking' has been much debated, but there is now general agreement that it was Mrs Vesey who helped establish the idea. In Bath, she invited a poor but brilliant scholar, Benjamin Stillingfleet, to one of her gatherings. Stillingfleet was the disinherited son of the Bishop of Worcester. He was also a failed poet, philosopher and botanist. He said he had no clothes suitable for such an assembly. 'Don't mind dress,' said Mrs Vesey, 'come in your blue stockings.' Stillingfleet turned out to be such a success at these gatherings that, according to James Boswell, 'such was the excellence of his conversation that it came to be said that we can do nothing without blue stockings, and thus by degrees the name stuck'. For some the name was a veiled insult at upstart women; for others it was worn as a badge of honour. Mrs Vesey covered her chairs in blue satin, she was so proud of the title.

She herself was no intellectual, but she was a genius at organising society gatherings. She was also helped by the fact that her husband, who rejoiced in the odd name of Agmondesham, was a member of Dr Johnson's Literary Club. So she was able to invite the Great Cham to her gatherings, which was quite a coup, because the Doctor was no great lover of society. Hannah More, one of the leading female intellectuals of the age, wrote, 'I know of no house where there is such rational society, and a conversation so general, so easy and so pleasant.' Mrs Vesey slowly faded from the social scene as her mind became confused. She died in 1791, the year Haydn arrived in London. A new 'Queen' of the bluestockings had taken her place. Mrs Elizabeth Montagu's gatherings were unashamedly highbrow. Among her guests were men like the politician Edmund Burke, the man who campaigned against slavery, William Wilberforce, and the president of the Royal Academy, Sir Joshua Reynolds. Samuel Johnson went for a time, but he and Mrs Montagu fell out. Perhaps she contradicted the dogmatic doctor once too often for his taste. Mrs Montagu, who was known as 'fidget' in her youth because of her passion for dancing, was widowed in 1775 and inherited a fortune derived from coal mining from her husband. Her conversazioni were much more organised than Mrs Vesey's and aimed for the highest possible intellectual content. Mrs Montagu even wrote and had published essays on Shakespeare. She died in 1800.

Rebecca's older neighbour, the ambitious Anne Hunter, had a lot of competition and some very high standards to live up to. She seems to have succeeded. In Boswell's journal for July 1787 we read, 'Attended a concert at Mrs Hunters.' According to a niece she entertained some notable people in her large house in Leicester Square, where she moved in 1783. They included Horace Walpole, Hester Thrale, Fanny Burney, as well as Mrs Vesey and Mrs Montagu. It is very likely that before his death the Schroeters would have been invited, with Johann giving a performance for the delight of the guests, or even playing a duet with his hostess, or possibly with his wife. Boswell was very pleased with his evening concert at the Hunters' because his daughter was asked to play.

After his arrival Haydn got to know the Hunters through Rebecca. Rebecca had been in contact with Haydn very early on his first visit to London in 1791. She, too, liked to organise little soirées – and in her letters she talks more than once about 'our friends' and thanks him on one occasion for entertaining them all so much. Haydn was always very good in this kind of gathering. He no doubt recalled his evenings in Vienna at Maria Anna von Genzinger's, where similar middle-class people with a passion for music got together to amuse themselves. Mrs Hunter was probably invited to just such a gathering at Rebecca's. She may have recited or sung her poems, including 'O tuneful voice'. Anne Hunter was a skilled lyricist, and her poems fitted the mood and style of the times. At the Royal College of Surgeons there is a corrected manuscript in Haydn's hand, and a copy of 'Dr Haydn's original canzonettas for the voice with an accompaniment for piano forte', published in 1791 and dedicated to Mrs John Hunter.

The fact that it was published so early on disposes of one theory that many have all too easily accepted as true. This is that Anne Hunter was Rebecca's main rival for Haydn's affections and that this poem was written specifically with Haydn in mind. In 1802 she published a small volume of poems dedicated to her son John, who was a soldier. 'O tuneful voice' is one of many 'songs', as she calls them, in the book and could well have been written with her absent son in mind. After Haydn left London in 1795 Mrs Hunter continued with her poetry and contributed a number of verses to George Thomson, a music publisher in Scotland, who also pursued Haydn pretty relentlessly for a decade or so. He enlisted the talents of

Beethoven as well. Thomson got in touch with Anne Hunter because another of his authors, Anne's niece Joanna Bailey, praised her work. Anne had become known as the poet whose work was set to music by the 'sublime' Haydn. In a gossipy age there is no mention anywhere, nor any hint, that their relationship was anything but proper.

The available evidence leads firmly to the conclusion that there was no gossip to be had. When Haydn came to London, Anne Hunter was nearly fifty – a decade older than Rebecca. She had two surviving children, two who had died in infancy. She had been married for twenty years to one of the most famous men in London. Even Haydn refers to her husband as the 'celebrated' John Hunter. He tells with relish the story of when Hunter tried to remove a polyp from his nose with four sturdy fellows suddenly trying to pin him down in a chair while the surgeon sharpened his scalpel. The story points to an easy intimacy between Haydn and the Hunter family.

Rebecca knew well that Haydn was susceptible to pretty women, especially those who understood and appreciated music. No one, least of all she, had anything bad to say about Anne Hunter. Even one of her husband's most bitter enemies, Jesse Foot, in a scathing biography of John Hunter wrote, 'To her he was directed not only by personal attractions, but also mental endowments, which she possesses in a very eminent degree. She exhibited specimens of poetry in sonnets, which for beautiful fancy, and pleasing harmony, are excellent in their style.' Anne Hunter not only wrote poetry but music too. She set her own, then quite famous, 'Song of the Indian' to music and astonished the not usually astonished Hester Thrale: 'I had no notion she could write so well.'

A lifelong friend of the family, the Venerable Robert Nares, wrote in her obituary, 'Native genius was never more pleasingly united in female delicacy than in Mrs John Hunter. With every grace that could make her interesting in society, she had every personal and social virtue that could command respect or attachment.' What may have started the rumour that she was more to Haydn than just a friend was Nares's remark, 'When Haydn passed a season in London, she became the Muse of that celebrated composer.' Haydn certainly had other muses. In the little volume of twelve canzonets published in 1791, six were by Anne, the other six were written by Charlotte Bertie who in that year married the fourth Earl of Cholmondeley, a nephew of Anne's friend Horace Walpole.

What comes across in Anne's poetry, and in what people say about her, is her gift for friendship. She was in the habit of writing little verses for her friends and her family. Many of them speak with deep feeling about the value of true friendship. The only critic seems to be Fanny Burney who met Anne Hunter at Mrs Thrale's and at the Pantheon: 'She is a fine woman, and highly accomplished, but with rather too much glare, both within and without.' If Rebecca was one of her friends, then it is impossible to think that Mrs Hunter, given her social and literary ambitions, would want to put them at risk with an affair with another very public man. With a full family life as well as her poetry to occupy her, she had little time or inclination for an affair with a foreign composer.

While Haydn was away in Vienna after his first visit, Anne Hunter's husband died of a heart attack at St George's Hospital where he was chief surgeon. Some claim it was almost murder. Hunter had been suffering from angina for years and himself recognised that any sudden emotion, like anger, could do for him. His surgical colleagues at St George's were intensely jealous of his success in attracting the best students. Hunter was refusing to share the fees he earned, arguing that they were his by right. He went off to a showdown with the surgeons committee, and it is said that he was goaded beyond the norm by their attitude. He left the room, collapsed and died. Without a moment's pause his colleagues are rumoured to have turned to 'other business' and pressed on with the meeting. In his career Hunter had earned a great deal of money, but he had also spent a lot, not least on the huge collection of medical and animal specimens which filled the rooms of his large house in Leicester Square, and his country house in Earls Court, then a small village a few miles out of town. At the time his household was truly massive, with upwards of fifty people employed there, from assistants in the laboratories to cooks, maids, servants, grooms and coachmen. He died in October 1793 and, by the end of the month, everything was sold off and Mrs Hunter retired from society. When Haydn returned in 1794 she was still in deep mourning and not receiving anyone outside her immediate circle. He could not but respect her privacy and her grief.

During Haydn's first London visit they collaborated closely on the songs. She and her husband had become part of that huge circle of friends and admirers whom the Kapellmeister of Esterháza gathered around him in the months he was in England. Years later, she was known only as the woman whose poetry Haydn set to music, nothing more nor less. And despite the 'glare' that she showed in her day, as Fanny Burney put it, she spent nearly thirty years a widow, living modestly and seeing only family and close friends, among whom she numbered Rebecca.

While Anne and Rebecca led the quietly patient lives of widows, Haydn, who was soon to lose his wife, was cut out for greater things. Prominent among them was the composition of *The Creation*, which was first performed in Vienna to a rapturous reception in 1799. Haydn was keen that it should also be played in England. When he first arrived in London in 1791, he had gone to see the Handel Com-memoration of that year, which was held in Westminster Abbey. In the last week of May, by order of Their Majesties, a triumphant festival was organised. One of the people who attended was William Gardiner, a Leicester factory owner who recalled the performance of *Messiah* in his memoirs published nearly forty years later.

On entering the Abbey I was filled with surprise at the magnitude of the orchestra; it rose nearly to the top of the west window and above the arches of the main isle. On each side there was a tier of projecting galleries and I was placed in one of these. Above us were the trumpeters and appended to their instruments were richly embossed banners worked in silver and gold. We had flags of the same description which gave the whole a gorgeous and magnificent appearance. The arrangement of the performers was admirable, particularly that of the sopranos. The young ladies were placed upon a framework in the centre of the band in the form of a pyramid, as you see flower pots set up for a show . . .

Gardiner also recalls one amusing incident when someone tripped over a double bass, which was lying on its side. He 'disappeared immediately, and nothing was seen of him but his legs protruding out of the instrument'. There was a huge demand for tickets and, says Gardiner, some single tickets even changed hands at £20 a time. It would have been difficult to pick out Rebecca from the crowd in the overblown fashions of the time. Gardiner noticed that

> The female fashions were found highly inconvenient, particularly the headdresses, and it was ordered that no caps should be admitted of a size larger than a pattern exhibited at the Lord Chamberlain's office. As everyone wore powder, not withstanding a vast influx of hairdressers from the country, such was the demand for these artists, that many ladies submitted to have their hair dressed the previous evening and sat up all night to be ready for early admission in the morning.

Haydn sat near the King's box and Gardiner watched him 'with the aid of a telescope', which had been placed on a stand near the kettledrums. There were said to be over 1000 performers – conducted from the organ by Joah Bates. Haydn burst into tears when the Hallelujah Chorus was sung. He was overwhelmed by the sight and sound of so many hundreds of musicians and singers giving their all in one of the most impressive ecclesiastical setting in Europe. Haydn had only recently left Esterháza, where his orchestra and little opera company never amounted to more than thirty or forty musicians. Here, in full voice, were nearly twenty times that number. For Haydn it was an awe-inspiring moment, and he immediately saw the musical possibilities. It was then that he conceived the idea of trying to do something like it when he had the time and after he had discharged his contractual obligations to Johann Peter Salomon. One could argue that much of what he wrote in London was a preparation for *The*

Creation. He got used to bigger orchestras and larger audiences. He was able to study the effect his music had. His twelve London symphonies are full of musical innovations, of drama and humour. It was Salomon who suggested the text, the Book of Genesis. The subject alone clearly shows the huge ambitions Haydn had to produce a masterwork that would stand for all time – as Handel's *Messiah* already did. Haydn did not conceive *The Creation* as a rival to *Messiah*, but more an acknowledgement of his debt to the man who, he said, as his eyes streamed with tears in Westminster Abbey that May day, 'is master of us all'.

Haydn had always been enthralled by the use of large numbers of players in English bands – often double what he had been used to in his days at Esterháza. Handel's *Messiah*, with a choir of hundreds, had such power over an audience that Haydn wanted to do something similar. There is still some dispute about who first suggested the text to him – was it his concert promoter, Johann Peter Salomon? He claimed as much. The original text was written by Baron Gottfried van Swieten, an Austrian diplomat and noted music lover who led a group of the nobility in Vienna that sponsored, among other things, private performances of oratorio. He was a great champion of Bach and Mozart. He translated, rather badly, his German text into English. By now Anne Hunter was beginning to write lyrics to Scottish airs for the Edinburgh publisher George Thomson. As he wrote to her, 'it is not the first time that your muse and Haydn's are united as we see from the beautiful canzonets. Would that he had been directed by you about the words to *The Creation*! It is lamentable to see such divine music joined with such miserable broken English.' Anne must have taken the hint, because she set to work on her own versions of the text.

That Haydn never saw, or even knew of, Anne's reworking of the text is further proof that they were no longer in touch. Anne was a serious poet. Haydn was a great composer. Her interest in him was intellectual, not emotional. Rebecca knew it and trusted her friend. When Charles Burney organised a subscription for Haydn's published manuscript, the King and Queen, Mrs Anne Hunter and Mrs Rebecca

Schroeter were among those who signed up. Burney, who kept closely in touch with the world of music and art, was always a diplomat. He would have known that asking both to subscribe did not in any way embarrass either. Whether Haydn would have succumbed to Anne Hunter had she been a willing widow is perhaps best left unanswered; but despite the attractions of Anne and the other young women in the brilliant circle of artistic Georgian London, Haydn and Rebecca remained united.

CHAPTER FIFTEEN

Fleeting Shadows of Delight

As the small cross-channel packet sailed towards France and the English coastline slowly disappeared behind the horizon, Haydn certainly knew that he would never return. His three-year stay in London had earned him 24,000 Gulden. It was more than enough money to keep him in comfort in his old age. Safely packed away in the various trunks carrying his belongings were his London notebooks in which he had copied twenty-three letters from Rebecca. Among the reams of manuscript paper and music he was taking back with him were concertos written by her late husband, Johann Samuel Schroeter. He kept them until the day he died.

At sixty-three years of age, that Haydn wanted to go home and live quietly on his hard-won laurels should have surprised no one. Given his complaints about noise and dirt, Rebecca probably guessed as much. The pressures of life in London were indeed becoming harder to live with – with his enthusiastic audiences wanting ever more new surprises from him. At heart the celebrated composer was a simple man and, with Europe in turmoil, he preferred to see out his remaining years in places he knew. London had made him rich and famous. London had given him a better sense of his own self-worth as an artist. London had given him a love affair that he had relished. But London also represented a kind of slavery.

Back in March 1792 he had written to Maria Anna von Genzinger, 'In order to keep my word, and to support poor Salomon I must be the victim all the time. But I do really feel it. My eyes suffer the most, and I have many sleepless nights.' In his mind's eye he already saw his pretty little one-storey house in Gumpendorf as home. It would be a much-needed sanctuary away from the pressures of everyday life. Here he would be able to house his servants, including the ever faithful Johann Elssler and his family. And there was a piano for him. Then Gumpendorf was a small village outside Vienna. Today to the visitor it seems very much part of that great city but even as a museum there is a sense of what a cherished refuge it must have been for him.

Another factor[31] in the composer's decision to leave London for good was that he knew that in his old age, when he could no longer write music, the family he had served through so many decades would ensure that he could spend his last years in comfort and free from worry. King George III tried hard to persuade him, promising him accommodation in Windsor Castle. His Majesty had even joked that he would not be jealous if the composer spent his time tête-à-tête with the Queen making music. He refused, much to the King's chagrin. It would have meant he would spend his last few years as a liveried servant, no matter how generous the King would be. Certainly Rebecca Schroeter would have cared for him, nursed him, even. Their friends would have rallied round, but he would never have been free and the prospect of spending his last years in noisy noisome London was very unappealing. At heart, Haydn was a simple man used to routine. He liked the quiet life. The peasant mentality, though, opted for the practical rather than the romantic.

Haydn was not planning to retire immediately. He had agreed to remain in the employ of the Esterházy family as their Kapellmeister producing at least an annual mass for them. These late masses are among his finest works. One, 'In time of peace and war', is overtly patriotic; while another, dedicated to Nelson, marks the occasion when the famous British admiral, his mistress Emma Hamilton and her husband, the British ambassador to the royal court in Naples, broke their overland journey to London at Esterháza for a couple of days. In Emma's effects, after her death, some of Schroeter's manuscripts were found.

[31] H. C. Robbins Landon, *Chronicle and Works*.

The Esterházy family were keenly aware that having Haydn as their Kapellmeister brought them reflected glory. The composer felt he still owed them loyalty after three decades in their service. To help him they appointed someone to carry on the day-to-day work and he was no longer required to live at their palace of Esterháza, which was a great relief to him. But he was determined to keep busy, because he dreaded the prospect of spending his declining years cooped up with his shrewish wife, 'the monster', as he called her. The idea had been made even less palatable after the joys of life with the caring and loving Rebecca. In the end, though, it was his art that made the decision for him. He felt he had more music in him – all he needed was peace and quiet to bring it out. Luckily for Haydn, Maria Anna, his wife, does not seem to have relished living with Haydn either. She spent most of her remaining years taking the cure in various European spas.

For Rebecca, adjusting to Haydn's departure was as hard as, if not harder than, the first time. Then she knew he was coming back. Now it was certain that he would never set foot in England again. For a time she might have hoped that the pull of their love would be enough to bring him back. It was a vague possibility that if his wife were to die, she could follow him over to Vienna, as soon as the political situation on the Continent made it possible for a woman to travel alone. But gone for certain was the sensation of being at the very centre of the musical world. Gone were the almost daily visits, the late-night billets-doux after the concert. How much easier it must have been to get her friends round for a musical evening when the incomparable Haydn was there to play for them on the piano. From her letters we know that she had built a life around him. They give the impression that only his presence made the day complete – whether it was a snatched moment during a busy day or 'dinner here as usual'. She found verses for him, copied music for him and, most of all, listened to him and appreciated him. She knew he was married, that he had to go back to Vienna, but still she assured him of her affection and her gratitude for his friendship. She must have seemed almost too good to be true to Haydn, whose relationships with women had rarely – if ever – been as perfect as this one. A decade later, as we know, he was to remember her as 'a beautiful English widow who loved me, whom I might have married had I been free to do so'.

Perhaps they had discussed marriage if and when his wife died. Maybe he had promised her, as he had promised Polzelli his mistress, that if he married again it would be her. Men in love will promise many things to the object of their affections. Haydn loved women. He was a practised charmer and flirt. If his correspondence with Maria Anna von Genzinger is any guide, he was always fulsome in his praise of the recipient of his attentions, but self-deprecating when it came to himself. Haydn had a becoming modesty, which while practised was quite sincere. These patent social stratagems were partly convention but charming nevertheless. Women, then as now, learned to their cost that men do not always mean what they say – or even say what they mean.

The widow Schroeter, at forty-three, had only her memories. Her brother's and brother-in-law's rise up the social scale, acquiring land and wealth and a host of fine and titled friends, made Rebecca feel increasingly marginalised. It was as if she had been widowed for a second time. But Haydn did not abandon her completely. Though no letters have been found, they still corresponded and mutual friends carried messages. As Haydn had done with his other great love, Maria Anna von Genzinger, Rebecca was entrusted with some commissions on his behalf. Her name figures as a witness on a contract that Haydn drew up with a London publisher, Frederick Hyde, in 1796, her fine copperplate standing out firm and clear in the lengthy document.

Haydn, far from England and with no contact with the English language, was finding it harder and harder to write his little notes to Rebecca. Even when he had been in England his grasp of the language had been rudimentary and his written English was usually a phonetic version of what he heard people say. No wonder that in 1797 he tells the flautist J. G. Graeff[32] that his English is no longer good enough to

---

[32] Graeff had featured in Haydn's early Hanover Square concerts as a solo flautist. He was also involved in the professional concerts organised after J. C. Bach's death and

write directly to Mrs Schroeter. This fragmentary letter, which only came to light in 1982, proves that he was still in touch two years after he had left London and, secondly, that mutual friends knew of the relationship. Furthermore, the fact that he bothered to let her know why he was not writing as often because his English was no longer good enough shows once again that he was a caring man who never wanted to hurt anyone if he could avoid it. Of course, the longer they were separated the less they had to tell each other, as their lives took different directions. Nevertheless, the steady musical traffic through London provided Rebecca, if she stayed in touch with the musical world, with plenty of opportunity to keep up to date with what her 'dearest love' was doing. She, as a respectable widow living a quiet life on the margins of society, would have little to tell him.

Haydn's unlamented wife died in March 1799. The news came to the musical world in London and to Rebecca. Even though Bonaparte in France was beginning to worry the whole of Europe, and the British were convinced that he would soon cross the Channel, the mails got through and some intrepid travellers still risked their lives on the roads. The number of musicians coming to London had dropped sharply, though, and after Haydn's departure in 1795 the rage for music that had gripped the upper classes in London for so long began to abate. The oboist John Parke recalled in his memoirs that the art of music in this period was superseded by the art of war. Thirty benefit concerts in 1792 shrank to only eleven in 1798.[33] Failing harvests badly dented the revenues of the landed classes, meaning there was also less money around to be spent on going to concerts or organising private performances for friends. Having spent so much time at concerts in the early nineties during Haydn's stay, all this made a significant dent in her precious social life.

Her friend Salomon was still putting on concerts. A month after Mrs Haydn had died, Salomon presented a largely Haydn programme

therefore would have known Rebecca's husband – he may even have played some of his concertos for piano, violin and flute.

[33] Simon McVeigh, *Concert Life in London from Mozart to Haydn*.

at Willis's Rooms – formerly Almack's Rooms – behind Pall Mall. Had Rebecca attended she would have seen Jan Ladislav Dušek play the piano. A few years earlier *The Gazetteer* had written of Dušek that his 'sonata on the piano forte, if it had less affectation of expression, would have resembled the affecting simplicity of the much lamented Schroeter'. Given the similarity of styles, Rebecca would have wanted to hear her husband's successor in what was called the 'singing allegro' style of playing. It would also be the last time she could see him. Dušek, who was a partner in a music publishing firm, was about to flee his creditors as the company went bankrupt – a reminder, if Rebecca needed reminding, of the vulnerability of musical careers. Also on the bill was the celebrated singer Gertrude Mara. Madame Mara had known Schroeter's sister Corona in Leipzig where they both studied under the great Hiller. Unless the generous Salomon gave her a free pass, 10s 6d was a small price to pay to hear Haydn's music, reminisce with Salomon and talk about Schroeter with Madame Mara.

The last direct link between them comes in 1800 when Rebecca's name figures in the list of subscribers to Haydn's monumental oratorio *The Creation*. Haydn worked hard on his oratorio when he returned to Vienna after his second and last visit in London. On completion of the work in 1798 he busily undertook to raise as many subscriptions as he could for the published score in both German and English. In England he wrote to Charles Burney asking him to contact as many of the influential and wealthy as he could. Burney took to the task with relish and in the end collected nearly ninety subscribers. He started at the top and sought the support of the royal family. The King and Queen graciously accepted. The Prince of Wales was among the subscribers, as were the royal Princesses. Johann Peter Salomon could hardly refuse; the oratorio had been his idea in the first place. Another name was Christopher Papendieck, with whom Rebecca's late husband had performed for the royal family nearly twenty years before. Mrs Anne Hunter was also among the subscribers. Although she was no longer a leading society figures, having retired to a quiet widow's life, everyone knew that Haydn had set many of her songs to music. And there was Rebecca's name as well. That fact alone would certainly suggest that her relationship with Haydn was well known – by any of the people just mentioned. Only the King and Queen would have been unaware of its true nature, knowing Rebecca as the respectable widow of a former music master to the Queen rather than the composer's mistress. Rebecca's decision to subscribe shows that even after five years she was as keen a supporter of Haydn and his music as ever. She received her copy in July 1800.

Salomon, the man who had worked so hard on Haydn's behalf, was desperately keen to be able to mount the first English performance. Sadly, he was thwarted in this because of a mix-up over manuscript copies. Salomon and John Ashley, who directed the Lent oratorios at Covent Garden, had both ordered a manuscript from Haydn. Ashley's copyist, Thomas Goodwin, proved to be a master of organisation and produced 120 parts in just six days. When he was congratulated he replied, 'We emulated a great example. It is not the first time *The Creation* has been completed in six days.' Ashley duly staged the first performance on 28 March; there is a certain symmetry that the Lenten oratorio series was inaugurated at the Opera House by none other than Handel and Haydn's great tribute should have played there first. Salomon had to wait until 21 April. Happily for him, the critics seem to have preferred Salomon's production. He had helped his case greatly by telling the papers that his concert performance had been 'authorised' by the great Haydn. Given his and Haydn's reputation, his performance was oversubscribed. For English audiences *The Creation* never achieved the status of Handel's great work. The English translation was not very good and this may have had much to do with the warm but not ecstatic reception the work received. In fact, as we now know, Mrs Hunter felt that she could improve on the English text and worked on a number of drafts, but they were never used. Perhaps she and Rebecca talked it over, but neither had the social clout or funds to promote the idea. In Vienna *The Creation* did achieve what Haydn had hoped for and it soon became the Viennese equivalent of Handel's *Messiah* in that city's musical calendar.

Haydn had but a handful of years to live. An Austrian writer, Adie Funk,[34] paints a charming word picture of the venerable master in his final years in Gumpendorf. The composer of the Austrian National Anthem, he said, played the tune every day on his quaint piano of only five octaves. 'In this house there came to see him the most famous men of the day, calling him Papa Haydn, and reverently kissing his hand as he sat in his easy chair, his head covered with a powdered wig with long side curls, otherwise clad in a white heavily embroidered waistcoat of silk, with rich lace jabot, white stock with a golden clasp, brown coat of state, embroidered cuffs, black silk breeches, white silk stockings, and large silver buckles on his shoes.' If this is a true portrait of the old man then he was still firmly dressed in the style of the previous century, largely in what he would have worn as the Kapellmeister of the princely Esterházy family. Haydn was certainly a man of almost rigid habit and discipline. This, above all, would be the memory of him that Rebecca treasured to the end. She would see Haydn sitting in her London house, his happy face beaming with joy as she played one of his late sonatas for him on her Broadwood box piano, the centre of attention for all their friends.

About this time Rebecca gave up her lease on the house in Buckingham Gate – where she and Haydn had spent so much time together, where she had given musical parties for their mutual friends, and where Haydn had played and sung for her and their guests. She moved out of town and into what was then countryside: modern-day Camden Town. The house, greatly altered, still stands. It is number 68 Crowndale Road,[35] which runs off Mornington Crescent. She was close enough to the home of William Napier, her husband's publisher in neighbouring Somerstown, to help him through the poverty of his later years. The kind and generous Mrs Schroeter would never have deserted one of her oldest friends, with whom she had been connected since the day of her marriage back in 1775. In 1806 she obtained

---

[34] In a pretty little book on *Vienna's Musical Sites and Landmarks*, published in 1927.
[35] This information comes from the indefatigable Tony Scull in his article in the *Musical Quarterly*, 'More light on Haydn's English Widow'.

probate on her late husband's will – eighteen years after he had died. The estate was valued at less that £300. Did she need the money? We will never know. From now on her life took on the usual slow decline. In those days families cared for the old. The end of one's life was usually a rather cluttered and cloistered existence, and normally marked more by bereavement than gaiety.

Rebecca's brother, Robert, and Charles Murray, her brother-in-law, both died in 1808. In the old church at Medmenham the memorial put up by Robert's grieving widow Emma is still there. Engraved in the white marble are the words 'To the memory of Robert Scott, Esq., of Danesfield, who died the 6th of February 1808, aged 61. To a manly understanding and an amiable disposition, he united the accomplishments of a Gentleman and the virtues of a Christian. His piety was sincere and unaffected; his liberality active, unostentatious, and unbounded. He was respected by the Rich; by the Poor he was blessed; by his Friends he was beloved and honoured; above all, by her who was most intimately acquainted with his real worth, his grateful and affectionate widow'. Rebecca must have struggled hard to recognise the man described in such a glowing encomium as the implacable brother she knew who had always opposed her marriage and made her pay for years for what she did to the family by restricting her income.

Her brother's will shows just how far he had come on the back of his father's money. At the time it was valued at around £400,000 which made him a millionaire many times over in today's monetary values. He left his wife Emma an annuity for life of £2000, and 'whatever house or lease of house he may have in London at the time of his death, plus furniture, plate, linen, china, wine etc; the house, lands and estate of Danesfield and Medmenham in Buckinghamshire, furniture, plate, linen, books, china, wares, wines liquors, horses carriages etc . . .' Two close friends and their families figure heavily among the beneficiaries. The first, Henry William Tancred of Lincoln's Inn, was married to his sister-in-law – he stood to gain £5000. The other friend, Henry Parnell, son of Sir John Parnell, was also left £5000. To his sister Elizabeth Murray he leaves an annuity of £2000 for life. His sister Rebecca gets a paltry £500 'over and above what she receives from me now ...' Even in death Robert sought to control family affairs – and keep Rebecca dependent. She would seem to have been made to go on paying for her impetuosity of twenty years before.

Since Robert Scott died without any children, the hopes of the Scott family passed to the only son of Charles Scott Murray, who received everything else under the will. Among the codicils was added 'Robert Scott confirms in all parts the will he made on 18th September 1804, but in case any doubt arises concerning its validity, or if there is any dispute about it on the part of either his sisters, or his nephew Charles Scott Murray, he revokes every legacy left by will to his sisters and nephew and leaves the whole of his estate to Henry William Tancred and Henry Parnell in equal shares ...' Twenty years after the bruising Chancery case, which set brother against sister and son against mother, Robert Scott was adamant that his last will and testament should not become a source of family strife – rather friends should inherit everything than there should be another destructive family quarrel.

Just over a month after Robert Scott died, Haydn made his last public appearance at a performance of *The Creation* at the old university in Vienna. The concert was arranged to celebrate the composer's next birthday – his seventy-sixth. He was carried into the hall in an armchair, which was placed next to Princess Esterházy who, when she saw Haydn shiver a little, immediately wrapped him in her shawl, only to be followed by many other ladies of rank until he was almost smothered in coats. One of the most exciting musical moments in Haydn's piece is when the singer says 'let there be light – and there was light'. Haydn looked up to heaven and murmured, 'Not from me, but from thence everything comes'. The oratorio, which was sung in Italian on this occasion, received a tumultuous ovation.

In the audience were some of the leading composers of the day then in Vienna: Ludwig van Beethoven, who was already ushering in the newer music that would push Haydn's works to the margins during the coming century; Antonio Salieri, Kapellmeister to the Austrian court; Johann Hummel, who was Haydn's new deputy at Esterháza; Adalbert Gyrowetz, who had helped Haydn in his work in London. The army was drafted in to keep order at the doors. All but one of the members of the highest nobility attended. The absentee, who pleaded urgent business, was Haydn's employer Prince Nikolaus Esterházy, who enjoyed the renown his Kapellmeister brought him but cared little for his music. He did, however, let Haydn travel to the university in his coach. In the Museum of the City of Vienna is a fancy box, on the cover of which is a painting of the scene specially commissioned by Princess Esterházy.

A year after losing her brother and her brother-in-law Rebecca heard the news she must have been dreading and expecting. On 31 May, shortly after midnight, Haydn went, his servant Johann Elssler reported, 'blissfully and gently' to sleep. In the morning he was found dead. The French had been besieging Vienna. The noise made by their heavy armaments was overwhelming. Typically, Haydn tried to reassure his frightened staff. 'Don't worry, my children,' he told them, 'no harm can come to you while Haydn is here.' Right up to the end he still received visitors and even sometimes played the piano. It was always the same tune now: the Austrian National Anthem, a small but defiant gesture by a weak old man in the face of the enemy. Ironically, one of Haydn's last visitors was a young French officer of the Hussars, Clement Sulemy,[36] who came to talk to the famous old man about *The Creation*. Before he left he asked if he could sing to him. Haydn listened with tears in his eyes as the young enemy officer sang 'In native worth' from the great oratorio.

Johann Elssler, Haydn's copyist and servant, who had been with him on his second visit to London – and would certainly have known Mrs Schroeter – wrote a moving letter of his master's last hours to Griesinger, one of the two original biographers. It was the almost

[36] Sulemy is believed to have died soon afterwards in the battle of Aspern, according to the Haydn scholar Schnerich quoted in Karl Geiringer's *Haydn: A Creative Life in Music*, p. 189.

daily bombardment of the city that sapped Haydn's energy and led to a rapid decline. The final twenty-four-hour bombardment shattered the old man's nerves. Given the grave political situation, he was buried later that day, attended only by his family of servants, in Gumpendorf church. He was seventy-seven years old, some twenty years older than his English widow. It has been said that Napoleon had given orders that during the siege no harm should come to Haydn. When he heard the news of the composer's death, the Emperor ordered a guard of honour to be placed at his house. Many French officers mounted guard at the memorial service which took place on 15 June in the Schottenkirche. As he was laid to rest, Viennese musicians played Mozart's *Requiem*. Haydn would have appreciated that choice. His remains were removed to Eisenstadt in 1820 and were buried beneath the choir in the little mountain church for which he wrote most of his great masses.

With European mail disrupted by the Continental wars, the news of Haydn's death at the end of May was not reported in Britain until late July. It would be some months before there was a fitting memorial service to him held in London. A year after his death Haydn's two biographers, Dies and Griesinger, published their respective books. Griesinger's, the slighter of the two, appeared in July in Leipzig, while Dies, who had managed to write over twice as many pages, was published first in Vienna in May 1810. Dies says with certainty that Mrs Schroeter was still living in London in 1810. Since he did not go to London Haydn must have been maintaining some kind of contact with her or was at least sentimental enough to want to know that she was well. If he was not writing directly to her, he was sending messages or letters for her via other correspondents. He had often used Maria Anna von Genzinger in this way. Despite the scant references to be found, there is no reason not to believe that they were in contact in some form or another. Her friendship, let alone her love, was something Haydn still cherished. As his biographer says, 'a happy look came over his face' when he talked about the letters. The most intriguing question of all is whether Rebecca knew that she was mentioned in the book. She was nearly sixty. It was something from her past of which she had no reason to be ashamed. Nor could she have stopped any mention of their relationship, since she did not know of Haydn's conversation with his biographer. As for the book, it was published in German in Vienna. Very few people would have read it in London. The English papers at the time were full of the war with Bonaparte and England's survival, so a love story between an English widow and a German composer, which had happened nearly fifteen years before, was hardly likely to excite their readers.

Rebecca outlived many of her husband's friends. In 1812 her husband's old publisher, William Napier, died in Somerstown. It had been planned as a pleasant suburb in the 1780s but many of the houses failed to sell and their half-built shells were left standing. When Napier lived there it had become very much an area for the working class and for crowds of poor émigrés from the French Revolution. Despite his poverty, Napier still rated an obituary in the *Scots Magazine* in July: 'At Somerstown, Mr William Napier, in the 72nd year of his age. He was distinguished for his musical skill and for the beautiful selections of Scotch ballads, which he edited. For many years he belonged to His Majesty's band, and to the professional concert; but was obliged to retire on account of the gout in his hands to which he became a victim.' The last link of Rebecca's life with Schroeter and Haydn, Johann Peter Salomon, died on 26 November 1815. He was thrown from his horse. He is buried in Westminster Abbey – where on his tombstone is written 'The man who brought Haydn to England'.

Rebecca had another eight years to live. When she had left town for St Pancras, it would have been largely open country. There was one inn, the Mother Red Cap, which she would never have frequented, and a manor house. It was the usual last move of an elderly widow: smaller, quieter, safer and above all cheaper. Yet she would have seen the countryside fast disappear in the building boom of the early years of the nineteenth century. Without any family responsibilities, women in Rebecca's position had to get used to a humdrum routine. There would have been some embroidery, reading, running the small household, and occasional evenings with friends or family visits and, of course, attending church. If her brother's will is anything to go by, both her sister and sister-in-law did but the minimum to keep in touch with the errant member of the family. She had become the classic poor relation, whose pride had brought about her fall many years before. Rebecca's memories, though, were a good deal richer. She had the music that had been written for her. She could play the gentle music of her husband's concertos when she was in a reflective mood, or the rousing bohemian themes of the *Gypsy* trio that Haydn had written especially for her before he left England.

In 1821 Anne Hunter, whose charm had competed with Rebecca's own, died. Ever since her husband's sudden death in 1793 she had withdrawn from society and lived a quiet, almost secluded life. She wrote to her niece Joanna Bailey, 'I am but a shabby person; however, we scramble on thro' weeks, and months, somehow or other, as well as we can.' For many years she had been living alone in a small house in Lower Grosvenor Street. Her second great sadness was estrangement from her son, who fled to France to avoid his creditors. But her brothers, nieces and her daughter gave her much to be happy about. In old age Anne Hunter had continued to write some songs which Haydn's Edinburgh publisher, George Thomson, had bought from her. And she had published her own slim volume of verses in 1802. One of them bemoans the loss of a lover and the passage of time. It would have meant a lot to Rebecca.

The season comes when first we met,
But you return no more;
Why cannot I the days forget,
Which time can ne'er restore?
O days too sweet, too bright to last,
Are you indeed for ever past?

The fleeting shadows of delight,
In memory I trace;
In fancy stop their rapid flight,
And all the past replace:
But, ah, I wake to endless woes,
And tears the fading visions close!

Rebecca probably lived alone with only a servant or two to care for her. Old age, in those days, was more often than not a very heavy cross to bear and with only laudanum to dull any pain, nor adequate medical treatment to alleviate the worst effects of chronic illness. The memory could begin to play tricks. According to the rate books she was still of the parish of St Pancras. For the first twenty-two years Rebecca attended the old and very small parish church in whose churchyard Johann Christian Bach, another old friend from her younger days, had been buried. In 1816 Parliament authorised the building of a new church, because the parish was expanding so fast. When it was consecrated in 1822 it had cost over £90,000 – the most expensive church built in London since St Paul's. She died, aged seventy-six, in April 1823.

Fine and expensive though her new parish church was, Rebecca did not want to be buried there. As a final gesture of defiance, perhaps, she said she wanted to be buried alongside her late husband in the burying grounds of St George's, Hanover Square. They were then set among open fields quite a way out of town just west of the execution grounds of Tyburn. There were few close male relatives to attend her funeral. Her brother and brother-in-law were long dead. The present head of the family, Robert Scott Murray, was a deeply religious man and his son would later convert to Catholicism. They may have been part of the funeral party. Rebecca could well have gone to her grave alone with only a couple of professional mourners for appearance's sake. There would be no women in attendance and what female friends she had might well have found it too much to travel up to town for any kind of gathering – they would all be in their seventies as well.

Today the Bayswater Road has swallowed up most of the old cemetery. The actual site where the Schroeters lie is covered by a twentieth-century block of flats. On the north side is a private garden used by a nursery school. This is all that remains of the old burying ground: a tiny garden set behind a high iron railing which looks across to Hyde Park. The Park is the only reminder of the countryside that used to be within a short walking distance of most Londoners.

There, if one can ignore the rush of traffic up to Hyde Park Corner, it is just possible to reflect quietly on what it must have been like on a showery April day in 1823 as a small horse-drawn hearse trundled out with its light load draped in black to the freshly dug grave.

For neither Johann nor Rebecca is there any record of memorials being raised to their lives. Unlike her brother, Rebecca does not leave behind a marble monument engraved with a catalogue of the great works she performed for the poor or how loyal and loving a wife she was, or how much she is missed. It is as if she had never existed. There is mention of a headstone being ordered for Johann Samuel, but there is nothing at all for Rebecca. All that remains is the entry in the register of deaths. How many people accompanied her to her last resting place? Were there any members of the family – and, if there were, what would they have made of seeing Rebecca once again being joined in death, as she was in life, with the German music teacher? Or did this small gesture of defiance preclude any possibility that they would make the long trek from their fine houses in the Home Counties to stand in silence and remember her?

The rest of her family prospered mightily down the years, becoming even richer, and important members of society as Members of Parliament, lord-lieutenants and magistrates. The Scott Murray family disappears early in the 1900s and the huge estate at Danesfield, the family seat for over a century, was sold. It still stands today, much changed, yet a potent example of the upward mobility of this Scottish family of merchants and traders. Among her descendants nothing is known of their connection with Rebecca Schroeter. Indeed, why should they have known of her? In old age she was relegated to the edge of the family's world. She had no fortune to leave, nor vast estate to keep the younger members of the family interested.

The bare outline of Rebecca's life exists in faded parchment in Chancery Rolls, in church registers, family wills and private letters. Yet from these alone it is obvious why Johann Samuel Schroeter and Joseph Haydn were so smitten by her. She comes across as a warm, vibrant person who, when she loved, loved completely. 'I will have no other man than Schroeter,' she shouted at her family that fateful weekend in July 1775 when confronted by her aunts, uncles, brother, sister, mother and family friends. More than once she had insisted, 'I will have no other.' Sixteen years later, a widow, she was capable of love again and, thanks to her impression on Haydn who copied twenty-three of her letters, we hear her voice once more. 'Dearest Love,' she would write by candlelight to 'my Haydn' late at night after coming home from a concert where he had been applauded to the echo by the nobility. Rebecca was so much more than just a woman who gave up everything for love.

In an age that modern feminists now see as the one that launched many of the twentieth century's ideas about individual freedom and gender equality, Rebecca Scott was one of many marginalised people who got on with her life. They are the unsung revolutionaries and trailblazers. Despite the restrictions imposed by the social conventions of the time, Rebecca did what she wanted and stood by all her decisions. She was not famous in the way Fanny Burney, Hester Thrale Piozzi, Mary Wollstonecraft and many of the other great female icons of the day were famous. Rebecca lived life to the full but in the shadows and according to her own needs. She may have loved famous men, but she was no empty-headed fan hooked on the celebrity status of her lovers.

She is closer to the heroines of Jane Austen's novels. Reading Jane Austen's letters to her sister Cassandra, written about the same time as Rebecca lived out her old age, it is easy to picture her worrying about nieces and nephews and great-nieces and great-nephews, making the most of the few social visits she was invited to make. Just like Jane Austen, she might constantly reuse pieces of material so as to continue to be in the fashion. When she made the long trek out to the mansion at Danesfield for a family visit, how was she received? Did her sister or her sister-in-law greet her with love and affection, or was she just tolerated as the woman who had shamed them once and shamed them still by proudly referring to herself as 'Mrs Rebecca Schroeter'? She never changed her name and that name reminded them all of what she had done by marrying so far beneath her that overcast July Monday morning in 1775. It seems Rebecca had no children. Two of Mrs Hunter's four children died young. The loss of an infant was not unusual in those risky days for women in childbirth. Searches so far have not found anything to suggest even this unfortunate possibility as far as Rebecca was concerned. Mrs Hunter at least had a daughter to comfort her in old age. Rebecca had no one so close.

Rebecca Scott was obviously a self-aware human being. Her life, in the best eighteenth-century tradition of literature, was an ambiguous model of how life can be lived if you take your own decisions and listen to your heart as well as your head. She displayed pride in her determination to get what she wanted and encountered prejudice when she won through. Rebecca was both sense and sensibility incarnate. I doubt she had any regrets about the choices she had made. But the last words in the story of her life should be Rebecca's. As she wrote to her 'Dear Haydn' on 24 April 1792, 'I can not leave London without sending you a line to assure you my thoughts, my best wishes and tenderest affections will inseparably attend you till we meet again . . .'

APPENDIX

Rebecca's Letters

In 1959 the great Haydn scholar, H. C. Robbins Landon, published *The Collected Correspondence and London Notebooks of Joseph Haydn* (Barrie and Rockcliff). It was the forerunner of his monumental five-volume *Chronicle and Works*, which give an almost day-by-day account of the composer's life. No one can write about Haydn without consulting Robbins Landon. Much of the detail in my book is thanks to his pioneering research. What follows are the twenty-three letters that Haydn copied into the second of his London notebooks. The handwriting is clearly Haydn's. Robbins Landon arranged the letters in a chronological sequence. First he explained the abbreviation: 'F' = Faithful; 'M.D.' = My dear; 'D.' = Dear; 'Dst' = Dearest , 'M.Dst' = My Dearest; 'H' and 'Hn' = Haydn; 'D.H.' = Dear Haydn.

Mrs Schroeter presents her compliments to Mr Haydn and informs him, she is just returned to town, and will be very happy to see him, whenever it is convenient to him to give her a lesson

James St. Buckingham Gate Wednesday
June the 29th 791

Wednesday Feb 8th 793
M.D. inclos'd I have sent the words of the song you desired – I wish much to know, HOW YOU DO to day, I am very sorry to lose the pleasure of seeing you this morning, but I hope you will have time tomorrow. I beg you my D. you will take great care of your health, and do not fatigue your self with too much application to business.

My thoughts and best wishes are always with you, and I ever am with the utmost sincerity M.D. your F etc

March 7th 92

My D. I was extremely sorry to part with you so suddenly last Night, our conversation was particularly interesting and I had thousand affectionate things to say to you, my heart WAS and is full of TENDERNESS for you, but no language can express HALF the Love and AFFECTION I feel for you, you are DEARER TO ME EVERY DAY of my life. I am very sorry I was so dull and stupid yesterday, indeed Dearest it was nothing but my being indisposed with a cold occasion'd my stupidity. I thank you a thousand times for your concern for me, I am truly sensible of your goodness, but I assure you my D. if anything had happened to trouble me, I would have open'd my heart, & told you with the most perfect confidence. Oh how earnestly I wish to see you. I hope you will come to me tomorrow. I shall be happy to see you both in the morning and the Evening. God Bless you my love, my thoughts and best wishes ever accompany you, and I always am with the most sincere and invariable Regard my D. your truly affectionate

My Dearest I cannot be happy till I see you if you know, do, tell me, when you will come

My D. I am extremely sorry I cannot have the pleasure of seeing you tomorrow, as I am going to Blackheath. If you are not engaged this Evening I should be very happy if you will do me the favor to come to me – and I hope to have the happiness to see you on Saturday to dinner. My thoughts and tenderest affections are always with you and I am ever most truly my D. Your friends and etc

April 4th 92

My D. with this, you will receive the Soap, I beg you a thousand pardons for not sending it sooner, I know you will have the goodness to excuse me. – I hope to hear you quite well, and have slept well – I shall be happy to see you, My D. as soon as possible. I shall be much obliged to you if you will do me the favour to send me twelve tickets for your concert, may all success attend you my EVER D. H. that night, and always, is the sincere and hearty wish of your invariable and truly affectionate.

James S April 8th 92

James St. Thursday April 12th
M.D. I am so truly anxious about you. I must write, to beg to know HOW YOU DO? I was very sorry I HAD not the pleasure of seeing you this evening, my thoughts have been CONSTANTLY with you, and indeed MY D. L. no words can express half the tenderness and AFFECTION I FEEL FOR YOU – I thought you seemed out of spirits this morning, I wish I could always remove every trouble from your mind, be assured my D. I partake the most perfect sympathy in ALL YOUR SENSATIONS, and my regard for you is STRONGER EVERY DAY, my best wishes always attend you and I am my D. H. most sincerely you faithful etc

M.D. I was extremely sorry to hear this morning that you was indisposed, I am told you was five hours at your Study's yesterday, indeed my D. L. I am afraid it will hurt, why should you, who have already produced so many WONDERFUL and CHARMING compositions, still fatigue yourself with such close application. I almost tremble for your health, let me prevail on you my MUCH LOVED H. not to keep to your study's so long at ONE TIME, my D.LOVE if you could know how very precious your welfare is to me, I flatter myself you wou'd endeavor to preserve it, for my sake, as well as your own pray inform me how you do and how you have slept, I hope to see you to morrow at the concert, and on Saturday. I shall be happy to see you here to dinner, in the meantime, my D. sincerest good wishes constantly attend you and I ever am with the tenderest regard your most

(J. S. April the 19th 92)

April 24th 792

My D. I cannot leave London without sending you a line to assure you my thoughts; my BEST WISHES and tenderest affections will inseparably attend you till we meet again. The bearer will also deliver to you the March, I am very sorry, I cou'd not write it sooner, nor better, but I hope my D. you will excuse it, and if it is not passable, I will send you the DEAR original directly: If my H. wou'd employ me oftener to write music I hope I shou'd improve, and I know I shou'd delight in the occupation. Now my D. L. let me intreat you to take the greatest care of your HEALTH I hope to see you on Friday at the concert and on Saturday to dinner till when and ever I most sincerely am and shall be your etc

M.D. I am very anxious to know HOW YOU DO, and hope to hear you have been in good health ever since I saw you – as the time for your charming concert advances I feel myself more and more interested for your success, and heartily WISH everything may turn out to your satisfaction. Do me the favor to send me six tickets more. On Saturday my D. L. I hope to see you to dinner, in the mean while, my thoughts, my best wishes, and tenderest affections, constantly attend you, I ever am my D. H. most sincerely and aff (etc)

J. S. May the 2nd 1792

James St Tuesday May ye 8th

My Dt. I am extremely sorry I have not the pleasure seeing you today, but I hope to see you tomorrow at one o'clock and if you can take your DINNER with me tomorrow, I shall be very glad – I hope to see you also on Thursday to dinner, but I suppose you will be obliged to go to the concert that evening, and you know the other concert is on Friday, and you go to the country on Saturday, this my Dt. Love makes me more solicitous for you to stay with me tomorrow, if you are not engaged, as I wish to have as much of your company as possible. God Bless you, my Dst H, I am always with the tenderest Regard your sincere and affectionate etc

May 17th

M.D. permit me to return you a thousand thanks for this evening's entertainment – where YOUR – SWEET compositions and your EXCELLENT performance combine, it can not fail of being the most CHARMING CONCERT, but independent of THAT, the pleasure of SEEING you must ever give me infinite satisfaction – Pray inform me HOW YOU DO? And if you have SLEPT WELL? I hope to see you to morrow my D. and on Saturday to dinner, till when and always I remain most sincerely my D. L. most Faithfully (etc)

M.D. If you will do me the favor to take your dinner with me to Morrow, I shall be very happy to see you, and I PARTICULARLY wish for the pleasure of your company MY Dr LOVE BEFORE our other friends come – I hope to hear that you have slept well to Night and that you are in GOOD HEALTH, my BEST WISHES and tenderest Regards are your constant attendants and I EVER AM with the FIRMEST Attachment My Dst Hn most sincerely and affectionately yours R S.

James S Tuesday Ev. May 22nd

My Dr I beg to know HOW YOU DO? Hope to hear your Head-ach is ENTIRELY GONE, and that you SLEPT WELL. I shall be very happy to see you on Sunday any time convenient to you after one o'clock I hope to see you my Dr L on Tuesday as usual to dinner (crossed out[37]) – and I shall be much obliged to you if you will inform me what Day will be agreeable to you to meet Mr Mrs and Miss Stone at my house to dinner, I shou'd be glad if it were either Thursday or Friday, whichever Day you please to fix, I will send to Mr Stone to let them know. I long to see you my Dr H, let me have that pleasure as

---

[37] Tony Scull in his article in the *Musical Quarterly* thinks the phrase was scored out so heavily because the original phrase was 'sleep with me'. H. C. Robbins Landon is more circumspect. He thinks the phrase is 'spend the night with me'. Whatever the phrase, the relationship seems to have gone beyond platonic.

soon as you can, till when and ever I remain with the firmest attachment My Dr L: most faithfully and affectionately yours (etc)

Friday June ye 1st 792

My D. I cannot close my eyes to sleep till I have returned you ten thousand thanks for the inexpressible delight I have received from your EVER ENCHANTING compositions and your INCOMPARABLY CHARMING PERFORMANCE of them. Be assured my D. H. that among all your numerous admirers, no one has listened with more PROFOUND attention, no one can have such high veneration for your MOST BRILLIANT TALENTS as I have. Indeed my D. L. no tongue can EXPRESS the gratitude I FEEL for the infinite pleasure your Music has given me, accept then my repeated thanks for it, and let me assure you, with heart felt affection, that I shall consider the happiness of your acquaintance as one of the CHIEF Blessings of my life, and it is the SINCER wish of my heart to preserve, to cultivate and to merit more and more. I hope to hear that you are quite well. Shall be happy to see you to dinner and if you can come at Three o'clock it would give me great pleasure, as I should be particularly glad to see you my D. before the rest of our friends come – God bless you my D. I am ever with the firmest and most perfect attachment your etc

Wednesday night June 6th 1792

My Dst Inclosed I send you the verses you was so kind as to lend me, and I am very much obliged to you for permitting me to take a copy of them. Pray inform me HOW YOU DO and let me know MY DT L. when you will dine with me. I shall be happy to see you to dinner either to morrow or Tuesday whichever is most convenient to you, I am truly anxious and impatient to see you, and I wish to have as much of your company as possible: indeed by Dst H. I feel for you the fondest and tenderest affection the human heart is capable of, and I ever am with the firmest attachment my Dt Love, most Sincerely, Faithfully and most affectionately yours (ETC)

Sunday Evening June 10th 1792

My Dearest

I hope to hear that you are in good health, and have had an agreeable journey, that you have been much amused with the race, and that every thing has turned out to your satisfaction pray my Dst love inform me how you do? EVERY circumstance concerning you my beloved Hdn is interesting to me – I shall be very happy to see you to dinner to morrow and I ever am with the sincerest and tenderest regard my Dst Hdn most faithfully & affectionately yours R. S.

James S. Thursday even. June ye 14th 1792

M.D. I was EXTREMELY SORRY, I had not the pleasure of SEEING YOU to DAY, indeed my Dr Love it was a very great disappointment to me, as every moment of your company is MORE and MORE PRECIOUS to me now your departure is so near – I hope to hear you are QUITE WELL and I shall be happy to see you my Dr Hn any time to morrow after one o'clock if you can come but if not, I shall hope for the pleasure of seeing you on Monday – you will receive this letter to morrow morning I would not send it today, for fear you should not be at home, and I wish to have your answer. God Bless you my Dr Love, once more I repeat let me see you AS SOON AS POSSIBLE. I am ever with the most INVIOLABLE ATTACHMENT my Dr and most beloved H – most faithfully and most affectionately Yours R Sch

Saturday June ye 16th 1792

My D. I hope you are in good HEALTH, and that you slept well last night. I shall be very happy to see you on Monday morning – permit me to remind you about Mr Frasers, and you will be so good as to let me know on Monday how it is settled – God Bless you my D. Love, my thoughts and best wishes are your constant attendants, and I am ever with the tenderest regard my D. H. most etc

June the 26th 1792

Haydn also copied out four undated letters as follows:

My Dearest I am quite impatient to know how you do this Morning, and if you slept well last night – I am much obliged to you for all your kindness yesterday and heartily thank you for it. I earnestly long to see you my Dt L. and I hope to have that pleasure this morning. My THOUGHTS and best REGARDS are incessantly with you and I am ever my Dst H. most faithfully and most affectionately yours etc

M.D. I was extremely sorry I had not the pleasure of your company this morning as I most ANXIOUSLY wish'd to see you – my THOUGHTS are continually with you, my beloved H and my AFFECTION for you INCREASES DAILY, no words can express the TENDER REGARD I feel for you – I hope my Dt L. I shall have the happiness of seeing you tomorrow to dinner, in the meantime my best wishes always attend you and I EVER am with the FIRMEST ATTACHMMENT MY D. L. most etc

I am just return'd from the concert, where I was very much charmed with your DELIGHTFUL and enchanting COMPOSITIONS, and your spirited and interesting performance of them, accept ten thousand thanks for the great pleasure I ALWAYS receive from your INCOMPARABLE MUSIC. My D. I intreat you to inform me, how you do, and if you get any SLEEP to night. I am EXTREMELY ANXIOUS about your health. I hope to hear a good account of it. God Bless you my H. Come to me tomorrow I shall be happy to see you both morning and evening. I always am with the tenderest Regard my D. your F. and Aff...

Friday Night 12 o'clock

M.D. I am heartily sorry I was so unfortunate not to see you when you call'd this morning, can you my D. be so good as to dine with me TO DAY. I beg you will if possible – you can not imagine how miserable I am that I did not see you – do come to DAY I intreat you – I always am M.D. with the tenderest regard most etc

These twenty-three letters were copied in 1792 and found by Dies in 1807. They were first published in full in 1958.

Sources

It is impossible to write about the eighteenth century without leaning heavily on all the work that has gone before. As Isaac Newton said about his life of study, he stood on the shoulders of giants to see further. I would not, could not, claim to have made as much use of the 'giants' in eighteenth-century studies as a Newton, but without their insights, this modest work would not be possible. Thanks to Amazon.co.uk and Abebooks.com, I have managed to get hold of a huge number of marvellous books about the period, whose own bibliographies became useful signposts to London in the 1770s. Wherever possible within the text, I have acknowledged my sources. I am not an academic historian, so my reading has been wide and varied – hoping that I might come across an idea, an image, a fact or a name which would add to the picture of the musical world in London in the second half of the eighteenth century. What follows is a selection of the books which I consulted most often. I have grouped these sources by subject, rather than by author.

Composers

Haydn scholarship these days is prospering, as the composer gains the recognition he deserves for his musical gifts. There is one man, above all others, who has helped to bring about Haydn's rehabilitation. H. C. Robbins Landon produced a monumental five-volume *Chronicle and Works*, an almost day-by-day, and sometimes hour-by-hour account of Haydn's life. Volume three, *Haydn in England 1791–*

1793, was obviously of direct interest, as was to a lesser extent the final volume, *Haydn: The Late Years 1801–1809*. The publisher is Thames and Hudson, 1978. H. C. Robbins Landon also translated Haydn's London Notebooks and his collected correspondence, which included the twenty-three letters the composer copied out in his own hand (Barrie and Rockliff, 1959).

Vernon Gotwals did immense service to non-German-speakers with his translations of Haydn's first two biographers, Albert Dies and George Griesinger. Both men knew Haydn and talked to him about his life and music. Their slim books were published in 1810. Gotwals' translation of the two, under the title *Haydn – Two Contemporary Portraits*, was published in 1969 by the University of Wisconsin.

Rosemary Hughes and Karl Geiringer are two of the most recent biographers worth reading. Karl Geiringer's *Haydn – A Creative Life in Music* was last published in 1982 by the University of California. Rosemary Hughes' *Haydn* was last published in 1974 by J. M. Dent.

For the chapter on German musicians and their impact on concert life in London, I quickly discovered that no one seems to have actually traced their effect on music and musicians in the capital. Musicologists often have the disconcerting habit of assuming that everyone knows such things and that they do not need to be explained. The first composer, of course, was George Frederick Handel. Since he took English nationality, and became one of the nation's favourite composers, I have given his English name. Christopher Hogwood's biography is the best, the most readable, and his publishers Thames and Hudson have reproduced some evocative illustrations. Equally useful and readable is Jonathan Keates' *Handel: The Man and his Music*, published by Victor Gollanz in 1985.

The most significant German composer in terms of the subject of this book is Johann Christian Bach, also known as 'the London Bach'. There is very little literature about his life. C. S. Terry wrote a biography, which was first published in 1929. There is, of course, a wonderful portrait of Bach by his friend Thomas Gainsborough which reveals the gentle sweet man his contemporaries thought him to be.

J. C. Bach not only sponsored Schroeter, but he was also an important figure in Mozart's young life. There is too much to read about
Mozart for a dilettante like me. *Mozart and the English Connection* by
John Jenkins, published in 1998 by Cygnus Arts, was the most directly
useful. If you read nothing else, Robert Gutman's 'cultural biography'
is a mine of insights. Ruth Halliwell's 'The Mozart Family' (Oxford)
provides an intimate portrait of the family life of professional musicians. *1791: Mozart's Last Year* (Thames & Hudson, 1988) by the indispensable Robbins Landon is most evocative of Vienna in the 1790s.
Another book, *Vienna's Musical Sites and Landmarks* by Addie Funk
and published in English in Vienna in 1927 by Knoch, is a very superior
if dated guide for the musically minded tourist.

THE EIGHTEENTH-CENTURY WORLD OF MUSIC

I have drawn heavily on the pioneering work of Simon McVeigh
whose *Concert Life in London from Mozart to Haydn* reveals so much
about the period and the 'rage for music' which so engrossed society
in the second half of the century. It was published by the Cambridge
University Press in 1993. Also from Cambridge University Press is
Richard Leppert's *Music and Image* (1989) which fully covers social and
gender attitudes to music, music-making and music-makers. William
Weber's *The Rise of Musical Classics in Eighteenth-Century England*
(Clarendon, 1992) was another useful guide to the musical tastes
of the period. Carl Ehrlich's *The Music Profession in Britain since the
Eighteenth Century – A Social History* (Clarendon, 1985) was well worth
the time it took to track it down. You cannot write about music in this
period without referring to Mrs Papendieck's two-volume journals of
Court and Social Life in the Time of Queen Charlotte, edited by her
granddaughter Mrs Vernon Delves Broughton in 1887. These
memoirs are not always accurate. They were after all written nearly
half a century after the events, but she, more than anyone, was smitten
by Johann Samuel Schroeter, and she has written more about him
than anyone. She also knew Bach and Haydn. Other books which
give some fascinating details are *Invitation to Ranelagh* by Mollie Sands

(John Westhouse, 1946), which describes the world of the pleasure garden, and *The World of the Castrati* by Patrick Barbier (Souvenir Press, 1996), which lists that odd phenomenon of the time whose voices so enchanted and sometimes disgusted English audiences. The full set of *Grove's Dictionary of Music* smoothes the path with the reassurance that any esoteric musical fact (or fiction) will be listed, explained and sourced. It is from Grove that I gleaned enough biographical material for some of the minor musical characters in this story.

Eighteenth-century Society

There are, of course, the well known histories of the century – A. S. Turberville's *English Men and Manners of the Eighteenth Century* (Oxford University Press, 1957), Dorothy George's *London Life in the Eighteenth Century* (Penguin, 1989). Everything written by the late and much revered Roy Porter is useful. For my purposes I gained most from his *English Society in the Eighteenth Century* (Penguin, 1990) and *Enlightenment* (Allen Lane, 2000) which won the Woolfson prize in 2001. *Dr Johnson's London* by Liza Picard (Weidenfeld, 2000) is a useful compendium of curious facts. The literature of the period provides the most authentic detail of daily life. The novel – or 'history' as they were often called – provides us with a contemporary analysis and critique which is quite staggering for a newcomer to the subject. Of the novels of Fanny Burney, the most immediately useful is *Evelina – or The History of a Young Woman's Entrance into the World* (Penguin Classics). The introduction and notes by the distinguished Burney scholar Margaret Anne Doody (as well as her own stimulating biography of the author) put so much of female life into perspective. Fanny Burney's diaries are also a delight to read.

Roger Lonsdale's *Dr Charles Burney: A Literary Biography* (Oxford, 1965) and James L. Clifford's *Hester Lynch Piozzi* (Columbia University Press, 1987) together provide that sense of period and of people who had intellectual ambition but were held back by their place in society. The novelist Beryl Bainbridge demonstrates how historical fact can be used with her exquisite *According to Queenie* (Little Brown, 2001) which looks at Dr Johnson's last years through the eyes of Mrs Thrale's petulant daughter. This book was an inspiration for a fellow time-traveller.

The Yale edition of Boswell's diaries, one of the greatest publishing achievements of the twentieth century, is indispensable. Boswell knew everyone and went everywhere in London, and like any enthusiastic tourist he wants to tell you everything he has discovered and which delights him. He even went to a dinner where Haydn was among the guests. As a fellow Scot he understood Rebecca's family very well, and had encountered the same English prejudice against his race.

The most unexpected source book was David Hancock's *Citizens of the World* (Cambridge University Press, 1996) which tells the stories of, as he puts it, the 'men who developed the British Empire'. It was unexpected because when I first looked into it, I expected just general background on City of London merchants. Dr Hancock, however, dwelt at length on Robert Scott, Rebecca's father. It explained so much about the family's violent reaction to Rebecca's unsuitable marriage plans and their attitudes to a mere musician. Many of Britain's most successful commercial imperialists were of Scottish descent. They quickly exploited the Act of Union in 1707 to come down to London and from there set out to conquer the emerging markets of the world.

Women's lives are being studied as never before. A lot of the work coming out from the gender-studies gurus in the United States tends to view the age through the distorting prism of the twentieth century. Home-grown studies are much more balanced. *Georgiana, Duchess of Devonshire* (HarperCollins, 1998) by Amanda Foreman, and Stella Tillyard's *Aristocrats* (Chatto & Windus, 1994) were fascinating insights into women's lives – albeit at the highest social levels. Then there was *Sheridan's Nightingale*, the story of Elizabeth Linley, by Alan Chedzoy (Alison and Busby, 1997). Norma Clarke had an unusual angle in her *Dr Johnson's Women* (Hambledon, 2000). Janet Todd's *Mary Wollstonecraft: A Revolutionary Life* (Weidenfeld & Nicolson, 2000) was a useful counterbalance to the aristocratic lives featured earlier.

There is now a vast resource of the biographies of notable eighteenth-century male figures such as Boswell, Johnson, Garrick, Gainsborough, Reynolds, Smollett and Hogarth. The political giants, Pitt the Younger and Fox, are well represented. And, of course, the Prince Regent demands attention. I particularly liked Saul David's *The Prince of Pleasure* (Little Brown, 1998).

These books more than satisfied the needs of this writer trying to reconstruct the life of a woman whose claim to fame was that she had loved Johann Samuel and Joseph Haydn – though she herself would have rightly valued her life as worth much more than the names of the two musicians she had loved.

Index

Morning Post, 163, 169
Morzin, Count Karl Joseph
  Franz von, 122
Morzin, Countess
  Wilhelmina von, 122
mourning, 113
Mozart, Costanze, 124
Mozart, Leopold, 24, 43, 101
Mozart, Nannerl, 24
Mozart, Wolfgang Amadeus
  in London, 24, 34, 42
  pianistic duel with
    Clementi, 28, 103
  admires Handel, 30
  and J.C. Bach, 34, 101
  impressed by Schroeter's
    music, 50
  relationship with Haydn,
    118
  marriage, 124
  brief references, 120, 128, 186
  Works:
  Le Nozze di Figaro, 26, 118
  Requiem, 199
Munich, 101
Murray, Charles (RS's brother-
  in-law)
  marries Elizabeth Scott, 9,
    19
  becomes consul of Madeira,
    9
  rents house in London, 10
  and RS's marriage, 56, 57–8,
    61, 89, 91–3
  official request for witness
    statement from, 87
  gives evidence, 90–3, 94, 101
  death, 196
  brief reference, 12
Murray, Charles (RS's
  nephew) *see* Scott Murray,
  Charles
Murray (née Scott), Elizabeth
  (RS's sister)
  birth, 67
  marriage, 12, 19, 20, 73
  RS stays with, 9, 14–15
  and RS's marriage, 91
  official request for witness
    statement from, 87
  birth of son, 88
  gives evidence, 93, 94

brother's legacy to, 196–7
brief reference, 70
Museum of the City of
  Vienna, 198
music
  English attitudes to, 16–17,
    85
  London scene, 2, 21–38, 40,
    41–50, 74, 97, 103–4, 105–6,
    116
  on Continent, 39–40, 115–16,
    117–18
  see also names of musicians

Napier, William
  publishes Schroeter's
    music, 45–6, 48, 49, 101,
    110
  Scottish background, 47
  and Schroeter's wedding,
    61, 92
  bankrupt, 149–50, 175
  Haydn composes music for,
    150, 175
  Haydn concerned about
    health of, 161
  RS lives near, 195
  death, 200
Naples, 32, 40, 126, 165, 189
Napoleon Bonaparte, 192, 199,
  200
Nares, Venerable Robert,
  182–3
Nelson, Lord, 50, 55, 189
New Daily Advertiser, 45
New England, 86
News Letter, 30
Nicolai, Mr, 105
Nicolini (Nicolo Grimaldi),
  38
Nixon, Parson, 96
Norweb (née Scott), Janetta:
  The Memoirs of Janetta, 69–
  71
Novello, Vincent, 149
novels, 13–14

Oatlands, 139
Opera House/Royal Opera
  House, London, 33, 133,
  194
oratorios, 30, 31, 194

The Creation (Haydn), 184,
  185–6, 193–4, 197, 198
Messiah (Handel), 30, 31, 157,
  184–5, 186
Oswald, Richard, 68
Oxford, 137, 166
Oxford Street, London, 44

Paisiello, Giovanni, 118
Pantheon, 25, 44 100, 134, 183
Papendieck (née Albert),
  Charlotte
  becomes Schroeter's pupil,
    46
  attends Haydn's benefit
    concert, 135
  memoirs as historical
    source, 48
  on J.C. Bach, 50, 100
  on clothes, 136
  on concerts, 105–6, 148–9
  on Schroeter, 17, 50, 99
Papendieck, Christopher, 46,
  48–9, 105–6, 193
Paris, 40, 45, 50, 101, 163
Parke, John, 192
Parke, W.T., 50, 97
  Musical Memoirs, 50
Parnell, Henry, 196, 197
Parnell, Sir John, 196
Peace of Utrecht, 27
Pepusch, Johann Christoph,
  29, 33
Pepys, Samuel, 38, 67–8, 72
Perahia, Murray, 50
piano, 17, 36, 49
Piccadilly, London, 27
Pilhofer, Babett (Barbara), 126
Piozzi, Gabriel, 85
Piozzi, Hester *see* Thrale (later
  Piozzi), Hester
Pleyel, Ignaz, 28, 139
Pocock, Sir George, 70
Polzelli, Aloysius Antonio
  Nikolaus, 127
Polzelli, Antonio, 126, 127
Polzelli, Luigia
  appearance, 126
  as singer, 126–7
  Haydn's relationship with,
    126, 127, 164
  birth of second son, 127